GIVING &
INHERITING

{ Your family's security, ensuring that the right people inherit and minimising tax are all important. It's a mistake to assume that everything will somehow turn out all right if you don't plan ahead. }

Jonquil Lowe

About the author

Jonquil Lowe trained as an economist and worked for several years in the City as an investment analyst before moving to *Which?* where she was head of the Money Research Group. Jonquil now splits her time between working as a Lecturer in Personal Finance at The Open University and as a freelance researcher and journalist. She holds the Diploma in Personal Finance and writes extensively on all areas of personal finance. She is author of over 20 books, including *Pensions Explained*, *Finance Your Retirement* and *Save and Invest*, all published by Which?; the *Personal Finance Handbook* published by the Child Poverty Action Group and used as a set text for financial capability courses; *Be Your Own Financial Adviser* and, with Sara Williams, *The Financial Times Guide to Personal Tax*, both from FT Prentice Hall.

GIVING & INHERITING

Jonquil Lowe

Which? Books are commissioned and published by Which? Ltd,
2 Marylebone Road, London NW1 4DF
Email: books@which.co.uk

Distributed by Littlehampton Book Services Ltd,
Faraday Close, Durrington, Worthing, West Sussex BN13 3RB

British Library Cataloguing in Publication Data
A catalogue record for this book is available from the British Library

Previous edition 2007, this edition 2011

ISBN 978 1 84490 118 0
1 3 5 7 9 10 8 6 4 2

Author's acknowledgements
I would like to thank the team at Which? Books, especially my editor, Emma, for their unstinting
support and guidance, and also the readers who have written in with their queries and experiences
over the years and so helped this book to evolve.

Edited by: Emma Callery
Designed by: Bob Vickers
Index by: Lynda Swindells
Printed and bound by Charterhouse, Hatfield

Tauro Offset is a totally chlorine free paper produced using timber from sustainably managed forests.
The mill is ISO14001 certified.

PEFC
PEFC/16-33-160

For a full list of Which? Books, please call 01903 828557, access our website at www.which.co.uk,
or write to Littlehampton Book Services. For other enquiries call 0800 252 100.

CONTENTS

INTRODUCTION

Inheritance Tax (IHT) is widely thought to be unfair, but this is not the only reason for planning your giving and inheriting.

A topic guaranteed to raise most people's hackles is that of IHT. Rightly or wrongly, it is widely thought to be unfair. It stands accused of being a double tax on homes and other assets built up out of hard-won and already heavily taxed income; a tax that hits middle Britain, while the truly wealthy can afford clever avoidance schemes.

The fear of IHT snatching a chunk of your wealth may be a powerful motive for organising your giving and inheriting. But, more importantly, planning ahead should be a top priority to ensure that loved ones are financially secure and that the inheritance you leave goes to the people you choose and in the way that you want.

THE POLITICS OF TAXING WEALTH

The distribution of wealth in Britain is heavily skewed. In the chart on this page, the straight line shows how wealth would be shared out if there was perfect equality (so that, for example, half of households would own half of all wealth, three-quarters would own three-quarters of all wealth, and so on). The bowed line reveals the actual distribution of wealth is far from equal. In fact, half of households own just 10 per cent of the nation's wealth and the richest 10 per cent of households own over 40 per cent. Given such inequality, it could be argued that there is a strong case for taxing wealth to reduce the amount going to the 'haves' so it can be used to benefit those who have less. The problem is that such taxes typically affect, not just the very rich, but also people who do not consider themselves to be wealthy at all.

In the UK, there are several ways in which wealth is taxed. First, if you save or invest, any interest or other income from this is usually taxed. Some countries levy a yearly tax on just owning wealth – the closest to this in the UK is Council Tax, which is related to the value of the home you live in. (But Council Tax is due even if you rent rather than own your home, so this is not a pure wealth tax.) Then

Distribution of wealth in Great Britain

— total wealth excluding pension wealth

y-axis: cumulative % wealth (0, 10, 20, 30, 40, 50, 60, 70, 80, 90, 100)
x-axis: cumulative % households (0, 10, 20, 30, 40, 50, 60, 70, 80, 90, 100)

Source: Office for National Statistics, 2009, *Wealth and Assets Survey 2006–8*.

there are taxes when you dispose of your wealth. IHT falls into this category and is a tax on some gifts you make during your lifetime and what you leave on death. Capital Gains Tax (CGT) applies when you sell, give away or otherwise dispose of assets during your lifetime (but not on death). And stamp duty is a tax on certain types of wealth – particularly homes – when they change hands. Although, as the chart below shows, the take from CGT and IHT seems relatively small (forecast to be £3.4 billion for CGT and £2.7 billion for IHT in 2011–12), it is these taxes that are the main focus when planning your giving and inheriting. Chapters 1 to 4 and Chapter 9 explain how these taxes work and the opportunities for making gifts that are tax-free.

Traditionally, Labour governments are more inclined to use wealth taxes – for example, introducing, in 1976, a comprehensive tax on most lifetime gifts as well as bequests on death. It was short-lived, because the following Conservative government created significant exemptions for lifetime gifts. To the surprise of many pundits, the Labour governments of 1997 to 2010 did not tighten up the IHT regime (but did make important changes to pension schemes to prevent them being used for passing on wealth). Then 2010 saw the formation of a coalition government, comprising Conservatives and Liberal Democrats. with very different ideological views about wealth. In its manifesto, the Liberal Democrat party had expressed its intention to introduce 'a mansion tax at a rate of 1 per cent on properties worth over £2 million, paid on the value of the property above that level'. By contrast, the Conservatives stated their intention to 'raise the inheritance tax threshold to £1 million to help millions of people who aspire to pass something on to their children'. At spring 2011, neither of these extreme policies had been adopted, but the Coalition Government had announced the repeal of the restrictions preventing pension

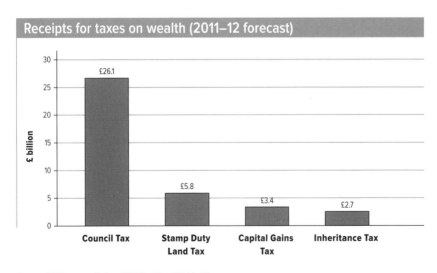

Receipts for taxes on wealth (2011–12 forecast)

£ billion

- Council Tax: £26.1
- Stamp Duty Land Tax: £5.8
- Capital Gains Tax: £3.4
- Inheritance Tax: £2.7

Source: HM Treasury, *Budget 2011 'Red Book'*, Table C3.

schemes being used for inheritance purposes – and you can find details of this in Chapter 7. These ideological tensions create an uncertain climate for planning your giving and inheriting.

Outlawing tax-avoidance

Another important source of uncertainty is the approach of the government tax-collection department, HM Revenue & Customs (HMRC). Even before the global financial crisis of 2007 and subsequent austerity measures, HMRC had been aggressively attacking tax planning, blurring the distinction between legitimate tax-saving arrangements and illegal tax evasion. A famous tax case in 1935 involving the Duke of Westminster established that *'every man is entitled if he can to order his affairs so that the tax attaching under the appropriate Acts is less than it otherwise would be'*. In other words, provided you are acting within the law, there is nothing wrong with arranging your affairs to minimise the tax you pay. Over the subsequent decades, these words have been much debated, in particular whether they should apply to complicated schemes set up wholly or mainly to save tax. There has been a growing body of new laws to outlaw specific tax-avoidance strategies. In addition, there has been a hardening of the way that HMRC interprets legislation, so that arrangements that appear to be legal are nonetheless being challenged. Since fighting HMRC can be a lengthy, costly and uncertain process, you should be wary about entering into any complex inheritance planning.

SHOULD YOU BE WORRIED?

Despite widespread anxiety that a lifetime's wealth could end up in the hands of HMRC, only around one estate in 23 paid IHT in 2007–8 (the latest year for which completed data are available). Moreover, IHT on your death (see Chapter 9) is a tax for your heirs to pay, not you. But you might be worried about IHT if:

- **You want to leave an inheritance.** Many people like to know that after they are gone, they are still able to help their family and friends, especially their children. IHT can take a big chunk out of what you leave. Broadly speaking, the first slice of an estate is tax-free (with the IHT threshold set at £325,000 from 2010–11 to 2014–15) – and up to double this in the case of a widow, widower or widowed civil partner. Above that, IHT takes a hefty 40 per cent bite. Chapters 5 to 7 look at planning your gifts tax-efficiently, including gifts to children and charity. Chapter 11 considers some issues that are important to the people who might receive your bequests.
- **You have a valuable home.** The boom in house prices during the 1990s and 2000s is a major reason why many middle-wealth households have found themselves drawn into the IHT net. Planning away an IHT bill is especially difficult if the bulk of your wealth is tied up in your home and Chapter 10, in particular, looks at the issues involved. The table opposite shows the average price of

a detached home (used here as a proxy for the value of homes that more mature households might have) compared with the threshold at which IHT starts. The table suggests that IHT is especially an issue for homeowners in the south and east of the UK. However, with the IHT threshold frozen until 2014–15, more people could be drawn into IHT if house prices start to rise again.

■ **Someone could face financial hardship when you die.** Anything you leave to your husband, wife or civil partner is normally free from IHT. But this exemption does not extend to other people who might depend on you financially. For example, an unmarried partner, brothers and sisters, children or a carer who lives with you might have to sell your home in order to pay IHT. You are likely to find Chapters 4 and 10 especially useful.

■ **You want to set up trusts during your lifetime.** You can arrange many lifetime gifts to be tax-free, but most gifts to trusts can trigger an immediate IHT bill. Trusts are not just for the very rich, but can be useful, for example, when an outright gift might be misused or the people you want to give to are not yet born. Chapter 4 explains the ins and outs of trusts.

> With the IHT threshold frozen until 2014–15, more people could be drawn into IHT if house prices start to rise again.

IHT threshold and average price of a detached house

	1989	1999	2009
IHT threshold	£118,000	£231,000	£325,000
Region			
North east	77,869	104,041	234,370
North west	98,326	120,386	289,131
Yorkshire and the Humber	82,171	112,346	279,924
East Midlands	90,576	107,969	247,304
West Midlands	98,567	128,846	284,491
East	137,522	151,253	353,000
London	190,997	258,757	585,369
South east	157,810	197,618	437,424
South west	120,107	137,891	326,018
Wales	84,227	105,587	246,993
Scotland	54,104	107,843	247,450
Northern Ireland	50,338	101,664	267,188

Sources: www.communities.gov.uk/housing/housingresearch/housingstatistics/; www.hmrc.gov.uk/rates/inheritance.htm

WHAT CAN YOU DO?

Everyone should carry out some basic inheritance planning as shown at the top the checklist below. The next step is to use Chapters 1 to 3 to check whether IHT and CGT are likely to affect you at all. If they might, in essence you have three options for reducing or eliminating a tax bill on your wealth: spend it, give it away or insure against the tax. But there are many ways you can put these options into effect as shown in the rest of the checklist. With *Giving & Inheriting* on your side, you can cross HMRC off your list of beneficiaries or at least relegate them to the bottom.

This edition of *Giving and Inheriting* is up to date as at March 2011 and includes changes announced in the March 2011 Budget.

> **!** If you are writing your own will, sorting out someone else's will, setting up a trust, considering tax avoidance schemes, or your situation is at all complex or involves large sums of money, please note that it is important to consult a legal and/or tax adviser. See Useful Addresses on pages 214–17.

Giving and inheriting checklist

Action	For information	✓ when complete
Essentials		
Make a will and keep it up to date	Chapter 8	
Nominate who should benefit from pension schemes if you were to die	Chapter 7	
Make sure life insurance is written in trust	Chapter 7	
Other actions to consider		
Plan lifetime gifts and bequests to make full use of the IHT tax-free limit	Chapters 2, 7 and 9	
Review how you share your home and assets	Chapters 7 and 10	
Make sure lifetime gifts are tax-free	Chapters 1, 2, 5 and 6	
Understand what tax-free gifts you can make in your will	Chapter 8	
Consider unlocking some wealth to spend and enjoy in your lifetime	Chapters 7 and 10	
Consider a trust if you think an outright gift would be unsuitable	Chapter 4	
Consider insurance if a tax bill is unavoidable	Chapters 3, 7, 9 and 10	
Watch out for tax pitfalls	Chapters 4, 9 and 10	
Be aware of your options if you receive an inheritance	Chapter 11	

LIFETIME GIFT PLANNING

Making gifts during your lifetime is the main way to reduce an inheritance tax (IHT) bill on your estate when you die, though you need to steer a course around other taxes that can hit lifetime gifts. Top priority is making sure you do not jeopardise your financial security by giving away more than you can afford. Giving something away now but retaining the right to use it during your lifetime might seem the answer, but the tax authorities have thought of that one too.

1

TAX AND LIFETIME GIFTS

A key way to avoid or reduce tax at your death is to give away your wealth during your lifetime. But you need to watch out for possible tax on your lifetime gifts.

WHAT'S IN THIS CHAPTER?

Although there are other and more important reasons for inheritance planning, such as protecting your family, saving tax is a strong motive. One of the most efficient ways to do this is to make lifetime gifts. Giving away your wealth – or income – during your life is the most straightforward and basic way of reducing the value of the estate that you leave at death. Lifetime gifts, provided they do not jeopardise your own financial security, can also be a good way to meet your other goals, such as helping children get established or supporting a charity. This chapter provides an overview of:

- How lifetime gifts fit into your overall inheritance planning (page 12).
- The tax treatment of lifetime gifts (page 13).
- Tax planning pitfalls you need to watch out for (page 17).

WHY MAKE LIFETIME GIFTS?

There are many reasons for making gifts – to help your children as they set out into adult life, to help other family members or friends and to support a charity are a few examples. Another reason is to reduce a potential IHT bill at your death.

It is important to appreciate that, unlike most other taxes, IHT is not a tax on a single transaction. You cannot simply look at a single gift in isolation to discover whether tax is due. IHT is charged on a rolling total of gifts you make over the last seven years. When you die, the estate you leave is treated as your final gift. Whether or not tax is due on your estate depends on whether the value of your estate plus other gifts you have made in the last seven years exceeds the IHT-free threshold.

Gifts you made more than seven years before death drop out of the calculation. It therefore follows that, provided you survive for seven years, any gifts you make now will reduce the value of your estate and so could save tax on the estate.

Some gifts are tax-free – such as gifts on marriage and up to £3,000 a year of gifts to anyone (see pages

Earlier years	9	8	7	6	5	4	3	2	1

Gifts in these years fall out of the calculation	Gifts in these years are added to your estate to see if tax is due on your estate	Year up to date of death

28–34) – and don't come into the calculation. You can make these at any time and, regardless of how long you survive, they reduce the value of your estate.

HOW LIFETIME GIFTS MAY BE TAXED

Although IHT is the main tax most people associate with giving and inheriting, it is not the only one. You need to be aware of two main taxes when making lifetime gifts: IHT and Capital Gains Tax (CGT). Some gifts affect your Income Tax position too. And, if you are giving away a property, in some situations Stamp Duty Land Tax (SDLT) could be an issue (see Chapter 10).

IHT and lifetime gifts

For IHT purposes, there are three types of lifetime gift:

- **Tax-free gifts** (also called 'exempt transfers'). There is no IHT on these.
- **Taxable gifts** (also called 'chargeable transfers'). Most gifts to trusts are taxable gifts. The gift is added to any other taxable gifts you have made during the last seven years. If the total comes to more than the tax-free threshold in force at the time of your latest gift, IHT at the lifetime rate of 20 per cent is due on the gift at the time it is made.
- **Potentially Exempt Transfers (PETs).** Gifts direct from one person to another count as PETs. A PET is tax-free provided you survive for seven years after making it. If you die within seven years, the PET is reclassified as a taxable gift.

IHT-free limit	
TAX YEAR	**TAX-FREE LIMIT**
2007–8	£300,000
2008–9	£300,000
2009–10 to 2014–15	£300,000

! Do not give away in your lifetime money or assets that you can't afford or might need later on.

CGT and lifetime gifts

CGT is a tax on the increase in value of something during the time that you have owned it. If you sell the thing at a profit, CGT is a tax on that profit. When you give something away, tax can be due on the potential profit you could have made.

Some things are always free of CGT, such as gifts of cash. Some types of transaction are CGT-free, such as gifts to charity. Even when something is taxable, there are various reliefs that reduce or even eliminate the tax bill. One of the most important is the yearly CGT allowance that everyone has. In 2011–12, the allowance is £10,600.

Income Tax and lifetime gifts

In some situations, you can be taxed on income from something you have given away. This applies, for example,

> **Trust** A legal arrangement where one or more people (the trustees) hold money or assets (the trust property) to be used for the benefit of one or more other people (the beneficiaries). The trust's rules can set conditions on how the trust property is held and used.

to gifts you have made to a trust if you can benefit from the trust and gifts you make to your dependent child if the income earned by the gift exceeds £100 a year.

In other situations, the Government encourages you to make gifts through tax incentives for you and/or the recipient. This applies to gifts to charities and certain gifts to children.

SDLT

SDLT is a tax on the purchase or transfer of land or property. But some transfers are tax-free, such as:

- Genuine gifts where no money changes hands. But be aware that, if the person receiving the gift takes over paying part or all of a mortgage against the property, this does count as money changing hands and so the exemption is lost.
- Property left in a will.
- Transfers where the purchase price is no more than £125,000.
- Transfers to a first-time buyer between 25 March 2010 and 24 March 2012 inclusive, where the purchase price is no more than £250,000.

There are more details in Chapter 10 and, if you think that SDLT might be due, you should seek advice from a solicitor (see Useful Addresses on pages 214–17).

For details of tax-free gifts, see Chapter 2. You can find out more about taxable gifts and PETs in Chapter 3.

MINIMISE IHT ON LIFETIME GIFTS

The following points are a round-up of straightforward ways to save IHT on lifetime gifts.

Make tax-free gifts

For a full list of tax-free gifts see Chapter 2. Here are three of the best:

- **Gifts that are normal expenditure out of income.** If you establish a regular pattern of giving that you can manage out of your income without reducing your living standards, the gifts are IHT free. The beauty of this exemption is that it can apply to gifts of any amount. It could cover, for example, monthly or yearly premiums you pay for a life insurance policy that, on your death, will pay out direct to the person you have chosen. It can also cover irregular payments made according to a regular pattern – for example, giving each of your children a set sum on their 18th birthdays.
- **Gifts to your husband, wife or civil partner.** Each of you has your own IHT, CGT and Income Tax allowances. If one of you holds most of the family assets, the other person could be wasting their allowances. To ensure those allowances are used to the full, consider spreading your assets more evenly between you (sometimes called 'equalising your estates'). Because gifts between husbands, wives and civil partners are normally tax-free, you can achieve this spreading without triggering a tax bill. Your gifts must be genuine, so you need to be confident that your relationship is sound.
- **Yearly tax-free limit.** Each year you can make tax-free gifts up to £3,000 that are not covered by any of the other IHT exemptions. If you don't use up the full allowance one year, you can carry the unused part forward to the next year (but no further), giving you a maximum tax-free limit of £6,000 for that year.

Use your tax-free limit

Any gifts you make that are not tax-free still will not trigger a tax bill provided your rolling total of gifts over the last seven years does not exceed the tax-free limit.

> If one of you holds most of the family assets, the other person could be wasting their allowances.

For more information about CGT on lifetime gifts, see Chapter 3. Chapter 4 includes information about gifts to trusts. See Chapter 5 for guidance on making gifts to children and Chapter 6 for gifts to charity.

MINIMISE CGT ON LIFETIME GIFTS

Here are some straightforward ways to save CGT on lifetime gifts.

Make tax-free gifts

For a full list of tax-free gifts see Chapter 2. Here are three of the best:

- **Give cash rather than assets.** There is no CGT on gifts of cash.
- **Give 'chattels' worth £6,000 or less.** Where you have a choice, consider giving away a painting, antique furniture or other collectibles rather than, say, shares. Provided they are worth £6,000 or less, possessions like these are exempt from CGT.
- **Use your tax-free limit.** Everyone can make a certain amount of gains tax-free each year. In 2011–12, the allowance is £10,600.

Make gifts to your wife, husband or civil partner

Each of you has your own IHT, CGT and Income Tax allowances. If one of you holds most of the family assets, the other person could be wasting their allowances. To ensure those allowances are used to the full, consider spreading your assets more evenly between you.

For CGT purposes, gifts between husbands, wives and civil partners are made on a no-gain-no-loss basis. This means there is no tax bill at the time of the gift. Instead the recipient takes over any gain that had built up and there could be tax on it when they eventually sell or give away the asset. Your gifts must be genuine, so you need to be confident that your relationship is sound.

LIFETIME GIFT PLANNING PITFALLS

To save tax, a gift must be genuine. If it's genuine, then you can't get it back later if your circumstances change. So think carefully before making lifetime gifts.

MONEY YOU NEED LATER ON

To save IHT, any gifts you make must be genuine. This means you completely give up the thing you give away. Check your current and future financial situation carefully to make sure you can really afford the gift. Be realistic about the future, for example:

- **Losing a partner.** If you are a couple, consider how your financial circumstances might change if you lost your partner through death or divorce.
- **Needing long-term care.** Think what resources you would have if later on you needed help with personal care, either in your own home or in a residential home. Under the rules that applied in 2010, the state may step in to pay for some or all your care needs if your income and savings are low. But be aware that you can be treated as still owning assets you have given away, if it seems that you made the gifts simply to qualify for state financial help. This is despite the fact that someone else is now the legal owner of the assets. So you could find yourself in a difficult position, where you may have to pay for your own care but might not be able to get the gifts back.
- **Inheritance.** Be wary of anticipating money or assets you expect to inherit from someone else. You might not be left the bequest after all or it might be worth less than you had expected.
- **Investment returns.** Use modest assumptions about how your savings and investments might grow in the future and the income they might generate for you.

GIFTS THAT DON'T COUNT FOR IHT

Especially if most of your wealth is tied up in your home, you might not have much spare wealth to give away. IYou might be tempted to give something away now but on condition that you carry on using it while still alive.

Gifts like this are called 'gifts with reservation' and, for IHT purposes, they continue to count as part of your estate and so do not save any tax at your death. Schemes that get around the gift-with-reservation rules are usually caught instead by the Pre-Owned Assets Tax (POAT) – see Chapter 4.

COMPLICATED TAX PLANNING

Not so long ago, the accepted view was: tax avoidance is legal, tax evasion is not. Tax avoidance was simply the clever but perfectly legal use of quirks in the law to save tax. But HMRC's attitude towards tax avoidance has become increasingly hardened over the years. Although exploiting loopholes in the legislation is not illegal as such, it is deemed to be unfair and a constant stream of new anti-avoidance legislation aims to close down complicated tax-planning schemes as fast as they appear. Therefore, you should approach any such scheme with caution.

If you are attracted to complicated tax planning, always ensure you get professional advice and bear in mind the following points:

- **Evasion.** Avoidance may be frowned upon but is not a crime. By contrast, breaking the tax rules is illegal tax evasion for which there are heavy penalties, including the possibility of a prison term.
- **Shams.** The courts are wise to attempts to dress up illegal tax arrangements to look like legal ones.
- **Associated operations.** Even where an arrangement seems to be within the law it may fall foul of the 'associated operations' rules. These have built up through case law and mean that a series of transactions can be looked at as a whole. If they do not have a bona fide commercial motive and have been devised primarily as a way of saving tax, they can be deemed to be artificial and the tax-saving effects nullified.

- **HMRC challenge.** HMRC is prepared to challenge schemes even when, according to the strict letter of the law, they might seem to be legal. To fight an HMRC challenge, you would need to pursue a case through the tax tribunal system and even ultimately the courts. Such disputes can be lengthy and costly with uncertain outcomes.
- **Changes in the law.** Even if the taxpayer wins a case against HMRC, the Government can change the law to close loopholes and ban schemes. Although such changes might not to be retrospective in the strict sense of the word, HMRC moved the goal posts when it introduced the POAT (see Chapter 4) and has made it clear that it is prepared to introduce further 'retroactive' measures if necessary. A retroactive change does not impose a tax bill for past tax years but does impose a tax bill now on actions you took in the past. So any action you take now which seems to save tax could give rise to a future tax bill if the law is changed.

SUMMARY

This chapter has given a quick overview of how lifetime gifts fit into inheritance planning and the range of taxes that you may need to take into account. Most important of these are IHT and CGT and the next chapter looks at possible gifts that are free of both these taxes.

TAX-FREE GIFTS

There are two key taxes to watch out for when you make a lifetime gift: Inheritance Tax (IHT) and Capital Gains Tax (CGT). This chapter looks at gifts you can make during your lifetime that are free of CGT, free of IHT or free of both.

TAX-FREE GIVING

Usually saving IHT means triggering a CGT bill or vice versa, but some gifts are free of both taxes.

WHAT'S IN THIS CHAPTER?

Lifetime gifts are an important part of inheritance planning. They can be especially efficient if you can arrange for your gifts to be tax-free.

- A summary of gifts that are free of both CGT and IHT (this page).
- In detail, the gifts that are free from CGT, a tax that applies to sales and other types of disposal as well as gifts (see opposite).
- In detail, the gifts that are free of IHT, including gifts that are tax-free only as long as you survive for at least a minimum time (page 28).

COMBINING THE TAX EXEMPTIONS

Some types of gift are specifically exempt from both CGT and IHT: for example, gifts to charities and museums and gifts of national heritage property. Other gifts will be completely tax-free as long as they fall within an IHT exemption and they comprise cash or other assets that are not liable for CGT. Chapter 3 describes other situations in which either CGT or IHT may not be payable. You can sometimes combine the CGT and IHT exemptions in these situations to ensure that your gifts are free of both taxes.

{ You can sometimes combine the CGT and IHT exemptions to ensure your gifts are free of both taxes. }

CAPITAL GAINS TAX

If something you own has increased in value up to the time you give it away, normally there would be CGT to pay. But some gains are tax-free.

When you give someone something that you own, you are treated for tax purposes as making a 'disposal' of an asset and the tax position is essentially the same as if you had sold it. This means that, if the asset's value at the time you give it away is greater than its value at the time you first started to own it, there could be a CGT bill. But don't panic. Often, you will not have to pay any CGT, because:

- Some assets are outside the scope of CGT.
- Gains from some transactions are always tax-free.

? **Asset** A handy shorthand word for something that you own. It could be cash, investments, a house, your personal possessions, or anything else.
Disposal Usually this means receiving a capital sum from an asset, for example, when you sell it or you receive an insurance pay-out because the asset has been lost or destroyed. But gifts also count as disposals for CGT purposes and you are treated as if you had received the market value of the asset.

CGT-free assets and transactions at a glance

The following gifts are either tax-free or there is no tax at the time the gift is made. Conditions may apply and are explained in this chapter.

- Money
- Chattels with a life of no more than 50 years
- Chattels worth £6,000 or less
- Motor vehicles
- Your only or main home
- Some National Savings & Investments (NS&I) products
- Individual Savings Accounts (ISAs)
- Enterprise Investment Scheme shares

- Venture Capital Trust shares
- Right to receive certain payments
- Gifts between husband and wife or civil partners
- Gifts to charities and some similar bodies
- Gifts of national heritage property
- Gifts if you move abroad for at least five years
- Gifts on death

THE SCOPE OF CGT

CGT is a tax on the disposal of assets. Assets cover virtually all types of possessions: land, buildings (including your home), stocks and shares, paintings, furniture, patents and copyrights, debts owed to you. But some assets are specifically free from CGT.

Money

Assets, for CGT purposes, do not include sterling currency – so a gift of money cannot result in a CGT bill.

Coin collections would not normally count as money. But, by an interesting quirk of the law, sovereigns minted after 1837 do still count as sterling currency and are therefore outside the CGT net.

PLANNING POINT

The special rules for taxing chattels mean that collecting antiques, rare books, paintings and similar items can be more tax-efficient than other investments and can make them particularly suitable as gifts. But bear in mind that the market for collectibles can be very fickle, making these high-risk investments, and the person you give them to is likely to incur costs storing and insuring these valuables.

(Sovereigns minted before then and other collectible coins count as 'chattels' – see below.)

There is no CGT on gains from buying and selling foreign money that you have obtained for your own use – for a holiday abroad, say, for buying or running a holiday home abroad or for use during a business trip.

Chattels

This means 'tangible, movable property' – basically your personal belongings, such as clothes, books, music collection and your household goods, as well as things such as jewellery, antiques, paintings and many other collectibles. An item in this category is exempt from CGT provided:

- It has a predicted useful life of 50 years or less and you have not used it in a business.
- It has an expected life of more than 50 years, but the value of the item at the time you dispose of it is no more than £6,000.

If you give away or sell a decoration awarded (e.g. to you or a relative) for valour or gallantry, there is no CGT on any gain, unless you had originally bought the decoration or exchanged something of value for it.

Chattels worth more than £6,000

If a chattel's value is more than £6,000, any gain can be worked out in a special way, which may reduce the CGT bill (see Chapter 3). There are rules to prevent you reducing the CGT payable by splitting up a set – for example, a set of chairs – and then giving all the parts of the set to the same person.

Motor vehicles

There is no CGT on gains from selling or giving away a private car (including vintage or classic cars), a motorbike or other private motor vehicle. This exemption can also apply to a vehicle used for business provided it was 'commonly used as a private vehicle'. However, the exemption does not stretch to vehicles that are not commonly used as private vehicles and are unsuitable for use in that way – so watch out if you are tempted by surplus Ministry of Defence tanks or similar exotica!

A vehicle you sell or give away might have a personalised or cherished number plate. The right to use the combination of letters and numbers shown on the plate is an 'intangible' asset that is not covered by the CGT exemption for motor vehicles. If the value of the vehicle you sell or give away includes an amount in respect of the personalised plate, you need to apportion the proceeds between the value of the vehicle and the value of the right to use the registration that is shown on the plate, and there could be CGT to pay on the latter.

Your home

There is normally no CGT to pay when you dispose of part, or all, of your only, or main, home.

This exemption automatically includes your garden provided your whole plot (house plus garden) comes to no more than half a hectare (about 1.25 acres). It covers giving away part of the garden while you retain the house, but not if it has ceased to be garden. For example, if you built a house in the garden and gave the house to your children, the gift would not be covered by the exemption. But you could give the children part of the garden free of CGT and leave them to develop the plot.

If your plot is larger than half a hectare, there is no automatic exemption and the garden is exempt only if its size is warranted by the nature of the house and deemed necessary for the reasonable enjoyment of the home. This can be hard to prove if you are disposing of part of the garden while keeping the home, since the act of disposal suggests that for 'reasonable enjoyment' you don't really need such a large garden after all. However, HMRC might accept that a gift of part of the garden is tax-free if made to a relative whose presence would not detract from your enjoyment of the rest of the garden.

If you have more than one home, you should nominate one as your main home for CGT purposes. A husband and wife or civil partners who live together can have only one main home between them. This is so even if they each spend a lot of time in separate homes, for example, because they live apart during the week for work purposes. Couples who are not married and not in a registered civil partnership can each have a separate main home even if they live mainly together in just one home.

You may lose part of the exemption if part of your home was set aside exclusively for business. The same applies if you let out part or all of your home, though in that case you might qualify for other reductions in your CGT bill. There may also be a CGT bill when you dispose of your home, if you have lived away for long periods.

■ PLANNING POINT ■

If you have more than one home and want to nominate one as your main home, you must make your nomination in writing to your tax office within two years of acquiring a second or further home. Once made, you can change the nomination if you want to. If you fail to make a nomination within the two-year time limit, your main home is determined on the facts – for example, where your post is sent, where you are registered to vote, and so on.

Case Study FRANK AND JANETTE

Frank and Janette have retired and plan to move permanently to their second home, which is in Devon and up to now they have just spent holidays and some weekends there. They want to give the family home in Kent to their only daughter, Marie.

The home is worth about £600,000 but there will be no CGT on the gift because the house has been Frank and Janette's main home throughout the whole time they have owned it. However, Frank and Janette will need to consider the IHT position of this gift (see Chapter 3).

{ There is normally no CGT to pay when you dispose of part, or all, of your only, or main, home. }

Enterprise investment scheme (EIS) A scheme to encourage investment in new and growing trading companies. You get Income Tax relief on the amount you invest and any gains are tax-free provided you hold the shares for at least three years. This is a high-risk investment and losses could outweigh any tax advantage.

Individual Savings Account (ISA) Scheme introduced by the Government in 1999 with tax incentives to encourage people to save more. Each year, you have an ISA allowance (£10,680 in 2011–12), which can be invested in stockmarket investments, like shares. If you choose, up to half of your allowance can be invested in cash (in other words, savings accounts offered by banks, building societies and NS&I). In 2011, the Government is due to launch a Junior ISA for children up to the age of 18, into which parents and others will be able to pay savings up to an annual limit.

Venture Capital Trust (VCT) A scheme to encourage investment in new and growing trading companies. It aims to be slightly lower risk than an EIS by spreading your investment across a range of different companies. You get Income Tax relief on the amount you invest provided you hold the shares for at least five years and any gains are tax-free.

Some investments

Gains on some investments are completely free from CGT: for example, NS&I products (including premium bonds), gilts, most corporate bonds, and investments held through an **Individual Savings Account** (ISA). ISAs can't themselves be transferred to someone else – you would need to sell the investments held within the ISA and give away the proceeds.

Provided certain conditions are met, gains on shares bought through an **Enterprise Investment Scheme** (EIS) or **Venture Capital Trust** (VCT) are also free of CGT.

Insurance policies

Payment from a life insurance policy, whether on maturity, early surrender or even through selling the policy to someone else, is usually exempt from CGT. The exemption does not apply, however, if you bought the policy from someone else, for example through an auction. And it does not apply to selling your direct holding of an investment fund that specialises in holding policies bought from other people (but if such an investment – often called a 'life settlement bond' – is offered by an insurance company, the proceeds will be subject to Income Tax rather than CGT).

Your rights to certain payments

If you dispose of your right to receive an income under an annuity or a covenant, say, there is usually no CGT on any gain you make as a result. Similarly, if you give away your right to benefit under the terms of a trust or your right to repayment of money you have lent someone, there is usually no CGT – but there could be, if in the first place you had bought these rights.

TAX-FREE TRANSACTIONS

Some types of transaction (regardless of the type of asset involved) are exempt from CGT or subject to other rules that mean there is no tax bill at the time of making a gift.

Gifts between husband and wife or between civil partners

Gifts between a husband and wife or between civil partners are free of CGT provided the couple are living together. The gift is not exempt but is treated as being made on a no-gain-no-loss basis – see Chapter 3 for an explanation of how this works.

> Gifts between a husband and wife or between civil partners are free of CGT provided the couple are living together.

Gifts to charities and certain other bodies

Donations and gifts to charity, and to various other institutions, including many museums and art galleries, local authorities, government departments and universities, and community amateur sports clubs are CGT-free.

Gifts of national heritage property

The sale or gift of certain property, such as works of art, to a museum, art gallery, the National Trust or similar

Case Study RASHEED

Rasheed wants to make a large donation to the local hospice which cared for his wife up to her death. He has some units in a unit trust on which he has made a substantial gain. If he sold the units and donated the proceeds to the charity, he would have to use part of the proceeds to pay CGT on the gain. But, if he transfers the units direct to the charity, this is a tax-free gift. There are also Income Tax advantages to making the donation in this way (see Chapter 6).

? **Resident** You will always count as resident in the UK if you spend 183 days or more of the tax year in the UK. You may still count as resident even if you spend fewer days here.

Ordinarily resident This normally applies if you live in the UK year after year, even if you are away temporarily.

Non-resident and not ordinarily resident
This is likely to apply if you go to work full-time abroad and the following conditions are met: your absence from the UK and your contract of employment both last at least a whole tax year; your visits back to the UK add up to less than 183 days in any one tax year; and your visits back to the UK average 91 days per tax year or less. (Your day of arrival, but not the day you leave count towards the 183- and 91-day tests.) By concession, a husband, wife or civil partner accompanying their spouse to work abroad can also count as non-resident. If you go abroad for reasons other than work – say, you retire abroad – to count as non-resident, you will need to convince HMRC that you have severed your ties with the UK.

body, university, local authority or government department, may be exempt from CGT. So, too, is the acceptance by HMRC of such property in lieu of IHT (see page 181).

Eligible property can include pictures, prints, books, manuscripts, works of art and scientific objects, provided they are 'pre-eminent' for their national, scientific, historic or artistic interest. Buildings and land of outstanding scenic, historic or scientific interest and items associated with them are also eligible.

A gift of eligible property to anyone else can be free of CGT if it also qualifies as conditionally exempt from IHT (see page 29) or would do so if it did not count as a Potentially Exempt Transfer (see Chapter 3).

To qualify, the person receiving the gift must agree certain conditions with HMRC including that the gifted property will stay in the UK, it will be properly maintained and preserved, and the public will have reasonable access to it. The exemption from CGT is lost if the property is subsequently sold, unless this is to a museum, art gallery, the National Trust or similar body, university, local authority or government department.

If the gift is not exempt, you might instead be able to claim hold-over relief (see page 58).

Gifts if you move abroad

If you leave the UK to take up residence abroad, you can give away assets you acquired while still in the UK without paying any CGT, provided you count as a non-UK-**resident** and not **ordinarily resident** for at least five complete tax years. (But check whether you will be subject to any foreign tax in the new country where you become resident.) If your time abroad comes to less than five years, capital gains realised while you were away are subject to CGT in the tax year you return to the UK.

The box opposite outlines the current rules that determine whether or not you are resident. These have built up, based on case law and HMRC guidance. However, in 2011, the Government is consulting on introducing a new statutory test of residence to be implemented from

Case Study **JENNY**

Jenny is a fashion designer, working for an international firm. Usually she is based in London but in March 2011 she is posted to New York. Her husband, Patrick, decides to go with her. The posting is due to last for a minimum of two years, but can be extended after that on a yearly basis. Provided they stay away for at least five years, this could be an ideal opportunity to give their son a piece of land that Patrick owns. The former paddock has been included as development land in the latest local plan, which has boosted its value from a few thousand pounds to £300,000. Despite its high value, there will be no CGT on the gift, provided Patrick remains non-resident and not ordinarily resident for at least five whole tax years.

April 2012. To keep track of the consultation and changes, visit the HMRC website.

Gifts on death

When you die, you are deemed to make a gift of everything you own to your heirs but, whatever, and however much, you leave, it is always free of CGT. Your heirs are treated as acquiring the assets at their market value at the time of your death, so any previous capital gains that had built up while the assets were in your hands are cleared.

When you die, however much you leave, it is always free of CGT.

For more information about residency status, see the Centre for Non-Residents section of the HMRC website at www.hmrc.gov.uk/cnr/ and its free printed guide HMRC6 *Residence, domicile and remittance basis.*

INHERITANCE TAX

Most lifetime gifts you make are either free of inheritance tax (IHT) or count as Potentially Exempt Transfers (PETs).

IHT is a tax on a 'transfer of value' from one person to another – in other words, a transaction that reduces the value of the estate of the person making the gift. In theory, IHT could apply to any gift but, as with CGT, there are exemptions. This means that on most lifetime gifts there is no IHT to pay, because:

- Various types of gift are always free of IHT.
- Some gifts, called PETs, are free of tax, provided the giver lives on for seven years after making the gift (see Chapter 3).

GIFTS THAT ARE ALWAYS FREE OF IHT

The scope of IHT is, on the face of it, wider than that of CGT because IHT covers all assets – including money, as well as houses, land, pictures, furniture and investments. Gifts made in certain circumstances or between certain people or bodies are free of IHT. This applies to the following gifts, whether you make them during your lifetime or as bequests in your will (see Chapter 8).

Inheritance-tax-free gifts at a glance

The following gifts are tax-free. Conditions may apply and are explained in this chapter.

Tax-free in lifetime and on death
- Gifts between husband and wife or civil partners
- Gifts to charities and some similar bodies
- Gifts of national heritage property
- Gifts to political parties
- Gifts to housing associations

Tax-free lifetime gifts
- Normal expenditure out of income
- Gifts for the maintenance of your family
- Lottery syndicates and similar arrangements
- Yearly tax-free exemption
- Small gifts
- Wedding gifts
- PETs if you survive seven years

> Most lifetime gifts you make are either free of IHT or count as PETs.

 For information about which gifts count as PETs and how they are taxed, see page 55.

Gifts between husband and wife or between civil partners

Gifts between husband and wife or between civil partners up to any amount are tax-free as long as the couple are not divorced (or the partnership hasn't been dissolved). Even a husband and wife or civil partners who are separated benefit from this exemption. If the husband, wife or civil partner receiving the gift is not '**domiciled**' in the UK, the exemption is limited to a total of £55,000. However, note that a person is automatically treated as UK-domiciled for IHT if they have been resident in the UK for 17 out of the last 20 years.

Gifts to charities and certain other bodies

This exemption from IHT is similar to the equivalent one for CGT (see page 26). It covers outright donations and gifts of any amount to UK charities, national museums and art galleries, universities, local authorities, government departments and a number of other bodies, including community amateur sports clubs.

Gifts of national heritage property

The gift of certain property, such as works of art, to a museum, art gallery, the National Trust or similar body, university, local authority or government department may be exempt from IHT. The transfer of

 Domicile Your place of domicile is broadly where you make your permanent home and intend to end your days. However, for the purposes of IHT, you are treated as still UK-domiciled during the first three years after you have acquired a domicile in another country, or if you have been a UK resident for 17 of the last 20 tax years.

such property to HMRC in lieu of paying IHT (see page 181) is also exempt.

Eligible property can include pictures, prints, books, manuscripts, works of art and scientific objects, provided they are 'pre-eminent' for their national, scientific, historic or artistic interest. Buildings and land of outstanding scenic, historic or scientific interest and items associated with them are also eligible.

A gift of eligible property to anyone else can be conditionally exempt from IHT. To qualify, the person who is receiving the gift must agree certain conditions with HMRC, including that the gifted property will stay in the UK, it will be properly maintained and preserved, and the public will have reasonable access to it.

You can't claim conditional exemption for a gift that is a PET (see page 55), but you can apply if the gift subsequently becomes chargeable because the giver died within seven years.

A claim for conditional exemption must be made within two years of the gift (or death in the case of a potentially exempt transfer). You (and/or your husband or wife) must have either owned the property for at least six years or inherited it on the death of the previous owner with a conditional exemption also applying to that transfer.

Gifts to political parties

A gift to a political party is exempt from IHT, provided the party has at least two MPs or polled at least 150,000 votes at the most recent general election.

Housing Associations

Gifts of land to a Registered Housing Association are exempt from IHT.

LIFETIME GIFTS THAT ARE FREE OF IHT

The following gifts are free of IHT only when they are made during your lifetime (so you can't get these exemptions for gifts you make through your will).

{ If you can show the gift you are making is one of a regular pattern, the gift will be exempt from IHT. }

Normal expenditure out of income

If you can show that a gift you are making is one of a regular pattern of similar gifts and that you are making it out of your income (rather than from your savings or other capital) and you have enough income left to maintain your normal standard of living, the gift will be exempt from IHT. For example, you might pay a regular sum each month into a grandchild's Child Trust Fund.

Normally, gifts under this exemption are cash. If you make gifts that are not cash, you will have to be able to prove that the things you are giving were bought out of your current income.

Gifts made under a legally binding agreement, such as a deed of covenant, will usually be treated as regular gifts. So too will premiums you pay for an insurance policy or contributions to a pension scheme that is for the benefit of someone else: for example, a policy on your life, which would pay out to your children in the event of your death. If the gifts are not made under any formal agreement but you intend that they will be regular gifts, they can still qualify for the exemption.

The gifts do not necessarily have to be regular payments to one person. They could form a regular pattern of giving to different people – for example, gifts to each of your grandchildren on their coming of age or large gifts to each of your children on their marriage (smaller gifts would be covered by the wedding exemption – see page 33).

HMRC decide each case on its merits. Usually it gets involved only after death when the personal representatives of someone who has died are claiming the exemption for gifts made within the seven years before death. But occasionally you might want to establish with HMRC during your lifetime that your gifts will form a regular pattern. If that is not clear at the time of the first few gifts, HMRC might agree provisionally to allow you the exemption, but they will review your case later on to see if you really have carried on making gifts as you intended.

The gifts must be made out of your current income and you must be able to show that you have enough income left to meet your day-to-day living expenses. HMRC's own guidance to its tax officers states that *'income is not defined but should be determined in accordance with normal accountancy rules; it does not necessarily coincide with income for income tax purposes'*. This is an example of HMRC interpreting a grey area of legislation in a particular way. It may result in some of the money you regularly live on being excluded from the measurement of your income for the purpose of this IHT exemption. Income definitely includes earnings from a job, interest from investments, dividends from shares. But, for example, if you have bought a purchased life annuity, part of the 'income' you get counts as return of your capital so cannot be used to fund gifts under this IHT exemption. Similarly, some life insurance-based investments (such as with-profits bonds and single premium bonds)

let you withdraw each year up to 5 per cent of the amount you have invested as an 'income', but again this is not income for the purpose of this IHT exemption. And if you have paid a lump sum to buy an immediate care plan to pay residential care home fees, the regular pay-outs from the plan do not count as income, even though the care home fees are counted as expenditure to maintain your normal living standards.

Immediate care plan A special type of annuity where, in exchange for a lump sum, a regular income is paid for the rest of your life. This income is tax-free if paid direct to a care provider.

Purchased life annuity An investment where you swap a lump sum for a regular income usually payable for the rest of your life but not the type of annuity you buy as part of a pension arrangement.

Case Study BAHIYA

Bahiya, who is in her 60s, shares her home with her son, Maalik. She realises that when she dies, there is likely to be an IHT bill on her estate and that Maalik might be forced to sell their home to pay it. To avoid this situation, Bahiya pays £270 a month for a whole life insurance policy that will pay out a lump sum direct to Maalik on her death. He will then be able to use the sum to pay the IHT due. Because the policy is for Maalik's benefit, the premiums count as gifts from Bahiya. They are exempt gifts for IHT because Bahiya pays them regularly as part of her normal spending out of her income.

For more information about how your regular gifts might be treated for IHT, call HMRC's IHT and Probate Helpline on 0845 302 0900.

Gifts for the maintenance of your family

Money or things that you give to provide housing, food, education, or some other form of maintenance, for your husband or wife, civil partner, ex-husband or ex-wife, ex-civil partner, children or a dependent relative are all outside the IHT net.

As far as husband and wife or civil partners are concerned, the normal exemption for gifts between married couples and civil partners (see page 29) would usually apply rather than this exemption. But if the recipient husband, wife or civil partner is domiciled (see page 29) abroad, this exemption could be useful. This exemption will usually cover maintenance agreements made as a result of a marriage breakdown or dissolution of a civil partnership.

The definition of children is very wide, covering stepchildren, illegitimate and adopted children, but it does not extend to grandchildren.

Usually a child is considered to be adult when he or she reaches the age of 18 but, if he or she goes on to full-time education or training after that age, the IHT exemption carries on. This means, for example, that money you give a student son or daughter to support them while at university is exempt from IHT.

A 'dependent relative' can be any relative of you or your husband or wife who is unable to maintain him or herself because of old age or infirmity. It also includes your mother or mother-in-law, even if not elderly or infirm, if they are widowed, separated or divorced. As a concession, this exemption is also extended to gifts to your mother if she is unmarried, provided she is financially dependent on you.

Lottery syndicates and similar arrangements

There is no IHT to pay on the transfer of winnings to members of a syndicate set up to share wins from schemes such as the National Lottery and football pools, provided the money is shared out according to an agreement that was drawn up in advance of the win. The agreement could be just oral but it is better to have a written agreement. So, if you and your family or friends often daydream about how you would give each other part of a really big win, it might be a good idea to draw up a formal arrangement now.

> Money you give a student son or daughter to support him or her while at university is exempt from IHT.

 HMRC have withdrawn all their information leaflets about IHT. Instead, their guidance is published on the internet at www.hmrc.gov.uk/inheritancetax/.

Case Study GRAHAM

Graham, 70, has played the National Lottery every week since it started. He often talked about how he would share a big win with his two children and his sister. Even so, he was stunned when he won over £900,000. He gave £200,000 each to his sister and children. This was in line with the plan he had discussed, but it would have been better if he had written it down. There will be no problem if he survives seven years after making the gifts, but, if he dies within that time, HMRC may query with his personal representatives whether the gifts really were exempt and argue instead that they should be treated as PETs (that become taxable gifts on death within seven years).

Every tax year you can give away £3,000-worth of gifts. This exemption is in addition to the other exemptions.

Yearly tax-free exemption

Every tax year, you can give away £3,000-worth of gifts without their counting in any way for IHT purposes. This exemption is in addition to the other exemptions, so a gift that qualifies for some other exemption does not count towards the £3,000 annual limit.

If you do not use up the full exemption one year, you can carry it forward to the next year – but not to any subsequent year. This means that, if you used none of last year's exemption, you could make up to £6,000-worth of gifts this year that qualify for the exemption. Gifts always use up the exemption for the tax year in which they are made first before using up any carried-forward exemption.

Small gifts

You can make as many gifts as you like totalling up to £250 to each person, and these will be exempt. You cannot combine the small gift exemption with another exemption to give more than £250 to one person but you can, say, give £3,000 to one recipient and gifts of £250 to any number of other people.

This exemption will generally cover birthday and Christmas presents, and any other small gifts you make during the year.

Wedding and civil partnership gifts

As a parent, you can give up to £5,000 to the happy couple free of IHT. A grandparent (or other ancestor) can give up to £2,500. Anyone else can give up to £1,000. The bride and groom or partners can give up to

For details of how PETs are taxed, see page 55.

£2,500 to each other, but this limit will not be relevant if both are domiciled in the UK, since the exemption for married couples and civil partners will apply – gifts between spouses and civil partners are tax-free.

The exemptions apply to each giver: for example, assuming both sets of parents of the bride and groom or partners were still living, the couple could receive a maximum of £20,000 from their parents IHT-free.

Usually, gifts under this exemption will be outright gifts. But the exemption can also apply to gifts put into trust for the benefit of the bride, groom or civil partners, their children or the husbands or wives of their children.

PETs

A PET (potentially exempt transfer) is a gift from one person to another (or to a few types of trust – see Chapter 4) that is not covered by some other IHT exemption. As long as the person making the gift survives for seven years after the date of the gift, there is no IHT to pay. If the giver dies

{ The couple could receive a maximum of £20,000 from their parents IHT-free. }

within seven years, there may be a tax bill. PETs are looked at in detail in Chapter 3.

SUMMARY

This chapter has considered the two main taxes that may affect your giving and inheriting: CGT and IHT. With both taxes, especially IHT, there are lots of exemptions that can help you to make tax-free lifetime gifts. The most useful IHT exemptions include gifts up to any amount, provided they are part of your normal spending out of income; gifts up to any amount to maintain children (for example, to help them through university); and your annual £3,000 exemption.

You need to choose your gifts carefully to ensure that they are free from CGT as well as IHT. There is no problem with gifts between husbands and wife or civil partners, since these are normally exempt from both CGT and IHT. Gifts of cash up to any amount and 'chattels' (such as antiques and paintings) worth up to £6,000 are free from CGT and so can be a particularly good choice.

It is important to bear in mind that there is no CGT on things that you leave on death. Where something you own has increased in value substantially, it may be more tax-efficient to pass it on in your will rather than give it away in your lifetime.

TAXABLE LIFETIME GIFTS

If you give away something not covered by any of the exemptions described in the previous chapter, there is a risk of tax on the gift. But, by timing your gifts to make best use of the various reliefs and allowances, you may be able to reduce the tax bill or eliminate it altogether. The two main taxes you need to worry about are Capital Gains Tax (CGT) and Inheritance Tax (IHT). They work in very different ways.

TAXES YOU NEED TO CONSIDER

I n some cases, you may want to make a lifetime gift but be unable to arrange it as a tax-free gift. Often the problem is CGT rather than IHT.

WHAT'S IN THIS CHAPTER?

Chapter 2 looked at arranging your giving so that it is tax-free, but this is not always possible. In that case, it is important to know how tax may affect your gifts, what you can do to minimise or eliminate the tax bill, and who will be responsible for paying any tax due. This chapter looks at:

- How CGT may affect your lifetime gifts, even when they are free of IHT (see opposite).
- How IHT may affect lifetime gifts and what you leave on death, even where CGT does not apply (page 48).
- Special rules that can protect business and similar assets from either or both of these taxes (page 59). These are just touched on briefly and you are recommended to get professional advice from an accountant or solicitor if you run a business.

WHEN TAX MAY BE A PROBLEM

Unless you are making a gift to a trust, there is considerable scope to arrange lifetime gifts so that they are free of IHT. But, to escape CGT as well often requires careful planning.

There is no difficulty if you are making a gift to your husband, wife or civil partner or to a charity since, as you saw in Chapter 2, these are CGT-free as well as normally being exempt from IHT. But, in other cases, to avoid CGT you need to think carefully about the type of asset you are giving away or the timing of your gift. For example, can you give cash or, say, a painting or possession that falls within the special rules for chattels? Can you give away something on which you will have made a loss rather than a gain? If not, is it possible to split a gift in two so that you can make use of two tax-free allowances rather than one?

With the few types of lifetime gift that could give rise to an immediate IHT bill, the key is to make good use of your tax-free limit.

An awareness of how these two taxes work will help you plan your way around them to make your gifts as tax-efficient as possible.

HOW CAPITAL GAINS TAX WORKS

C apital gains are the profits you make as a result of something increasing in value during the time you have owned it. You are taxed on these gains when you dispose of the asset, which includes giving it away.

CGT has, in the past, been an extremely complicated tax but was greatly simplified from 6 April 2008. Where you make gifts (or other disposals) on or after that date, you calculate whether any tax is due and how much following the steps in the illustration overleaf.

NO TAX TO PAY?

Chapter 2 looked at gifts that are specifically exempt from CGT. But even if your gift is not exempt – for example, if you are giving away shares, a second home or a valuable heirloom – there could still be no tax to pay, because of:

- **Special reliefs.** You may be able to deduct part or all of the value if, say, the asset has been your only or main home at some time (see page 40) or this is a business asset (see page 59).
- **Losses.** You reduce gains by deducting losses that are made on other assets.

- **Tax-free limit.** Everyone can make several thousands of pounds of gains each year, which are automatically tax-free.

See the illustration overleaf, which shows how the taxable gain on something you give away can be reduced.

Your first step in working out what tax might be due is to calculate the basic gain on the asset you are giving away – use the calculator on page 39.

{ Everyone can make several thousands of pounds of gains each year, which are auto-matically tax-free. }

CGT: an overview

For gifts on or after 6 April 2008, use this illustration to see how the value on which CGT is levied can be reduced

| The asset you give away | Value of the asset at the time you started to own it | Increase in value during the time you have owned the asset |

| There may be tax on this part | Increase in value during the time you have owned the asset |

| You take away any special reliefs, eg if the asset is your home or business | Special reliefs |

| And you subtract any losses you've made on other assets in the same year | Losses |

| You also subtract any losses on other assets carried forward from earlier years | Losses |

| Last, you subtract your yearly tax-free allowance | Tax-free allowance |

If there is nothing left, there is no tax

Basic gains calculator

Final value of the gift (A)

This will usually be the price you would have received if you had sold the asset on the open market.

A £ _____

Initial value of the gift (B)

This is the price you originally paid for it or its market value at the time you first became the owner.

B £ _____

Allowable expenses (C)

These are costs you incurred in acquiring and disposing of the asset (for example,

commission paid to a broker, the cost of an expert valuation or solicitor's fees, stamp duty paid on the purchase of a property or shares) and any expenses associated with enhancing the value of the asset (e.g. adding an extension to a property), but not spending on maintenance and repairs.

C £ _____

THE BASIC GAIN (D)

Work out A − B − C to find the basic gain.

D £ _____

Case Study CAROLE

Carole bought a holiday cottage in May 1998 for £65,000. The buying costs amounted to £1,200. In August 1998, she added a conservatory at a cost of £1,700. In March 2011, Carole gave the cottage to her niece. It was then valued at £125,000 and the costs incurred in making the transfer amounted to £1,500. Carole is deemed to have made a basic gain on the gift as follows:

Final value of the cottage	£125,000
less initial value	£65,000
less allowable expenses (£1,200 + £1,700 + £1,500)	£4,400
Basic gain	£55,600

SOME SPECIAL RULES

If you are giving away something that you started to own on or before 31 March 1982, any gains that built up before that date are, in effect, tax-free. This is because you set the initial value equal to the item's value on that date. You can still deduct any allowable expenses incurred after 31 March 1982, but none that arose before then.

If the item you are giving away now was originally a gift to you, check whether you and the original giver claimed holdover relief (see pages 58 and 59). If so, your initial value will not be the value on the date you acquired the item. Instead it will be the initial value of the person who gave you the item. If that person acquired the item on or before 31 March 1982, the initial value using the holdover relief rules will be the value on that date.)

If you are giving away just part of something – for example, half a holiday home that you own – you will need to work out the relevant proportion of the initial value and allowable expenses. If expenses clearly relate to the part you are keeping or the part being given away, you simply claim those expenses relating to the gift but not those relating to the part you are keeping. If it is impossible to divide up an expense in this way, you split the expense by multiplying by the following fraction:

$$\frac{\text{Final value of the part given away}}{\text{Final value of the whole item}}$$

For example, suppose you are giving away a flat worth £130,000 in a property valued at £390,000 and you spent £9,000 adding solar panels to the roof of the whole property. You would be able to deduct from the value of the gift this much of the cost of the solar panels as an allowable expense: £130,000 ÷ £390,000 × £9,000 = £3,000.

But there are different rules for splitting the initial value and allowable expenses for shares, unit trusts and similar investments – see page 44.

SPECIAL RELIEFS

You have already seen how any gain when you give, sell or dispose of your only or main home is usually free of CGT (see page 23). This exemption is called 'private residence relief'. But in some circumstances, you may qualify for relief on just part, but not all, of such a gain. This might occur, for example, if the property was not your home for all of the time that you owned it. However, some periods of absence are ignored:

- **The first year** (sometimes up to two years) if you cannot live there because of building work, provided you do then move in.
- **Up to four years in total** during which your employer requires you to work away from home in the UK, provided you lived there before the first spell away and after the last.
- **Unlimited periods** while you are required to work abroad, provided that you lived there before the first spell away and after the last.

- **Up to a total of three years** of absences for any other reasons, provided you lived there before the first spell away and after the last.
- **The last three years of ownership,** as long as this has genuinely been your main home at some time.

Any other periods of absence can give rise to a capital gain. To work out whether there is tax to pay, you calculate the basic gain as normal and then multiply it by:

$$\frac{\text{Number of complete months of absence}}{\text{Number of complete months you owned the property}}$$

If you have rented out the property during your absence, as long as the property was your main home at some time, you may be able to reduce a gain on which tax would otherwise be due by claiming 'letting relief'. Letting relief is a deduction set equal to the lower of: £40,000, the amount of the gain, or the amount of private residence relief you get. This sounds complicated, but the case study for Bill, right, illustrates how this works.

Part of the gain from giving away a home could be taxable if you have used part of the home exclusively for business.

Another important special relief, called entrepreneur's relief, may apply if you are giving away a business or assets used in your business – see page 60 for information about this.

Having worked out the amount of any special reliefs you can claim, you deduct them from the basic value that you calculated above.

Case Study BILL

Bill bought his home in Dorset in May 1988 for £70,000. In September 1999, he moved to Sheffield and bought a new home there. Rather than selling his Dorset home, he let it. But, in February 2011, he gave the property to his daughter, Angela. At the time of the gift, the Dorset property was valued at £225,000.

Bill owned his Dorset home from May 1988 to February 2011, a period of 273 complete months. He lived there from May 1988 to September 1999, a period of 136 complete months. Adding in the last three years of ownership, 172 months qualify for private residence relief.

The basic gain on the property is £225,000 – £70,000 = £155,000. Bill can also claim a variety of allowable expenses that reduce the basic gain to £130,000. Of this, 172 ÷ 273 × £130,000 = £81,905 is covered by private residence relief and so tax-free. The remaining 101 ÷ 273 × £130,000 = £48,095 is potentially taxable. However, the home has been let, so Bill can claim letting relief. This will be set equal to the lower of: £40,000; the otherwise taxable gain, which is £48,095; or the private residence relief, which is £81,905. The lowest of these three amounts is £40,000.

Therefore, in total Bill can claim special reliefs of £121,905 and has a taxable gain of £130,000 – £81,905 – £40,000 = £8,095. From this, he can deduct any losses and his yearly tax-free limit.

To find out more about private residence relief and letting relief, see the HMRC Helpsheet 283 *Private residence relief* available from www.hmrc.gov.uk or the Revenue Orderline 0845 900 0404.

ALLOWABLE LOSSES

If you have given away, sold or disposed of more than one item during the tax year, you carry out the calculations described above for each item and then add together all the gains on which tax may be due. The next step is to subtract any allowable losses. This is done in two stages.

First you subtract any losses you have made in the same tax year. If your losses for this year come to more than your gains, your gains are reduced to zero and you can carry forward the unused losses to future years. (You cannot carry losses back to earlier years, although on death your executors may be able to do so.)

If your losses come to less than your gains for this year, next you subtract any losses that you have been carrying forward from earlier tax years. But you deduct only so much of these earlier losses as is needed to reduce your gains to the amount of your tax-free limit for the year (see opposite). Any losses not used up continue to be carried forward to future years.

As you can see, losses made in the same tax year can reduce your gains below the amount of your tax-free limit, meaning that the allowance could be wasted. Therefore, you might want to plan the timing of your gifts and sales to make the best use of your allowance each year – see the case study for Elspeth.

If you don't know the initial value of the item you are giving away, a professional valuer may be able to help, for example, a member of the National Association of Valuers and Auctioneers (see www.nava.org.uk). For quoted shares, use a historic share price service (for example, www.londonstockexchange.com). There is a charge for these services.

HOW MUCH TAX?

There is just one more allowance to consider, then you can work out your final tax bill.

Yearly tax-free limit

If you are deemed to have made a taxable gain on an asset you gave away, there could be some tax to pay, but not necessarily. Everyone has a tax-free limit. This means the first slice of taxable gains that you make each year is tax-free. In 2011–12, you can have net taxable gains of £10,600 before any CGT becomes payable. The tax-free limit for earlier years is shown in the table, below.

Yearly CGT allowance

TAX YEAR	TAX-FREE LIMIT
2008–9	£9,600
2009–10	£10,100
2010–11	£10,100
2011–12	£10,600

{ In 2011–12, you can have net chargeable gains of £10,600 before any CGT becomes payable. }

Working out the tax bill

Since 23 June 2010, CGT has been charged at two rates: 18 per cent and 28 per cent. To find out which rate applies to your gain, add your taxable gains to your taxable income for the year and look up the rate in the table overleaf.

If your taxable income is below the threshold for the 28 per cent rate but adding the gain takes the total above the threshold, you pay 18 per cent CGT on the part of the gain below the threshold and 28 per cent on the part of the gain above the threshold. For example, suppose in 2011–12, your taxable income is £34,000 and you have a taxable gain of £3,000. Your taxable income is £1,000 below the higher-rate threshold, so £1,000 of the gain is taxed at 18 per cent and £2,000 at 28 per cent. This gives a tax bill of (18% × £1,000) + (28% × £2,000) = £740.

You can also view CGT rates and allowances on the HMRC website at www.hmrc.gov.uk/rates/cgt.htm.

Tax rates on chargeable gains

IF YOUR GAINS PLUS TAXABLE INCOME EQUAL:			THIS TAX RATE APPLIES:
Band	2010–11 [1]	2011–12	
Up to the higher-rate threshold	Up to £37,400	Up to £35,000	18%
Above the higher-rate threshold	Over £37,400	Over £35,000	28%

[1] From 23 June 2010 onwards. Between 6 April and 22 June 2010, a single rate of 18 per cent applied to all gains.

Note that, although tax on the gain is worked out using information about your taxable income, the CGT bill does not in any way affect the way your income is taxed.

Case Study **PAUL**

In the 2011–12 tax year, Paul has net chargeable gains of £15,000. He deducts the tax-free limit of £10,600, leaving taxable gains of £4,400. Paul's taxable income for the year is £34,000. The tax on his gains is worked out as follows:

Part of gains below £35,000 threshold	£1,000
Part of gains in excess of £35,000 threshold	£3,400
CGT at 18% on £1,000	£180
CGT at 28% on £3,400	£952
Total CGT bill	£1,132

{ Special rules are needed to identify which shares you are disposing of. }

SPECIAL RULES FOR SOME TYPES OF ASSETS OR GIFTS

There are some additional rules to take into account if you are giving away shares, unit trusts or chattels, or you are making a gift to your husband, wife or civil partner.

Shares and unit trusts

If you give away identical shares, unit trusts or other securities that you acquired all at the same time, the CGT rules apply in the same way as for any other asset. But suppose you own shares in one company, all of the same type but bought at different times. Special rules are needed to identify which shares you are disposing of, so that you can use the correct initial value and allowable expenses.

For gifts and other disposals made on or after 6 April 2008, the shares you give away are matched to the ones you own in the following order:

- **Shares you bought on the same day.**
- **Shares purchased within the following 30 days.** This rule was introduced to curb a practice called 'bed-and-breakfasting'. You used to be able to realise a capital gain or loss by selling shares one day and buying them back the next. Such a move could be very tax-efficient – for example, crystallising enough gain each year to use up your tax-free limit. Now, you need to leave at least 30 days between selling the shares and buying them back.
- **All the rest of your shares.** These are pooled together and treated as if they were a single asset. If you give away some of the shares, you are treated as if you are giving away part of the asset, using the rule

described on page 40 to work out the appropriate proportion of the initial value and allowable expenses. The case study for Connie, overleaf, demonstrates how this works.

> The 30-day rule does not apply if you sell shares you own direct and buy them back within an ISA ('bed-and-ISA').

Planning point

The 30-day share-matching rule means you cannot crystallise a capital gain or loss by selling shares one day and buying them back the next. But the 30-day rule does not apply in the following circumstances: you sell shares you own direct and buy them back within an Individual Savings Account ('bed-and-ISA'); you sell shares you own and your spouse or civil partner buys the same shares; you sell shares in one company and buy shares in a different but very similar company. Using these techniques could help you wipe out some or all of a taxable gain before making a gift of the assets.

It is doubtful that using, say, the bed-and-ISA arrangement above to crystallise a loss to set against your

capital gains for the same year and so reduce CGT would work. In 2006, a new tax-avoidance law was introduced that prevents you claiming as an allowable loss, any loss that results from an arrangement where the main purpose is to save tax. This is a very widely drawn piece of legislation and it has been left to the Revenue to say that, in its opinion, it should not apply to, for example, timing your losses to set against your gains, or giving assets to your husband, wife or civil partner so they can sell at a loss to reduce their gains. Provided there is a genuine change of ownership or you are exposed to a real commercial risk (by, for example, being out of the stock market for 30 days), it seems that any resulting loss should be allowable.

Connie was given 300 shares in an information technology company in April 1997 and she bought further shares in the company in 1998, 1999 and again in 2000, as shown in the table below.

Date of purchase	Number of shares	Share price	Total paid	Allowable expenses
4 April 1997	300	15p	£45	£0
9 April 1998	1,700	34p	£578	£17
2 November 1999	500	105p	£525	£17
16 July 2000	700	67p	£469	£15
TOTALS	3,200		£1,617	£49

Connie chose well as this company proved to be one of the survivors when the dot.com bubble burst. In October 2010, when the total shareholding was valued at £10,000, she gave a quarter of the shares (800 shares) to her niece, Harriet.

The final value of the shares she gave away was deemed to be 800 ÷ 3,200 × £10,000 = £2,500. The initial value was deemed to be 800 ÷ 3,200 × £1,617 = £405 and the allowable expenses 800 ÷ 3,200 × £49 = £13. This produced a basic gain of £2,500 – £405 – £13 = £2,082 (which was easily covered by Connie's tax-free limit, so there was no tax to pay).

After the gift, Connie holds 3,200 – 800 = 2,400 shares with an initial value of £1,617 – £405 = £1,212 and allowable expenses of £49 – £13 = £36.

Chattels

'Chattels' means personal possessions, such as pictures, furniture, antiques, jewellery and other collectibles.

There is no CGT on gifts of chattels with a predictable life of 50 years or less or on more durable chattels where they are valued at £6,000 or less (see Chapter 2). For chattels worth more than £6,000, special rules apply that can reduce the tax you pay. The chargeable gain is the lower of either five-thirds of the excess of the disposal value over £6,000 or the gain worked out in the normal way.

Gifts between husband and wife or between civil partners

There is no CGT on a gift between a husband and wife or between civil partners (see Chapter 2) and the transfer is said to be made on a no-gain-no-loss basis. What this means becomes important if the recipient subsequently sells or gives away the asset, because in order to work out any CGT bill, you need to know about the two points described on the next page.

- **Date of acquisition.** For CGT, the spouse or civil partner receiving the gift started to own the asset from the date of the gift.
- **Initial value.** The recipient is treated as if the value on that date is the initial value which applied to the spouse or civil partner making the gift plus any allowable expenses the giver qualified for. In effect, the recipient has taken over the giver's initial value and allowable expenses.

Case Study **SAMIR**

Samir bought a paddock for £5,000 in May 1996. He incurred allowable expenses of £315. In October 2007, he gives the paddock to his wife, Mel. In June 2011, Mel sells the paddock for £12,000. To work out whether CGT is due, Mel needs to do the following calculations:

- Final value: £12,000.
- Deduct initial value: £5,315 (Samir's initial value plus Samir's allowable expenses).
- Deduct Mel's allowable expenses: £300 in solicitor's fees.
- This gives a gain of:
  £12,000 – £5,315 – £300 = £6,385.

TELLING HMRC

If you have taxable gains and you receive a full-length tax return, you need to complete the capital gains supplement. If your tax affairs are fairly straightforward, you may instead be sent a short four-page tax return. There is no place on the short return to report capital gains. You need either form R40(CG) or the full return instead.

To avoid penalties, file your 2011 tax return no later than 31 January 2012 if you use the online filing service or 31 October 2011 if you are sending in a paper return. (You can either use the HMRC's free online service or buy commercial software.) 31 January 2012 is also the deadline for paying any CGT. Your tax office will work out your tax bill for you, provided you get your return back by 31 October. Alternatively, the online software should tell you how much tax you owe.

If you don't get a tax return, you must tell your tax office about any taxable capital gains by 5 October following the end of the tax year in which you made the gains. There is no need to report disposals if you have no tax to pay.

You must keep records of the information that backs up your return for one year following the date on which you filed the return (longer if you are in business). Your tax office can ask to see these records and fine you if you can't produce them.

To find out about filing your tax returns online, visit the HMRC website at www.hmrc.gov.uk/sa/file-online.htm. The HMRC site includes a list of commercial tax software suppliers at www.hmrc.gov.uk/efiling/sa_efiling/soft_dev.htm.

HOW INHERITANCE TAX WORKS

M ost lifetime gifts escape IHT. But some are taxable when they are made and many become taxable if the giver dies.

Chapter 1 listed lifetime gifts that are always free of IHT. Other gifts you make will be either:

- **Taxable gifts** (more formally called 'chargeable transfers'). This includes gifts to most types of trust. This chapter explains how taxable gifts are treated for IHT. See Chapter 4 for information about using trusts, or
- **PETs (potentially exempt transfers),** which mainly covers outright gifts to people (but also gifts into trust for a disabled person – see Chapter 4).

The value of a gift for IHT is the loss to the giver (which may differ from the value to the recipient).

TAXABLE GIFTS

The main lifetime gifts that are taxable are most gifts to trusts. When you make a taxable gift there may be a tax bill at the time you make the gift. If you die within the following seven years, the recipient could also be charged extra tax.

How taxable gifts are taxed

IHT does not apply to each gift you make in isolation. It is based on all the taxable gifts you have made over the last seven years. Adding all these gifts together gives you a 'cumulative total' – called your 'running total' in this book. The first slice of the running total – up to £325,000 in 2011–12 and fixed at this level until 2014–15 – is tax-free. You pay tax only on a gift (or part of it) that spills over the tax-free limit – see the illustration on page 50.

The tax-free limit is normally increased each tax year broadly in line with price inflation but, as part of the austerity measures following the global financial crisis of 2007, the Government pre-announced that the limit would be frozen until April 2015.

The IHT rate on lifetime gifts is set at half the rate of tax that may apply to your estate when you die. The death rate for the 2011–12 tax year is 40 per cent; so the lifetime rate is 20 per cent.

 HMRC have withdrawn all their information leaflets about IHT. Instead, their guidance is published on the internet at www.hmrc.gov.uk/inheritancetax/.

IHT tax-free limit

The tax-free limit for IHT used to be increased in line with inflation, but changes have been erratic in recent years. From 2009–10 until 2014–15, the limit is frozen at £325,000. The rates of IHT (40 per cent on death and 20 per cent on lifetime transfers) have been unchanged since 1988.

Married couples and civil partners can pass on any of their IHT allowance that is unused when they die to their surviving spouse or civil partner (see page 126). To establish if there is any unused allowance, you may need to know the IHT limits for an earlier tax year in which a spouse or civil partner died. The limits going back to 1986 (when IHT started) are shown below. For earlier years (when Capital Transfer Tax and Estate Duty applied), visit the HMRC website at www.hmrc.gov.uk/rates/iht-thresholds.htm.

Who pays the tax?

IHT due on a lifetime gift at the time the gift is made can be paid either by the person or trust making the gift or by the person or trust receiving the gift. If the giver pays, the tax itself counts as part of the gift, increasing the value of the transfer to be taxed. A gift where the giver pays the tax is called a '**net gift**'; if the recipient pays the tax, it is called a '**gross gift**'. You can work out how much tax is due on a net or gross gift using the calculators on pages 52–3.

> **Gross gift** A gift where the person receiving the gift pays any tax due.
>
> **Net gift** A gift where the person making the gift pays any tax due.
>
> **Nil-rate band** Another name for the IHT-free limit.

Death within seven years

Tax on a lifetime gift that is a chargeable transfer is usually charged at a rate of 20 per cent (in 2011–12). But, if the person making the gift dies within seven years, the gift is reassessed and tax is recalculated using the tax-free limit and death rate current at the time of death (£325,000 and 40 per cent for 2011–12). If the giver dies more than three years but less than seven years after making the (continued on page 54)

IHT tax-free limits, 1986–2015

TAX YEAR	TAX-FREE LIMIT	TAX YEAR	TAX-FREE LIMIT	TAX YEAR	TAX-FREE LIMIT
1986–87	£71,000	1996–97	£200,000	2006–07	£285,000
1987–88	£90,000	1997–98	£215,000	2007–08	£300,000
1988–89	£110,000	1998–99	£223,000	2008–09	£312,000
1989–90	£118,000	1999–2000	£231,000	2009–10	£325,000
1990–91	£128,000	2000–01	£234,000	2000–11	£325,000
1991–92	£140,000	2001–02	£242,000	2011–12	£325,000
1992–93	£150,000	2002–03	£250,000	2012–13	£325,000
1993–94	£150,000	2003–04	£255,000	2013–14	£325,000
1994–95	£150,000	2004–05	£263,000	2004–15	£325,000
1995–96	£154,000	2005–06	£275,000		

IHT: an overview

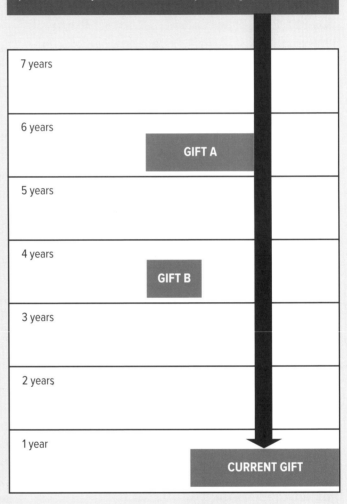

The asset you give away

This may be a lifetime gift or your estate at death
(On death, what you leave is treated as your final gift)

If your current gift is taxable, it is added to any other taxable gifts you have made during the seven years up to the time of this gift

7 years

6 years

GIFT A

5 years

4 years

GIFT B

3 years

2 years

1 year

CURRENT GIFT

{ IHT is based on all the taxable gifts you have made over the last seven years. }

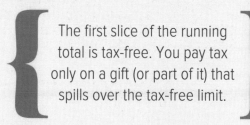

The first slice of the running total is tax-free. You pay tax only on a gift (or part of it) that spills over the tax-free limit.

You have a tax-free limit

──────────── Tax-free limit (the nil-rate band) ────────────

Taxable gifts over the last seven years use up the limit in the order the gifts were made

| GIFT A | GIFT B | CURRENT GIFT |

──────────── Tax-free limit (the nil-rate band) ────────────

If the current gift falls within the limit, no tax is due

| GIFT A | GIFT B | CURRENT GIFT |

──────────── Tax-free limit (the nil-rate band) ────────────

If part or all of the current gift falls above the limit, tax is due

| GIFT A | GIFT B | | CURRENT | GIFT |

──────────── Tax-free limit (the nil-rate band) ────────────

Taxable part of gift

TAXABLE LIFETIME GIFTS

A net gift is when the giver pays the tax.

Running total before your latest gift (A)
Add up all the taxable gifts you have made during the last seven years. If you paid the IHT on any of those gifts, include the tax you paid.

A £ _____

Tax on your running total (B)
If amount A is £325,000 or less, tax is £0. If amount A is greater than £325,000, tax is 20% of the excess, in other words, 20% × (A − £325,000).

B £ _____

Your net running total (C)
Work out A − B.

C £ _____

Your current gift (D)
Enter the value of the gift you are now making. Use the amount that the recipient will receive.

D £ _____

Your new net running total (E)
Work out C + D.

E £ _____

Tax on your new running total (F)
If amount E is £325,000 or less, tax is £0. If amount E is greater than £325,000, tax is 25% [1] of the excess, in other words, 25% × (E − £325,000).

F £ _____

TAX ON THE CURRENT GIFT (G)
Work out F − B to find the amount of tax to be paid by the giver on the current gift.

G £ _____

[1] This percentage is derived as follows. The gross value of the gift is found by dividing the net gift by (1 − 20%): a process called grossing up. To find the tax due on the gift, the grossed-up value is multiplied by the lifetime IHT rate of 20%. But 20% ÷ (1 − 20%) = 20% ÷ 80% = 25%, so we can simply multiply the net gift by 25%.

A gross gift is when the recipient pays the tax.

Running total before your latest gift (A)

Add up all the taxable gifts you have made during the last seven years. If you paid the IHT on any of those gifts, include the tax you paid.

A £ _____

Tax on your running total (B)

If amount A is £325,000 or less, tax is £0. If amount A is greater than £325,000, tax is 20% of the excess, in other words, 20% × (A – £325,000).

B £ _____

Your current gift (C)

Enter the value of the gift you are now making. Use the amount that you are giving.

C £ _____

Your new running total (D)

Work out A + C.

D £ _____

Tax on your new running total (E)

If amount D is £325,000 or less, tax is £0. If amount D is greater than £325,000, tax is 20% of the excess, in other words, 20% × (E – £325,000).

E £ _____

TAX ON THE CURRENT GIFT (F)

Work out E – B to find the amount of tax to be paid by the recipient on the current gift.

F £ _____

gift, the full death rate is reduced by IHT taper relief – see below.

Various factors influence whether any extra tax might be due:

IHT taper relief

YEARS BETWEEN GIFT AND DEATH	% OF FULL DEATH RATE WHICH APPLIES (AT 2011–12 RATES)	% RATE OF TAX ON THE GIFT
Up to 3	100	40
More than 3 and up to 4	80	32
More than 4 and up to 5	60	24
More than 5 and up to 6	40	16
More than 6 and up to 7	20	8
More than 7	0	no extra tax

■ Tax on the reassessed gift is worked out using the tax-free limit and death rate at the time of death. The tax-free limit will normally be higher than the limit that applied at the time of the gift. The death tax rate will normally be higher than the lifetime rate but this will not necessarily be so if the Government has since changed the rates.

■ PETs made within seven years of death are reclassified as taxable gifts (see opposite). If they were made before the taxable gift being reassessed, the PETs will now use up part of the tax-free limit that had previously been available for the taxable gift.

Case Study FREDERICK 1

Frederick wants to set up a discretionary trust to make sure that his two grown-up children and any future grandchildren will have a 'last resort' emergency fund to help them out if the need arises. (For more about discretionary trusts, see Chapter 4.)

Frederick sets up the trust on 1 October 2011 with a gift of £70,000. He will pay any tax due on this, so it is a net gift. As Frederick has not used any of his annual exemption of £3,000 for 2011–12 (see page 33), only £67,000 is taxable. Over the seven years from 2 October 2004 to 1 October 2011, he has made other taxable gifts of £300,000. He uses the calculator for net gifts on page 52 to work out his IHT position as follows:

■ **Amount A:** Frederick's running total before making the gift is £300,000
■ **Amount B:** The running total is less than £325,000 so the tax on it is £0
■ **Amount C:** The net running total is £300,000
■ **Amount D:** He enters the value of the gift, using the amount the trust will receive: £67,000
■ **Amount E:** Adding C and D gives a new net running total of £367,000
■ **Amount F:** Tax on the new running total is 25% × (£367,000 – £325,000) = £10,500
■ **Amount G:** Subtracting B from F comes to £10,500 – £0 = £10,500. This is the amount of tax to be paid by Frederick on the gift to the trust.

Frederick's gift to the trust is made up of the £70,000 plus the £10,500 he pays in tax, making £80,500 in total.

 As well as extra tax on the gift, death within seven years may increase tax on your estate. See page 168 for an example of how lifetime gifts can affect tax on your estate at death.

Case Study FREDERICK 2

Suppose, in the previous case study, Frederick decided to give £70,000 to the trust, but leave the trust to pay any tax. The taxable gift of £67,000 would be a gross gift. Using the calculator on page 53 for gross gifts, the IHT position would be:

- **Amount A:** Frederick's running total before making the gift is £300,000
- **Amount B:** The running total is less than £325,000 so the tax on it is £0
- **Amount C:** He enters the value of gift, using the amount he is giving: £67,000
- **Amount D:** Adding A and C gives a new net running total of £367,000
- **Amount E:** Tax on his new running total is 20% × (£367,000 − £325,000) = £8,400
- **Amount F:** Subtracting B from E comes to £8,400 − £0 = £8,400. This is the amount of tax to be paid by the trust

The trust would receive £70,000 but £8,400 would have to be used to pay the IHT bill due on the transfer, leaving £61,600 in the trust fund.

Any extra tax due will be charged to the person who received the gift but, if they cannot or will not pay, the giver's estate must pay. There is no refund if the reassessed tax bill is lower than the original amount of tax paid.

the seven years before death, so extra tax might become due on them (see opposite).

- **The estate.** The PET becomes part of the running total of gifts made in the seven years before death, so may cause extra tax on the estate (see Chapter 7).

PETs

Gifts that are neither exempt (see Chapter 2) nor taxable are PETs. They are initially treated as exempt but, if you die within seven years, the clock is turned back and the PET reassessed as a taxable gift. This can have several effects:

- **The gift.** There may be a tax bill on the PET itself.
- **Other gifts.** The PET may become part of the running total of other PETs and taxable gifts made in

How the PET is taxed

If the giver dies within seven years, the PET is treated as if it had originally been a taxable gift. This does not necessarily mean tax becomes due, because of:

- **The yearly tax-free exemption.** If the exemption (see page 33) has not already been used, up to £3,000 (or £6,000 if the previous year's exemption is also unused) of the reclassified PET is tax-free.

 Either the giver or the recipient of a PET can take out insurance to cover a tax bill expected to arise if the giver dies within seven years – see Chapter 7.

How IHT taper relief reduces tax on a reassessed PET

YEARS BETWEEN MAKING THE PET AND DEATH	% OF FULL DEATH RATE WHICH APPLIES (AT 2011–12 RATES)	% RATE OF TAX ON THE GIFT
Up to 3	100	40
More than 3 and up to 4	80	32
More than 4 and up to 5	60	24
More than 5 and up to 6	40	16
More than 6 and up to 7	20	8
More than 7	0	no extra tax

■ **The tax-free limit.** Only if the running total of gifts in the seven years up to the PET exceeds the relevant tax-free limit will any tax become due. In the case of a reassessed PET, the relevant tax-free limit is the amount in force at the time of death (not at the time the gift was made). The limit is £325,000 if the giver died in the 2011–12 tax year.

If the running total up to the making of the reassessed PET does come to more than the tax-free limit, IHT is due at the rate current at the time

Case Study **GODFREY**

Godfrey dies on 1 January 2012. He made the following gifts during his lifetime (assume the annual tax-free exemption has already been used each year):

1 January 2002	Taxable gift	£129,000 to a discretionary trust
1 January 2004	Taxable gift	£70,000 to a discretionary trust
1 February 2005	Taxable gift	£68,000 to a discretionary trust
1 June 2007	PET	£80,000 to his nephew, John

On his death, taxable gifts and PETs made within the last seven years (2 January 2005 to 1 January 2012) are reassessed as follows:

■ **Taxable gift on 1 February 2005.** Tax was originally paid in 2004–5 on a running total of £129,000 + £70,000 + £68,000 = £267,000. The tax-free limit then was £263,000 and the trust paid tax at 20 per cent on the £4,000 of the gift that exceeded the limit: 20% × £4,000 = £800. When the gift is reassessed on Godfrey's death, there is no extra tax due because the running total of £267,000 is less than the tax-free limit of £325,000 in force at the time of death.

■ **PET on 1 June 2007.** No tax was charged on the PET at the time it was made. When it is reassessed on Godfrey's death, the PET becomes the top slice of £80,000 on a running total of £129,000 + £70,000 + £68,000 + £80,000 = £347,000. As the tax-free limit is £325,000, this leaves £22,000 of the PET to be taxed at the death rate of 40 per cent. So tax is initially calculated as 40% × £22,000 = £8,800. However, taper relief applies because the PET was more than three years before Godfrey's death. Only 60 per cent of the tax is payable – i.e. 60% × £8,800 = £5,280.

of death (40 per cent in 2011–12). However, if the giver died more than three years after making the gift, tax is reduced by IHT taper relief – see the table, opposite.

Any tax that becomes due on a reassessed PET is first charged to the person who received the gift. If they don't pay, the late giver's estate must pay the bill.

Note that PETs in the *seven years before death* are reassessed. Taxable gifts in the *seven years up to the making of the PET* are looked at in deciding whether tax is due. This means that gifts made during the 14 years before death could be relevant.

> **!** Taper relief only reduces any tax on the reassessed PET. If there is no tax on the PET (for example, because the running total including the PET, is less than the tax-free limit), then taper relief has no relevance. Taper relief cannot be used to reduce tax on the estate of the deceased giver.

FALL IN VALUE OF A TAXABLE GIFT OR A PET

There is some tax relief if the value of a reassessed PET or taxable gift has fallen since the time it was first made. (This applies regardless of the type of gift – for example, land, chattels, shares, and so on.) Whoever is paying the tax is allowed to deduct the fall in value from the original value of the gift. Bear in mind that the original value of a gift was the loss to the giver not the value to the recipient, so even a large percentage fall in the value of the item in the recipient's hands might have only a small impact on the value of the item for IHT purposes.

Case Study **DOROTHY**

In September 2009, Dorothy gave her niece, Charlotte, one of a pair of antique vases. As a pair, they had a market price of £110,000 but individually were each worth only £40,000. Therefore the value of the gift was £110,000 – £40,000 = £70,000. The gift counted as a PET.

In February 2012, Dorothy dies and Charlotte receives a demand for tax on the gift. She has the vase valued and it is now worth £35,000. Charlotte agrees to the reduced value of the gift which is £70,000 – £5,000 = £65,000.

Dorothy's running total of gifts up to September 2009 was £265,000. Adding the value of the vase brings the total to £265,000 + £65,000 = £330,000. This is £5,000 more than the 2011–12 tax-free limit of £325,000, so Charlotte must pay tax of 40% × £5,000 = £2,000. As fewer than three years have passed since the gift, taper relief does not apply.

If you need to get an item valued, you may need the help of a professional valuer, for example, a member of the National Association of Valuers and Auctioneers (see www.nava.org.uk).

CGT HOLD-OVER RELIEF

With some gifts, you could face bills for both CGT and IHT at the time that you make them. Hold-over relief lets you avoid a double tax bill, by, in effect, giving away your CGT too. Gifts that qualify for this include:

■ Gifts that count as taxable gifts for IHT.

■ Gifts that would count as taxable if they were not covered by the yearly tax-free exemption (see page 33) or the tax-free limit (see page 48).

■ PETs if they become chargeable because the giver dies within seven years.

The chargeable gain you have made on the gifted asset is deducted from your total chargeable gains for the year, so you pay no CGT on the gift. The chargeable gain is also deducted from the recipient's initial value, which increases the likelihood of a chargeable gain when the recipient comes to dispose of the gift. The recipient's taper relief is calculated from the date they became the new owner of the asset.

You can't claim hold-over relief if you are making the gift to a trust in which you have an interest which is called a 'settlor-interested trust' (see Chapter 4).

TELLING HMRC

You do not have to tell the tax authorities about lifetime gifts you make that count as PETs, but you should keep a record of them. Put the record where it would be found by whoever would handle your estate if you were to die, since they will be required to check what gifts you have made in the seven years prior to death and to report them for tax purposes.

If you make a taxable gift (which, in nearly all cases, means a gift involving a trust), you need to report this on form IHT100 – there are several versions, so either check which one you need on the HMRC website or explain the type of gift you are making if you order the form from the Probate and Inheritance Tax Enquiry Line (see below).

Normally you must send in the form within 12 months of the end of the month in which you made the gift but any tax due must usually be paid before this. With a lifetime taxable gift, tax is normally due within six months of the end of the month the gift was made. But if the gift was made in the period 6 April to 30 September, tax is due by 30 April of the following year.

If tax is due on a PET or taxable gift following the death of the giver within seven years, the tax is due within six months of the end of the month in which death occurred.

 Form IHT100 can be downloaded from the HMRC website at http://search2. hmrc.gov.uk/kbroker/hmrc/forms/ihtforms.jsp or ordered from the Probate and Inheritance Tax Enquiry Line 0845 302 0900.

GIVING AWAY BUSINESS ASSETS

Some investments count as business assets for CGT and IHT and so benefit from favourable tax treatment.

Advice on giving away your business, farm or woodland is outside this book's scope, so seek professional advice from a solicitor or accountant. But some fairly ordinary investments count as business assets. This is how they are taxed when you give them away.

CGT AND BUSINESS ASSETS

A gift of business assets may qualify for extra reliefs from CGT.

Hold-over relief

Gifts of business assets qualify for hold-over relief. This applies even if there is no immediate IHT bill on the gift (see opposite). The effect is that you give away your CGT liability with the gift. The definition of business assets includes shares in unlisted trading companies. Importantly for investors, a company counts as unlisted even if it is quoted on the Alternative Investment Market (AIM). 'Trading company' specifically includes letting

Alternative Investment Market (AIM) A junior section of the London Stock Exchange designed for companies that do not qualify for the main market, for example, because they are too small or do not have a long enough track record. Generally, AIM companies tend to be relatively new, small and/or growing so tend to be high-risk investments.

Furnished holiday letting For your holiday home to qualify as a business asset, it must be available for commercial letting for at least a minimum period (210 days from 2011–12 but 140 before then) and actually let for at least a minimum period (105 days from 2011–12 but 70 days before then). Furnished holiday lettings may be situated in the UK or any other member state of the European Economic Area.

out furnished holiday accommodation on a commercial basis, which could be useful if you want to give away a holiday home to your children, say.

Entrepreneurs' relief

This relief reduces a CGT bill when you give away or otherwise dispose of

For information about hold-over relief and a claim form, see the HMRC Helpsheet 295 *Relief for gifts and similar transactions* available from http://search2.hmrc. gov.uk/kbroker/hmrc/forms/viewform.jsp?formId=3190 or the Revenue Orderline 0845 900 0404.

your business if you are a sole trader, partner or have shares in your own personal trading company. Gains are taxed at a special low rate of 10 per cent. There is a lifetime limit (£10 million from 6 April 2011) on gains that can qualify. See HMRC Helpsheet 275 for details.

IHT AND BUSINESS ASSETS

Business assets may also qualify for extra IHT relief. If you give away something that counts as business property and you have owned it for at least two years immediately prior to making the gift, you can claim a 100 per cent relief to eliminate your IHT bill – this is called business property relief.

The definition of business property includes holdings of unquoted shares of eligible companies, including those traded on AIM. Relief does not apply to companies that are wholly or mainly engaged in dealing in shares or securities, dealing in land or buildings, or making and holding investments. Unlike the CGT rules, the definition

of business property does not include furnished holiday lettings.

A gift of business property might count as a PET and become taxable if you die within seven years. Business property relief can then be claimed, provided:

- The recipient still owns the asset, or
- The recipient no longer owns it but has fully reinvested the proceeds in other assets that also qualify for business property relief.

Similar 'agricultural property relief' is available where farms are passed on. Special treatment may also be available for timber growing on woodland – broadly, if neither business nor agricultural property relief apply, it may be possible to defer IHT on the value of the trees (but not the land) when woodland is passed on at death. IHT may become payable when the timber is sold.

SUMMARY

This chapter has looked at the way CGT and IHT are worked out and the interaction between the two taxes. The rules are complex and it has not been possible to cover every detail, but you should have enough information now to be able to work out the likely tax CGT and/or IHT bill on a lifetime gift and the IHT that may be due at death on earlier gifts as well as on the estate.

{ Business assets may qualify for extra IHT relief. The definition of business property includes shares traded on AIM. }

 If you are planning to give away your business, farm or woodland, you should seek advice from an accountant and solicitor.

LIFETIME GIFTS WITH STRINGS ATTACHED

It could be useful to make a gift but keep some rights to use it yourself. This is unlikely to save you Inheritance Tax (IHT) and could even land you with a yearly Income Tax bill. More positively, you might want to make a gift but put some conditions on how it is used. Trusts let you do just that and can still be set up efficiently despite recent changes to the way trusts are taxed.

LESS THAN OUTRIGHT GIFTS

When you make an outright gift, you give up all rights to use the thing you have given away or to dictate how it is used by the recipient. In some situations you may want to retain those rights.

WHAT'S IN THIS CHAPTER?

You may be tempted to 'give away' things on condition that you can carry on using them for now. While such gifts do legally transfer ownership to someone else, they are not recognised for IHT purposes. A quite different problem arises where you want to make a gift, but you are reluctant to do so if you feel the recipient would not be able to manage the financial responsibility involved or the people you want to receive your gifts are not all born yet.

Therefore, this chapter looks at:

- How lifetime gifts are treated for tax if you retain the right to carry on using them (page 64).
- Which gifts are not caught by these rules (page 66).
- How gifts could be caught by pre-owned assets tax (POAT) and your options for dealing with it (see page 68).
- How using 'trusts' (special legal arrangements) enables you to put restrictions on how and when the intended recipients can use your gifts (page 74).
- How tax affects different types of trust (see page 78).

{ It is worth pausing to question whether you can really afford the gift. }

WHEN THESE ISSUES MIGHT ARISE

Giving something away but carrying on using it may seem particularly attractive if most of your wealth is tied up in your home. In that case, you may have little spare cash or other assets out of which to make lifetime gifts. As you will see in this chapter, you cannot save IHT this way and can even create extra tax bills for yourself. Whenever you want to make a gift of something but hang on to it as well, it is worth pausing to question whether you can really afford to make the gift at all. Bear in mind, too, that it is not a good idea to make gifts that jeopardise your own financial security.

While insisting on your own continuing use of a gift is not good planning, there is nothing to stop you specifying other types of condition. Using trusts rather than outright giving lets you put conditions on your gifts. This strategy can be particularly useful if the recipient would not be able to manage your gift, perhaps because they are young, have a disability, have a tendency to act irresponsibly or might easily be influenced in an adverse way by other people. It can also be a useful strategy where you want to give to a group of people, some of whom are not yet born or where you are not sure which of them might in future be in most need of help. Trusts can also let you make gifts that are contingent on some event that may or may not happen, such as making a gift on marriage or on reaching a specified age, or stopping a gift on remarriage.

{ Using trusts rather than giving lets you put conditions on your gifts. }

GIFTS YOU RETAIN THE RIGHT TO USE

Most gifts of this sort can't save your estate IHT and might even trigger an Income Tax bill in your lifetime. But there are some exceptions.

GIFTS WITH RESERVATION

Problems can arise if you give something away but continue to benefit from it in some way. Special IHT rules apply to gifts like these:

- **The person receiving the gift does not really take possession of it.** For example, you might give a valuable painting to someone but carry on hanging it in your home.
- **You carry on deriving some benefit** from the thing you give away unless you pay a full market rate – or the equivalent in kind – for your use of the asset. This might happen if, for example, you give your home to your children but you retain the right to live in all or part of the property rent-free.

These are 'gifts with reservation'. A gift with reservation still counts as part of your estate when you die and so does not escape IHT. A gift can stop being a gift with reservation if your use or benefit stops and you survive seven years after that. A gift might not be a gift with reservation at the time you make it, but can become one later on if you subsequently start to use it or benefit from it. For example, suppose you give someone a painting that continues to hang in your house but pay a full commercial rent to the owner for your use of the picture, this would take the gift outside the gift-with-reservation rules. But if the rent is not reviewed and, after say five years, it ceases to be a commercial amount, at that stage, the gift would become a gift with reservation and the painting would once more form part of your estate for IHT purposes.

! The gift-with-reservation rules have no impact on Capital Gains Tax (CGT). For CGT purposes, your gift is effective at the time you make it, even if it is a gift with reservation for IHT. The gifted asset is not part of your estate at death for CGT purposes, so the exemption from CGT at death cannot apply. Any increase in the value of the asset between the time you gave it away and the time you die is a capital gain built up in the hands of the recipient and tax may be due when he or she eventually disposes of the asset.

How a gift with reservation is taxed

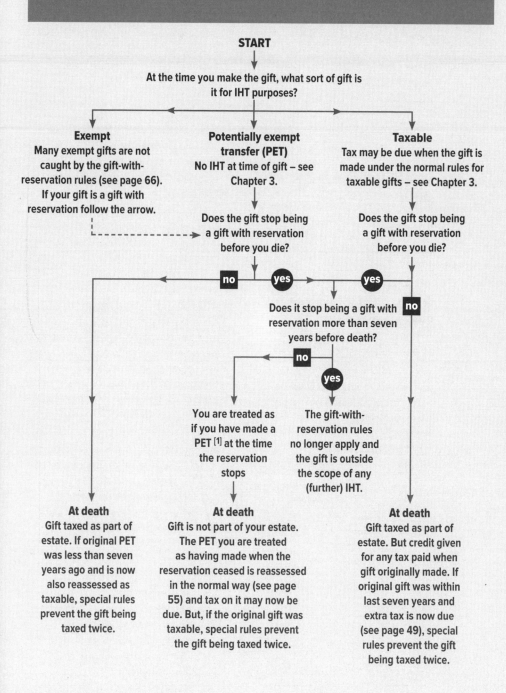

START

At the time you make the gift, what sort of gift is it for IHT purposes?

Exempt
Many exempt gifts are not caught by the gift-with-reservation rules (see page 66). If your gift is a gift with reservation follow the arrow.

Potentially exempt transfer (PET)
No IHT at time of gift – see Chapter 3.

Does the gift stop being a gift with reservation before you die?

Taxable
Tax may be due when the gift is made under the normal rules for taxable gifts – see Chapter 3.

Does the gift stop being a gift with reservation before you die?

no **yes** → **yes**

Does it stop being a gift with reservation more than seven years before death? **no**

no

yes

You are treated as if you have made a PET [1] at the time the reservation stops

The gift-with-reservation rules no longer apply and the gift is outside the scope of any (further) IHT.

At death
Gift taxed as part of estate. If original PET was less than seven years ago and is now also reassessed as taxable, special rules prevent the gift being taxed twice.

At death
Gift is not part of your estate. The PET you are treated as having made when the reservation ceased is reassessed in the normal way (see page 55) and tax on it may now be due. But, if the original gift was taxable, special rules prevent the gift being taxed twice.

At death
Gift taxed as part of estate. But credit given for any tax paid when gift originally made. If original gift was within last seven years and extra tax is now due (see page 49), special rules prevent the gift being taxed twice.

[1] HMRC's view is that you cannot set the £3,000 yearly tax-free exemption (see page 33) against the PET or claim the exemption for normal expenditure out of income (see page 30).

GIFTS THAT ARE NOT CAUGHT

Some gifts with strings attached are not caught by the gift-with-reservation rules and so they are effective in reducing your estate for IHT purposes.

Gifts made a long time ago

The gift-with-reservation rules do not apply to any gifts made before 18 March 1986.

Gifts that are exempt from IHT

If the original gift is covered by certain of the exemptions outlined in Chapter 2, the gift-with-reservation rules do not apply. The exemptions are:

- Gifts between husband and wife and, from 5 December 2005 onwards, gifts between civil partners (but see below)
- Gifts to charities and certain other bodies

> { There is no gift with reservation if your husband, wife or civil partner rather than you benefits. }

- Gifts of national heritage property
- Gifts to political parties
- Gifts to housing associations
- Small gifts (up to £250 per person)
- Wedding gifts.

Note that the above list does not include all types of exempt lifetime gift. In particular, the gift-with-reservation rules can apply even though a gift is exempt at the time it is made because it is 'normal expenditure out of income' or covered by the £3,000 yearly tax-free exemption.

For gifts made from 20 June 2003 onwards, the law was changed so that the gift-with-reservation rules do apply to gifts between husbands and wives or gifts between civil partners in the following circumstances:

- The gifted asset(s) are put into a trust giving your spouse or civil partner an interest in possession.
- The interest in possession later ends before the giver's death, and
- The spouse or partner then neither becomes the outright owner of the property nor gets a further interest in possession in it.

These 2003 rules were introduced specifically to stop complex tax avoidance arrangements known as 'Eversden schemes'. For general information about trusts and what an 'interest in possession' is, see page 76 onwards.

Gifts that benefit your spouse or civil partner

There is no gift with reservation if your husband, wife or civil partner rather than you uses or benefits from the item you give away. But you must make sure there is no way in which you could potentially benefit. For example, if it is a gift of money, it should not be paid into an account that your spouse or civil partner holds jointly with you.

Gifts you pay to use

A gift of land or chattels is not a gift with reservation if you pay the full market rent (or full payment in kind) for using it or benefiting from it. For example, you might give a son or daughter a piece of furniture but continue to keep it at your home. If you pay to insure it and pay your child an appropriate rent based on an independent, professional valuation of the item, you should normally be outside the gift-with-reservation rules.

Gifts you share without benefiting by more than your share

Without triggering the gift-with-reservation rules, you are allowed to give away part of land or property – for example, your home – and share it with the co-owner(s), provided you do not benefit in any way from the bit you've given away. For example, you

would have to bear your full share of the bills. See Chapter 10 for more information.

Gifts that are separated from the part you keep

If you can carve up a possession which you intend to give away and keep a distinct part of it that forms a separate asset in its own right (a process called 'shearing'), you can give away the remainder without the part you retain counting as a gift with reservation.

However, these days you will be caught by the gift-with-reservation rules if you apply shearing to gifts of land or property by, for example, splitting your ownership into a lease that you keep and a freehold that you sell (called a lease-carve-out or 'Ingram scheme'). This is because of anti-avoidance rules that came into effect in 1999. Ingram schemes set up before 9 March 1999 continue successfully to fall outside the gift-with-reservation rules.

Case Study **SYBIL**

Sybil invests a lump sum in a school fees plan designed to pay fees for her grandson, Harry. The arrangement allows for the policy to return a lump sum to Sybil if Harry were to die before finishing his education at the school. The payment of school fees is the gift from Sybil to Harry and the right to the refund is not deemed to be part of the gift (and is essentially a separate asset that Sybil keeps), so there is no gift with reservation.

See page 74 onwards for information about trusts. See Chapter 10 for things to consider if giving away or sharing your home.

Reservation of benefit due to infirmity

The gift-with-reservation rules will not apply if the benefit or use you derive from land you gave away has arisen because of unforeseen changes that mean you can no longer take care of yourself because of old age, illness or disability. This could apply if, say, you give the family home to your children and move out – perhaps to somewhere smaller and more manageable. If later, you have to move in with the children so they can care for you, this will not trigger the gift-with-reservation rules. For this exception to apply, the person who receives the gift must be a relative of you or your husband, wife or civil partner.

PRE-OWNED ASSETS TAX (POAT)

Tax advisers are clever people and, over the years, a variety of schemes have grown up to get around the gift-with-reservation rules. Two – Ingram schemes and Eversden schemes – have been briefly mentioned earlier in this chapter. For many years, these and other avoidance schemes were typically used only by people with fairly substantial wealth. But, as rising house prices during the 1990s and 2000s brought many 'ordinary' people potentially into the IHT net, some schemes started to be marketed more widely.

HMRC typically countered each avoidance scheme as it arose with challenges in the courts and changes to the law. But generally each Revenue success in stopping future use of a scheme has left a trail of successful tax avoiders who had bolted before the stable door was closed. HMRC decided on a new tack and, from April 2005 onwards, introduced the POAT.

What is POAT?

POAT is a yearly Income Tax charge on the benefit you are deemed to get from something you used to own, or provided the money for, for example if you sell your home to your children but carry on living there, or you give them cash to buy a home and then they let you move in. 'Benefit' includes, for example, occupying land, using an asset or receiving income from it. POAT is mainly aimed at gifts that escape the IHT gift-with-reservation rules, but its scope is much wider.

A tax with a past

POAT is an extremely unusual tax for two reasons:

- **It is an Income Tax** being used to plug loopholes in a completely different tax, namely IHT.
- **It is 'retroactive'.** The government of the day pointed out that POAT does not go back and reassess you

 See page 74 onwards for information about trusts generally. See page 89–93 for trusts for children.

for tax for previous years and so insists this is not a 'retrospective' tax. But the point is debatable. New tax measures normally apply only to actions taken on or after the date the measures come into effect. By contrast, POAT can impose a tax charge now on actions you took in the past.

Who has to pay POAT?

Three types of assets are affected: land (meaning buildings as well as just land), chattels (for example furniture, paintings, jewellery, books) and intangible assets. In the case of land or chattels, POAT may affect you if you can benefit from:

- An asset you have disposed of at any time on or after 18 March 1986 (called the 'disposal condition'), or
- An asset owned by someone to whom you have given money

> **?** **Arm's length** The term HMRC use to describe the sort of commercial deal you would make with someone you did not know on the open market as opposed to a special arrangement you might strike with a friend or family member.

> **Intangible asset** Something you own that has no physical presence, such as cash, shares, insurance policies or other financial assets. You may be caught by POAT if you put cash, insurance policies or other intangible assets into a trust where, under Income Tax rules, any income from the trust is taxed as if it is yours. Under the POAT rules, 'trust' does not include a 'bare trust' (see page 76). You are not caught if the trust benefits your husband, wife or civil partner but not you.

within the last seven years in order to directly or indirectly fund their acquiring the asset (called the 'contribution condition').

POAT does not just apply to gifts but other types of disposal too, such as sales.

There are a number of exemptions from POAT – see the table on page 71. In addition, POAT does not apply if the person who made the gift and receives the benefit is not resident in the UK. If you are resident in the UK but your domicile (the place you consider to be your permanent home) is elsewhere, POAT can apply only to assets you have in the UK not elsewhere in the world.

> **!** The Labour government that introduced POAT warned that it was prepared to make further use of retroactive legislation so that actions you take now that successfully save tax cease to be effective once the law is changed. There is no reason to think that the current government would take a different approach. This means that the scope for complicated lifetime IHT planning is now severely restricted because any scheme that is successful in saving IHT on your estate is likely to draw HMRC's attention and may result in some other compensating tax charge.

■ PLANNING POINT

You are not caught by the POAT contribution condition if you only acted as guarantor for a loan.

How POAT works

The benefit you are deemed to receive from an asset you have given away or contributed towards is added to your other income for the year and Income Tax is charged in the normal way.

POAT works in a similar way to Income Tax on the value of fringe benefits you get through a job. The benefit you are deemed to get depends on the type of asset:

- **Land.** The full market rent you would otherwise have to pay. If you benefit from only part of the property, the benefit is a proportion of the full market rent. You can deduct any rent you actually pay to the owner.
- **Chattels.** The market value of the asset multiplied by an official interest rate set by HMRC (used also in connection with valuing loans from employers to employees). The interest rate is usually set for a year at a time and in 2011–12 is 4 per cent. For example, if the item was valued at £50,000, the yearly benefit would be 4% × £50,000 = £2,000. The benefit is scaled down if you use only part of the possession and you can deduct any amount you actually pay the owner for your use of the asset.
- **Intangible property.** The market value of the trust property multiplied by the official interest rate (4 per cent in 2011–12) less any Income Tax or CGT you already pay on the property.

The value of an asset is generally the value it could be expected to fetch if sold on the open market. Assets must be valued on the first day of the tax year (6 April) or, if later, the date on which the asset first came within the POAT regime. Land and possessions are valued only once every five years with each valuation applying unchanged for the whole five-year period.

For answers to frequently asked questions about POAT, see the HMRC website at www.hmrc.gov.uk/poa/poa_faqs.htm.

Transactions to which POAT does not apply

A transaction involving: Land, possessions or intangible assets
Is not caught by POAT if any of the following apply:

- The yearly benefit from all your transactions caught by POAT, before deducting anything you pay the owner(s), comes to no more than £5,000. (If it exceeds £5,000, the whole amount not just the excess is taxable.)
- The asset is still part of your estate for IHT.
- It is a gift with reservation for IHT.
- It is a gift where you have opted to be treated as if it were a gift with reservation (see page 72).
- It is a gift exempt from IHT and also the gift-with-reservation rules (see page 66).
- You pay full market rent for your benefit.
- You share the asset and benefit no more than your fair share.

A transaction involving: Land or possessions
Is not caught by POAT if any of the following apply:

- You disposed of the whole asset at **arm's length** or on arm's length terms. You can retain rights for yourself if they can be carved out as a separate asset in the same way as applies under the gift-with-reservation rules (see page 67).
- You disposed of part of the asset at arm's length to someone not connected with you. [1] This exempts, for example, an equity release scheme (see page 192) where you sell part of your home to a commercial company.
- You disposed of part of the asset to someone who is connected with you [1] on arm's length terms, but only if the transaction took place before 7 March 2005. This exemption could cover an informal equity release scheme where you had sold part of your home to a relative in return for cash or income.
- You disposed of part of the asset on arm's length terms on or after 7 March 2005 where the amount paid to you is not in cash or assets readily convertible to cash. This could cover a situation where you gave part of your home to someone who had moved in to be your carer in recognition of their caring services to you.
- It is a transfer to your husband, wife or civil partner or to a trust giving them an interest in possession (see page 76) for life.
- It is a transfer under a court order to a former husband, wife or civil partner or to a trust giving them an interest in possession (see page 76) for life.
- The reason for the disposal is the maintenance of your family.
- The disposal is an outright gift covered by the IHT-free yearly allowance (see page 33) or the small gifts exemption (see page 33).
- It is an outright cash gift used to buy land or possessions where the gift was made more than at least seven years before you started to benefit from the asset.
- Your use of the land started only because you were no longer able to care for yourself because of old age or infirmity.

[1] For the purpose of POAT, a 'connected person' includes your husband, wife, civil partner, child, brother, sister, grandparent (and their parents, grandparents and so on), grandchild (and their children and so on down the line), uncles, aunts, nieces, nephews and trusts of which you are the settlor.

Your options under POAT

If you have a transaction that is caught by POAT, you have four options:

- **Pay the yearly POAT charge.** POAT is a charge on benefit you are deemed to get not actual income, so to pay POAT you will need to have income or other resources you can dip into.
- **Pay the full market rent** to the owner of the asset for your use of it. Again, you need to have enough income or other resources to afford this option.
- **Unscramble the transaction** so that it returns to your estate or becomes subject to the IHT gift-with-reservation rules. No POAT is due, but IHT may be payable on the asset when you die. Unscrambling might not be possible. Under the transaction, legal ownership has normally passed to someone else. They may be unwilling or unable to give the property back. In addition, unscrambling may incur costs and CGT charges.
- **Without unscrambling the transaction, opt to be treated as if the IHT gift-with-reservation rules apply.** This means no POAT is payable but IHT may be due when you die. You have until 31 January following the end of the tax year in which you first became subject to POAT to make this election. However, HMRC may agree to accept a late election, if you miss the deadline. Once the election is made, the election is irreversible, so you can't change your mind later on and decide you would rather the gift-with-reservation rules didn't apply after all.

Electing to be treated as if the gift-with-reservation rules apply affects only the IHT position. For CGT, you continue to have disposed of

■ PLANNING POINT ■

If the benefits you get from all the assets caught by POAT come to no more than £5,000, there is no POAT to pay. In that case, you might decide to stay within the POAT regime, but consider how the value of the asset concerned might change in future.

Paying the owner a full market rent could be a good option if you can afford it and you would, in any case, like to pass on more of your wealth to the owner. For example, you might have given your home to your children under a scheme that got around the gift-with-reservation rules and you can now pass them a regular sum each year in the form of rent. However, the rent will count as taxable income in the hands of your children.

Coming back within the gift-with-reservation rules (either by unscrambling or election) would not cause an IHT problem if your estate at death would in any case be less than the tax-free limit (£325,000 in 2011–12).

To check the current official rate of interest, see the HMRC website, www.hmrc.gov.uk/rates/interest-beneficial.htm. Valuing the benefit from intangible property is a complex area. Contact any adviser who set up or helps you run the trust for further information.

the asset on the date the transaction took place. Any increase in the value of the asset between then and the date of death accrues in the hands of the new owner and may be liable to CGT when they dispose of the asset. By contrast, if the asset had been part of your estate, any taxable gain would have been wiped out by the exemption from CGT for assets given away on death.

Telling HMRC

It's up to you to realise if you are caught by POAT and declare any liability on your tax return. If you do not receive a tax return, tell your tax office by 5 October following the end of the tax year in which the liability started and you will be sent a form.

If you want to opt out of POAT by electing to be treated as if the gift-with-reservation rules apply, use form IHT500 available from HMRC and send it in no later then 31 January following the year in which the liability to POAT starts. For example, if you started to be liable for POAT in 2011–12, you must make the election by 31 January 2013.

> It's up to you to realise if you are caught by POAT and declare any liability on your tax return.

Case Study MOLLY

Molly, like many pensioners, is 'cash-poor, asset-rich'. She struggles to manage on her pensions but lives in a valuable home. She has been thinking about taking out a home reversion scheme (see Chapter 10), whereby she would sell part of her home to a company for a lump sum but retain the right to live in the home until she dies (or, if necessary, moves permanently into care).

Her grandson, Dan, suggests that instead of going to a reversion company, he could buy a share of her home and give her a better deal than a company. If Molly and Dan had made such an arrangement before 7 March 2005, there would have been no problem. But, from that date onwards, such arrangements are caught by POAT and Molly will become liable to tax each year on her benefit from living in the part of the home she sells to Dan if it exceeds the £5,000 threshold at which POAT becomes due. They work out if this will be the case.

Molly's home is worth £300,000. Dan is willing to pay her the full £150,000 for a half share. A local estate agent advises that the rent they could charge if they let out the home would be £750 a month. This comes to £9,000 a year and so Molly's benefit from using the half the home that was sold would be 50% × £9,000 = £4,500. This is less than the POAT threshold, but it would not take much of a rise in market rents to draw Molly's deemed benefit over the £5,000 limit.

Dan and Molly decide to look at an alternative option, which would be for Dan to lend Molly £150,000. It is important that the loan is arranged so that Dan can require it be repaid on demand at any time so that there is no reduction in the value of his estate (and so no gift for IHT purposes). Although not a condition of the loan, Molly intends to leave her home to Dan. Molly and Dan seek advice from a solicitor in order to get the detail of these arrangements right.

GIFTS USING TRUSTS

Y̶ou can retain some flexibility about who benefits from your gifts and how they are used by setting up trusts.

Trusts let you give away assets but retain some control over how they are used. Trusts can be set up during your lifetime or in a will. They are sometimes used as part of tax planning schemes that aim to save IHT. However, in Budget 2011, the Government announced that IHT avoidance schemes involving trusts will in future need to be disclosed to HMRC. This increases the likelihood of such schemes being closed down.

WHAT IS A TRUST?

A trust is an arrangement where the legal owners of assets (which can be things like money, land, buildings) hold the assets and must use them for the benefit of someone else. There are three conditions that must be met for the creation of a trust:

- The intention to create it must be clear from the words used.
- The trust property must be identified.
- It must be clear who is to benefit from the trust.

(In Scotland, there is a further requirement that trust assets or evidence of their ownership is physically delivered to the trustees or, alternatively, that the trust is registered in the Books of Council and Session.)

It is usual to set out this information and other conditions in a written deed, but trusts can come into being without anything being put into writing.

 Settlement Term used in tax legislation to mean most arrangements or agreements that transfers assets with some element of 'bounty' (meaning some element of gift to the recipient). Trusts are sometimes referred to as settlements but 'settlement' includes many other types of arrangement as well.

{ Trusts let you give away assets but retain some control. }

Trusts are complex and need to be drawn up by a solicitor (or insurance company, which will use its own solicitors) – see page 78.

WHY USE TRUSTS?

Trusts can be useful in many situations, for example:

- **Giving to children.** You might want to make a gift now to a child to be available to him or her later, for example, when they reach an age you specify.
- **Maintaining control.** The person you want to benefit might not be good at handling money. For example, they have learning difficulties or a tendency to be a spendthrift.
- **Giving to a group.** Maybe you want to give to a group of people that is not yet complete – for example, your grandchildren including those yet to be born.
- **Retaining flexibility.** Perhaps you're not sure at this stage who should benefit from your gift or you want to be able to change who benefits or the amount they get if circumstances change. Provided you specify the range of potential beneficiaries now, you can leave these decisions until later.
- **Separating income from capital.** This lets you specify that someone will have your assets in the end but, in the meantime, someone else has the income from them or the use of them. This can be particularly useful in family situations – for example, if you want a widow or widower to be financially secure but ultimately want your children (maybe from a former marriage) to benefit.
- **Giving on special occasions or in set circumstances.** You might want to make a gift only on the occasion of some possible but indeterminate event, such as a marriage or birth. Similarly, you might want someone to benefit now but for your gift to pass to someone else if, say, the first beneficiary goes bankrupt.
- **Maintaining confidentiality.** A beneficiary does not have to know that you have arranged a gift to be made at some future time. Similarly, a beneficiary in receipt of income or capital from a trust does not have to know who the settlor was.
- **Tax-efficiency.** Sometimes a gift into trust can save you tax, or avoid tax problems that would arise with an outright gift. But the scope for saving tax was reduced by changes from 2006 onwards.

Who's involved in a trust?

- **The settlor** (called the truster or granter in Scotland). This is the person who gives away the assets to be placed in the trust. A trust may have more than one settlor and this does not have to be an individual. For example, the settlor could be a company or another trust.
- **The trustees.** There is usually more than one trustee and these are the legal owners of the trust property. So the property is registered in their names, and they are responsible for holding it safely and accounting for it. The settlor can be a trustee, so too can a beneficiary.
- **The beneficiaries.** There might be one beneficiary or more. These are the people who will – or might – share the trust property and any income from it. Beneficiaries can be individuals, companies, charities or other bodies. Different beneficiaries may have different rights. The settlor can be a beneficiary of the trust, but this has tax implications – see page 83.

THE MAIN TYPES OF TRUST

There are three main types of trust. Which is suitable for your needs depends on what you are trying to achieve.

Bare trust

How does it work? A bare trust (also called an absolute trust or simple trust) is a very simple type of trust. Someone holds assets as nominee for someone else – for example, a parent holds investments for their child. Once the beneficiary is aged 18 or more (or is married if younger), he or she can call for the income and/or capital at any time and the trustee has no right to withhold it. For tax purposes, the beneficiary – not the trustee – is treated as the owner of the trust property.

A bare trust is easy to set up and administer. But watch out if you are a parent making a gift to your child to be held in a bare trust as any income may be taxed as yours not the child's – see Chapter 5. Income from gifts from other sources – for example, from grandparents – and any capital gains count as those of the child. This can make a bare trust more tax-efficient than other trust options in suitable cases. Against this, you must balance the drawbacks. Once the trust is set up, you cannot change the beneficiaries or the shares in which they own the trust property. The settlor has no control at all over the use of the trust property once a child has reached their majority. The trust property is part of the beneficiary's estate when he or she dies – if the beneficiary is under the age of 18 (12 in Scotland) at the time of death, they would die intestate (see Chapter 8) since they would be too young to have made a will.

Possible uses

- Making a gift of property to a child – e.g. a share in a family business – which the child does not yet have the legal capacity to hold because of his or her young age.
- Building up a nest-egg for a child to have on reaching 18 years of age. But see Chapter 5 for other options.

Interest-in-possession trust

Also known as a 'life-interest trust' or 'fixed-interest trust'.

How does it work? One or more beneficiaries have the right to receive income earned by the assets in the trust as that income arises or they have the right to use the assets held by the trust, for example, the right to live in a house. This is called a 'life interest'. Eventually the assets in the trust are distributed. This might happen, for example, on the death of the life-interest beneficiary or at a specified date or when a specified event, such as marriage, occurs. The person or people who then receive the assets are said to hold the 'reversionary interest'. You could give the same person both interests (the life interest from one date and the reversionary interest from a later date).

Possible uses

- Where you eventually want to pass on assets to one or more people but need to provide for someone else in the interim.
- Where you do not want the beneficiary to have full control of the assets in the trust or you want to defer handing over control until a later date.

Discretionary trust

How does it work? If a trust is not a bare trust or an interest-in-possession trust, it is by default a discretionary trust. A distinguishing feature is that generally income can be accumulated within the trust to be paid out later or at the discretion of the trustees. Usually there is more than one beneficiary. Often there will be a 'class' of beneficiaries, such as your children or your grandchildren, not all of whom have to be born at the time the trust is set up.

Possible uses

- Where you want the ability to alter who will benefit under the trust.
- Where you want to be able to alter the proportions in which the beneficiaries share in income and/or capital from the trust.

 See page 78 onwards for how trusts are taxed.

Case Study **DAVID**

David's will stipulates that, on his death, a large part of his assets should be placed in trust. The trustees would invest the assets as they saw fit and the income from them (and use of his former share of the family home) should go to his wife during her lifetime. On his wife's death, the assets are to be shared equally between their three children. David has drawn up his will in this way, first, to guard against his widow being short of money during her lifetime and, secondly, to ensure that his children will eventually receive his assets even if his widow remarries.

Case Study **JOHN**

John had been ill for some time and, knowing that he did not have long to live, he checked his will and brought it up to date. He was a widower with three adult sons. One had a good, secure income, another had not settled down to a career yet but had only minor financial problems, while the third son was generally in financial difficulties – largely of his own making. John wanted to be fair to all his boys but was not happy with the idea of just sharing out his assets between them. They did not all have the same need and the youngest son in particular would be likely to squander any inheritance. John decided to set up a discretionary trust in favour of all the sons. He appointed his own two brothers (the sons' uncles) as trustees and gave them discretion to make payments and loans from the trust fund to the sons if or when, in the trustees' opinion, such help was warranted. After ten years (by which time John felt the boys should all take responsibility for themselves), the remaining trust assets were to be distributed equally among them.

SETTING UP A TRUST

A bare trust can be set up very easily – for example, by simply stating on an application form that you are holding savings or investments on behalf of someone else.

With other trusts, it is best to use a formal, written deed that makes your intentions crystal clear. Get professional help setting up a trust from a solicitor either direct or through an accountant, tax adviser or independent financial adviser (IFA). Depending on the complexity of the trust and the value of the assets concerned, creating a trust can be expensive (costing hundreds, even thousands, of pounds), so it is important to check that the benefits warrant the financial outlay.

Life insurance products are very often used in conjunction with trusts.

Many life insurance companies can provide you with off-the-peg trust documents that let you very simply, and usually at no extra cost, opt to have a life policy written in trust – though you need to check the IHT implications (see page 133). You can either arrange this direct with the insurance company or through an IFA.

HOW TRUSTS ARE TAXED

There are three taxes to consider when looking at trusts: Income Tax, CGT and IHT. The IHT rules changed from April 2006 onwards and divide trusts into three categories:

- **Relevant property trusts,** which are generally subject to IHT.
- **Qualifying trusts** for disabled people and bereaved children, which escape IHT.
- **A hotch-potch of other trusts** that are treated leniently for IHT.

Trusts in any of these three categories could be interest in possession trusts or discretionary trusts.

Bare trusts fall outside the normal tax rules for trusts and are subject to a very different regime.

The lists that follow describe the tax rules for bare trusts, relevant property trusts and those trusts that benefit from more favourable IHT treatment. Page 83 looks at special Income Tax rules that apply to 'settlor-interest trusts'. Turn to page 93 in Chapter 5 for a discussion of the Income Tax treatment of 'parental trusts for children'.

? **Qualifying trust** A trust set up to benefit a person who is disabled or who has a health condition expected to lead to disability, or a trust set up in the will of a parent who has died or under the laws that step in where there is no will (see Chapter 8) for the benefit of a child of the deceased. In general, no IHT charges apply to this type of trust.

Relevant property trust A trust that does not qualify for any special IHT treatment. Therefore, putting money or assets into the trust counts as a taxable gift. There may be an IHT charge at 10-yearly intervals throughout the life of the trust and there may be IHT to pay when money or assets are paid out of the trust.

Case Study **SEB**

Seb is the beneficiary of a bare trust containing £10,000 capital. This was a gift from his grandmother. The capital has earned approximately £400 a year income and some small capital gains. Both are well within Seb's Income Tax and CGT allowances. On reaching 18, Seb intends to ask the trustee, his dad, to carry on acting as trustee but to advance Seb regular sums to support him while at university. On finishing university, Seb intends to take outright possession of the remaining trust property (if any). As he is already treated as the outright owner, no transfer takes place and so there will be no IHT.

Bare trusts

Putting a gift into trust Unless you can use one of the exemptions described in Chapter 2, your gift into a bare trust normally counts as a PET (see Chapter 3), so there is no IHT to pay provided you survive for at least seven years. No special rules apply regarding CGT – check the ordinary rules in Chapter 3 to see if any CGT will be payable on the gift.

The trust's tax position Income and gains from the trust property are treated in the same way as if the property was owned directly by the beneficiary. This means that income is taxed at the beneficiary's top rate after taking into account allowances and any other deductions. The exception to this is where the assets in the trust are a gift from a parent to a child, in which case income may be taxed as that of the parent – see Chapter 5. Gains are taxed at the beneficiary's top rate after taking account of the yearly CGT tax-free limit.

Payments to beneficiaries Where, as is usual, tax has already been paid as income and gains arose, there is no further tax to pay when payments are made to the beneficiary or used for his or her benefit. But see Chapter 5 regarding gifts from a parent.

When the bare trust ends The trust property has been treated as owned by the beneficiary throughout. Therefore there is no change when the beneficiary takes outright possession of the trust property.

> Creating a trust can be expensive, so check that the benefits warrant the financial outlay.

 The taxation of trusts is complicated. Get advice from the firm you are using to set up your trust.

Putting a gift into trust This is a taxable gift for IHT, unless you can claim one of the exemptions in Chapter 2. So the gift can create an immediate tax bill (see Chapter 3), unless when added to other taxable gifts you have made within the last seven years, it is within your tax-free limit (£325,000 in 2011–12). CGT may be due, if you are giving assets other than cash, but you can claim hold-over relief (see page 58).

The trust's IHT position There is a 'periodic charge' on the value of the trust property. This is made on each tenth anniversary of the setting-up of the trust. Tax due is worked out as shown in the calculator opposite. If money or assets are paid out of the trust, an exit charge must be paid by the trustees. The charge is worked out by multiplying the full ten-year charge by 1 ÷ 40 for each three-month period during which the property was in the trust since the last periodic charge. The tax charge is scaled down similarly if the property was added to the trust after the start of the relevant ten-year period.

The trust's Income Tax position: discretionary trusts Tax on income is paid at the 'rate applicable to trusts' (RAT), which is 42.5 per cent on dividends and 50 per cent on other income. All trusts liable for the RAT on income benefit from a basic-rate band (£1,000 in 2011–12). Income falling within the basic rate band is taxed at 10 per cent (dividends), or 20 per cent (other income).

The trust's Income Tax position: interest-in-possession trusts Income from the assets in the trust may be paid either direct to the beneficiaries or first to the trustees who then pass it on to the beneficiaries. The trustees are responsible for tax at different rates depending on the type of income. The 2010–11 rates are 10 per cent on dividends and 20 per cent on savings income.

The trust's CGT position CGT on any taxable capital gains is also payable by the trustees at the RAT of 50 per cent in 2010–11, though the trust can set a tax-free limit (usually half the amount individuals get, so £5,300 in 2011–12) against the first slice of gains.

Income payments to beneficiaries: discretionary trusts Income is all paid out with tax at a notional rate of 50 per cent already deducted. You receive the net income plus a 50 per cent tax credit. The sum of the two counts as your gross income against which you can set the tax credit. This means, unless you are an additional rate taxpayer, you can claim a refund of part or all of the tax.

Income payments to beneficiaries: interest-in-possession trusts Income paid out to beneficiaries is broadly treated as if it had been received directly by them. Two different treatments may apply, depending on the type of income:

- Dividends are received net of tax at 10 per cent and accompanied by a tax credit. Non-taxpayers cannot reclaim this tax credit. Starting- and basic-rate taxpayers have no further tax to pay. Higher-rate taxpayers must pay further tax of 22.5 per cent on the grossed-up amount of the dividend. Additional-rate taxpayers must pay a further 32.5 per cent of the grossed-up amount.
- Other income is paid net of tax at 20 per cent. Non-taxpayers can reclaim this. Starting-rate taxpayers can reclaim half the tax deducted. Basic-rate taxpayers have no further tax to pay. Higher-rate taxpayers must pay extra tax of 20 per cent on the grossed-up amount of the interest. Additional-rate taxpayers must pay a further 30 per cent of the grossed-up amount.

Capital payments to beneficiaries If you receive a payment of capital from the trust, there is no CGT for you to pay and you cannot reclaim any CGT paid by the trust. Note that, once income has been accumulated within the trust, the payment of it to a beneficiary will normally count as a payment of capital.

When the trust ends An IHT exit charge is made on the whole of the trust property as if it were any other payment from the trust (see above).

Calculator: working out the first periodic charge

			Example (2011–12)
Value of trust at time of periodic charge	**A**	£	A £310,000
Value of gifts in seven years up to the date the trust was set up	**B**	£	B £90,000
Add A and B	**C**	£	C £400,000
Tax-free limit for year of periodic charge	**D**	£	D £325,000
C minus D	**E**	£	E £75,000
Multiply E by lifetime IHT rate of 20%	**F**	£	F £15,000
Divide F by A to find the effective rate of tax	**G**	%	G 4.938%
Multiply G by 30%	**H**	%	H 1.452%
Multiply H by A to find periodic charge now due	**I**	£	I £ 4,500

Working out the periodic charge

The calculator above will help you work out the first 10-year periodic charge for a relevant property trust, for a straightforward case. (There are additional steps if, say, the trust includes business property.) For more detailed guidance, you can download a worksheet from the HMRC website (see below), but you do not have to do the calculations yourself. If you report the relevant information, the Revenue will calculate the tax due for you.

▌PLANNING POINT ▌

A reversionary interest in an interest-in-possession trust is treated as a separate asset from the interest in possession and counts as 'excluded property' outside the IHT net. This means the gift of a reversionary interest cannot create an IHT bill. There is no CGT either provided you are the beneficiary for whom the interest was created or, if not, you did not buy the interest.

 For more information about the taxation of trusts, see the HMRC website at www.hmrc.gov.uk/trusts/types/index.htm. Download the form (IHT100), worksheet (IHT100WS) and guidance for reporting the periodic charge at http://search2.hmrc.gov.uk/kbroker/hmrc/forms/viewform.jsp?formId=3337#help.

QUALIFYING TRUSTS

Bereaved minor's trust A trust set up on the death of a parent to use assets from the parent for the benefit of their child (or children). For details, see Chapter 5.

Disabled person's trust This is a trust set up either in life or in a will for the benefit of someone who has a permanent mental or physical incapacity – for example a trust set up by parents to provide lasting support for a disabled child. It can also be set up by someone with an existing health condition – for example, in the early stages of Alzheimer's disease – for their own benefit later on if they expect their condition to worsen. When the trust ends, IHT may be due on any remaining assets. In addition, the trustees and disabled person may jointly elect to have income and gains made by the trust treated as if they were received direct by the disabled person, so making use of their tax allowances and bands. The election must be made by 31 January falling one year and ten months after the first tax year from which the election is to apply (for example, by 31 January 2014 for the 2011–12 tax year). Once made the election cannot be reversed.

OTHER TRUSTS

Immediate post-death interest (IPDI) trust

This is an interest-in-possession trust that starts up on someone's death. It gives one or more people – for example, a surviving partner – a life interest. The person with the life interest is treated as if they own the assets outright. If the interest ends during their lifetime, the person with the life interest is treated as if they have made a PET to the recipient of the assets. If the interest ends on their death, the trust assets count as part of their estate and IHT may be due.

Interest in possession trust set up before 22 March 2006

This is a trust set up in lifetime or on death that gave someone the right to income from the trust or use of the trust assets, while typically other people have a right to the assets when the life interest ends. If the trust continues unchanged, or the interest-in-possession has been transferred to someone else, but this took place before 5 October 2008, the same rules as for immediate post-death interest trusts (see above) apply.

18-to-25 trust

A trust usually either set up in a parent's will or created through an amendment to an 'accumulation and maintenance trust' [1] for the benefit of a child or young person. The young person must take over the trust property on or before age 25 years. There are no IHT charges up to their reaching age 18, but an exit charge applies to withdrawals between ages 18 and 25 (see Chapter 5 for details).

[1] An accumulation and maintenance trust is a type of trust that before 22 March 2006 benefited from lenient IHT treatment. Such trusts could be used to build up savings for one or more children and/or pay for their education and general upbringing.

Settlor-interested trusts

A settlor-interested trust is one in which the settlor has a 'retained interest'. If this applies, income made by the trust will be taxed as that of the settlor. Often this will mean a higher tax bill.

You will be treated as having a retained interest if you or your husband, wife or civil partner can in any circumstances benefit from the trust, either now or at some future time.

The definition of retained interest is very wide, so you will be caught by the rules not simply if you or your husband, wife or civil partner is a named beneficiary of the trust, but even if you or they might become a beneficiary because of some seemingly unlikely circumstances, for example:

- The trust says your grandchild will become entitled to the trust property provided he or she reaches age 25 but you fail to say what happens if he or she does not reach that age. In that case, the property would automatically revert back to the settlor, so you are a potential beneficiary and have a retained interest.
- A trust is set up for grandchildren but the trustees have the power to give the trust property to any other trust that includes the grandchildren as beneficiaries. This would not exclude a trust that also included you or your husband, wife, civil partner or child as additional beneficiaries, so again you are deemed to have a retained interest.

Note, too, that if you are both the settlor and an actual or potential beneficiary under the trust, the IHT gift-with-reservation rules apply (see page 64). The trust property will then continue to count as part of your estate. (Unlike the retained interest rules, the gift-with-reservation rules do not apply if your husband, wife or civil partner is a beneficiary.) If you have an interest in the trust but have managed to set it up using a scheme that avoids the gift-with-reservation rules, the POAT – see page 68 – might instead apply.

See Chapter 5, page 93, for similar Income Tax treatment where a trust has been set up by a parent for a child.

(see page 64)

> **!** Most gifts to trusts are now taxable gifts for IHT, which generally opens the possibility of claiming hold-over relief from CGT (see page 58). But hold-over relief is not allowed where you make a gift to a settlor-interested trust.

{ Income made by the trust will be taxed as that of the settlor. }

SUMMARY

This chapter has looked at the problems that arise if you give something away but continue to use it. You can find more information in Chapter 10, which includes details of how the gift-with-reservation rules apply if you want to give away part or all of your home.

This chapter has looked at using trusts to help you retain some control over how your gifts are used. This has included an introduction to the tax rules that apply to trusts, but the rules can get very complex if your affairs are not straightforward. You are strongly advised to take advice from a solicitor or accountant if you are thinking about setting up a trust.

 For more information about tax and settlor-interested trusts, see the free HMRC leaflet HS270 *Trusts and settlements – income treated as the settlor's* available from http://search2.hmrc.gov.uk/kbroker/hmrc/forms/viewform.jsp?formId=3189 or the Revenue Orderline 0845 9000 404.

GIVING TO CHILDREN

There are many reasons for wanting to make a gift to a child. You might want to build up a nest-egg that the child can draw on when, say, he or she goes to university or buys his or her first home. Alternatively, you might want the money to be available sooner to help with education costs or as a tool to help the child learn how to handle money.

HOW TO ORGANISE YOUR GIFT

There are two main concerns when considering gifts to children: the tax-avoidance rules that may affect gifts from a parent to a child, and how to arrange the gift, given that the child may be too young to hold an investment or to use the gift wisely.

WHAT'S IN THIS CHAPTER?

Gifts to children, before they reach adulthood, can be particularly tricky to arrange. First, you may want to restrict access to the money or assets you give until you feel the child is sufficiently mature to use the gift wisely. Second, gifts from parents can be caught by rules that aim to stop tax avoidance. This chapter considers:

- How parents can arrange gifts to their children tax efficiently (see right and opposite).
- Precautions to take when other family members and friends make gifts to your children (page 88).
- Options for preventing children from accessing money and assets too soon (page 88).

GIFTS FROM PARENTS

Every person, however young, is within the tax system and so benefits from the basic tax allowances, in particular the personal allowance for Income Tax (£7,475 in 2011–12 for anyone under 65) and yearly tax-free limit for CGT (£10,600 in 2011–12).

In theory, families could save tax by spreading their income and assets across all family members including the children. But in the case of Income Tax, rules devised to stop tax avoidance prevent this.

The rules work like this. If a parent makes gifts to a child who is under the age of 18 and unmarried, and such gifts produce more than £100 a year income, the whole of the income (not just the excess over £100) is taxed as that of the parent who made the gifts. This applies both to outright gifts and gifts made using trusts (see page 89).

 For more information on NS&I children's bonus bonds and other investments for children, see page 94.

The anti-avoidance rules do not apply to capital gains produced by a gift from a parent, nor do they apply to some types of tax-free income. So by choosing the investments carefully a parent can still make tax-efficient gifts to their child.

Investing for a tax-free income

If you invest a gift you have made to your own child and it produces tax-free income, in most cases the anti-avoidance rules do not apply so it will not matter if the gift produces more than £100 income. The exception until 2010–11 has been cash Individual Savings Accounts (ISAs).

Cash ISAs have not been an option for most children because you had to be aged at least 16 to be eligible (and 18 for stocks and shares ISAs). There is no tax on income from an ISA so you might think there would have been no problem if parental gifts to a teenager were invested in cash ISAs. But, unusually for tax-free income, the anti-avoidance rules specifically apply to these pre-2011 cash ISAs so, if the income from the parental gifts exceeded £100, it would be taxed as that of the parent. This problem may disappear from 2011–12, because the Coalition Government has announced that, from autumn 2011, new 'junior ISAs' will be available. These will be open to all children under 18 who do not have a Child Trust Fund (see page 98). The Government has said that tax treatment will be the same as for normal ISAs. It has not yet confirmed that the anti-avoidance rule will be relaxed for Junior ISAs. But the Government has made clear that the key purpose of introducing these new ISAs is to give parents a way of investing on behalf of their children.

Until the new junior ISAs come on stream, the main investments that parents can make for their children without being taxed on the income are National Savings & Investments (NS&I) children's bonus bonds, friendly society tax-efficient savings plans, Personal Pensions and, for children born between 1 September 2002 and 31 December 2010, the Child Trust Fund.

Investing for gains instead of income

The £100 rule applies only to income from parental gifts, so you can get around it by giving your child investments that are expected to produce capital gains instead.

Suitable gifts might be growth-oriented unit trusts and open-ended investment companies (OEICs), and capital shares in split-capital investment trusts – see 'Investments for children' on page 94 for details. You could also consider collectors' items, such as paintings and antiques.

■ PLANNING POINT

The £100 limit applies to each parent and each child, so two parents could jointly make gifts to each child, which would produce up to £200 a year income without triggering the anti-avoidance rule.

Gifts from other people

The £100 rule applies only to parental gifts. It does not affect gifts from grandparents, uncles, aunts, friends of the family or anyone else.

To avoid confusion with HMRC, it is important to be able to distinguish these gifts from any parental gifts. It would be sensible to invest the two types of gifts separately – for example, you could put small parental gifts in a building society account and gifts from other people in another account. It is also a good idea to ask people who give money to your child to accompany it with a brief note stating the amount of the gift and who it is from. Keep such notes and letters in a safe place in case HMRC need to see them.

Where a child is young, money is often given to the parents to invest or use on the child's behalf rather than being given directly to the child. This may in effect create a bare trust (see pages 79 and opposite) with the parent as the trustee who must use the money as instructed by the person who made the gift. Even though the parent may then open an investment in the child's name, the gift should not count as a parental gift and so should not be caught by the anti-avoidance rules.

{ Ask people who give money to your child to accompany it with a brief note. Keep if safely in case HMRC need to see it. }

THE TYPE OF GIFT

Before deciding which investments to choose for a child, you first need to decide how to arrange your gift.

Outright gift now

The most tax-efficient option is usually to make an immediate gift to the child. Often this means asking the child's parents (if you are not yourself the parent) to manage the investment on his or her behalf, but children can operate their own bank and building society accounts and NS&I investment accounts (usually from around age seven). They can also hold tax-efficient friendly society plans in their own names.

Earmarking your own savings to give later

You could invest money now in your own name and later on give the proceeds to the child. If you are not already making full use of your yearly ISA allowance, you could use this to invest for a tax-free return.

This option has the advantage of flexibility because you choose the precise timing of the gift and in the meantime you have the freedom to change your mind, for example, if you run short of money.

The main drawback is the failure to make use of the child's own tax allowances, since any income and gains will be yours. In addition, the investment remains part of your estate until the gift is finally made. So if you die before handing over the gift, there could be IHT to pay.

Giving to a trust

Instead of making a gift direct to a child, you could put it in trust. An explanation of different types of trust is given in Chapter 4, but here we look at the trusts that you are most likely to consider if you are making gifts to children.

USING TRUSTS

This section looks at the range of trusts that you may create or that may come into existence because of particular circumstances, which aim to provide benefit for children. It considers:

- Bare trusts
- 18-to-25 trusts (and old accumulation and maintenance trusts)
- Disabled trusts
- Bereaved minor trusts, and
- Other trusts you might choose.

The section also alerts you to the tax pitfalls of setting up a 'parental trust for children'.

Bare trusts

There is no formal paperwork involved in setting up a bare trust (also called a simple trust or absolute trust). It comes into being where you hold money or assets on behalf of someone else, in this case a child.

The assets are treated as belonging to the child who has the right to any income and can take possession of the assets as soon as they reach age 18 (age 16 in Scotland). You, as trustee, have no discretion to withhold the income and assets.

Gifts to the child, which are then held on bare trust, are treated in the same way for IHT as an outright gift, so this is a Potentially Exempt Transfer (PET) and so free of IHT, provided the giver survives for seven years. Alternatively, this could be an IHT-free gift if one of the exemptions described in Chapter 2 can be used. The giver would not pay any CGT if they gave cash, but might if they gave something else (see Chapters 2 and 3 for how the CGT exemptions and rules work).

The rules about gifts from parents described on page 86 apply, so if the

 To arrange for a child to receive a tax return, in the first instance contact the Self-assessment Helpline 0845 900 0444.

income from your gifts is greater than £100, you will need to include the income on your own tax return. Where gifts into the bare trust are from other people – for example, grandparents, uncles, aunts and family friends – any income earned by the gifts counts as the child's income. Whatever the source of the gifts, any capital gains are taxed as those of the child. Where income and gains exceed the child's tax-free limits for any year, the child is responsible for declaring the amounts and paying tax. Therefore, parents (or whoever is holding the assets in the bare trust) will need to complete a tax return on behalf of the child.

However, many children have income and gains well below their tax-free limits and so are non-taxpayers. This means there will be no need to send in a tax return and you may be able to register the child to receive income without tax deducted (see page 97) or claim back some or all of any tax deducted. You need to re-check the position each tax year.

18-to-25 trusts

An 18-to-25 trust is a discretionary trust for a child where the young person becomes entitled to all the income and trust property no later than age 25. It qualifies for some favourable IHT treatment.

In the past, a popular route for making gifts to children was via an 'accumulation and maintenance trust'. This was a type of discretionary trust (see page 77) intended particularly to build up some wealth for children and/or provide funding for their education and upbringing.

Accumulation and maintenance trusts received favourable IHT treatment, provided various rules were met. However, subject to some transitional rules, accumulation and maintenance trusts came to an end from March 2006 onwards. The very many existing trusts were given two choices: amend the rules before 6 April 2008 to become an 18-to-25 trust, in which case some favourable IHT treatment would continue; or, do nothing, in which case the trust reverted to being a normal discretionary trust, classified as a 'relevant property trust', so that the normal IHT rules apply (see page 80).

18-to-25 trusts may also be created under the will of a parent who has died or be set up by a court under the Criminal Injuries Compensation Scheme to provide for a child whose parent has died ('bereaved minor's trust').

There was no IHT when assets effectively passed into an 18-to-25 trust because of a change in the rules of a previous accumulation and maintenance trust and, provided the rules are met (see page 92), there is no IHT on assets passing into a bereaved minor's trust.

Discretionary trusts must normally pay IHT in the form of 10-yearly periodic charges plus 'exit charges' on payments out of the trust (see page 81). By contrast, with an 18-to-25 trust, up to age 18, there are no 10-yearly periodic IHT charges and no exit charges. If the child does not take control of all the income and assets by age 18, then an exit charge will apply to payments out of the trust between ages 18 and 25. The charge is based on the amount paid out, the number of three-month periods that have passed since the child's 18th birthday and the amount originally paid into the settlement. The case study, Alice (below), describes how this charge works in straightforward circumstances.

Normal Income Tax and CGT rules for discretionary trusts (see page 80) apply to the 18-to-25 trust, unless it is a bereaved minor's trust, in which case, see page 92. Also see Parental trusts for children on page 92.

GIVING TO CHILDREN

Case Study **ALICE**

Alice's grandfather set up an accumulation and maintenance trust for Alice in 2000, paying in £400,000. He had made no other gifts in the seven years up to that time. In 2007, the trust rules were changed so that it became an 18-to-25 trust. Alice had reached age 18 on 31 December 2006, but the trustees did not feel she was ready to take over the trust assets. On 31 March 2011, the trustees pay out £200,000 to Alice to enable her to buy a home. There is an IHT exit charge to pay, which is worked out according to the following formula:

Exit charge = Amount paid out × Relevant fraction × Settlement rate

The amount paid out is £200,000. The relevant fraction is the number of calendar quarters since Alice reached 18 as a proportion of the 40 quarters that would make up a 10-year period. This comes to 17 ÷ 40. The settlement rate is the notional IHT that would have been payable when the trust was set up using current IHT rates, expressed as a percentage of the original sum paid into the trust and then multiplied by 30 per cent. So the notional tax would have been (£400,000 − £325,000) × 20% = £15,000. As a percentage of the £400,000 originally paid in, this comes to £15,000 ÷ £400,000 = 3.75%. But only 30% of this rate applies, which comes to: 3.75% × 30% = 1.125%. The trustees can now work out the exit charge as:

£200,000 × 17 ÷ 40 × 1.125% = £956.25

If Alice pays the tax, the IHT remains at £956.25, but Alice will then have only £200,000 − £956.25 = £199,043.75 after tax. More likely, the trustees will pay the tax for her, in which case the tax, as well as the £200,000, are both gifts from the trustees for IHT purposes. To find out the value of this gross gift and the amount of tax due, the trustees need to gross up the £200,000 paid out. This is done by dividing the amount paid out by:

1 − (Relevant fraction × Settlement rate)

So the trustees work out 1 − (17 ÷ 40 × 1.125%) = 0.99522. Dividing £200,000 by 0.99522 comes to £200,960. The exit charge is then recalculated using this grossed up amount: £200,960 × 17 ÷ 40 × 1.125% = £960.84. Alice receives £200,000 and the trust assets are reduced by £200,960.84.

Disabled person's trust

A disabled person's trust is one where the beneficiary has a physical or mental disability and broadly the assets in, and income from, the trust are used solely for the benefit of the disabled person (for example, this could include providing for their care, living costs, and so on). It could be a good option if you are concerned to provide for a disabled child. (However, this type of trust can be used to provide for a disabled person of any age and can also be set up by someone who has a condition that they expect will lead to disability later on.)

This type of trust counts as a trust for a vulnerable person and can qualify for favourable tax treatment – see the box, below.

Bereaved minor's trust

This is a trust set up either in your will or as a result of the laws that apply if you have made no will (see Chapter 8) to pass assets to your dependent child in the event of your death. A dependent child is under age 18 and unmarried. The assets going into the trust can only come from a parent and not, for example, a grandparent.

This type of trust can count as a trust for a vulnerable person and can qualify for favourable tax treatment – see the box, below. Provided the child takes over the trust assets on or before age 18, there is no IHT periodic or exit charge. However, you might be reluctant to think of your child taking control of substantial assets at such an early age, in which case the trust can be set up to delay the transfer of assets

Trust for a vulnerable person

Trusts to benefit disabled people or bereaved children can count as 'qualifying' for IHT purposes and so receive favourable IHT treatment. They are also treated favourably for Income Tax and CGT. You have to claim to have a trust recognised as a 'trust for a vulnerable person'.

Payments into the trust count as PETs for IHT and so become tax-free provided the person making the gift survives seven years (see page 55). There is no 10-yearly periodic charge and no exit charge. If the disabled person or child dies, the trust assets count as part of the person's estate and are then taxed in the normal way (see Chapters 3 and 9).

For Income Tax and CGT, the trustees first work out tax using the normal rules. These rules are different depending on whether this is an interest-in-possession trust or discretionary trust (see page 76). But the trustees also work out what tax would have been if the disabled person or child had directly received the income and gains, in which case their tax-free limits and tax bands would have determined the tax due. Usually this results in a lower tax bill and the trustees can claim the difference as a reduction in the amount of tax they hand over to the Revenue. The special treatment for Income Tax does not apply if the trust is a 'settlor-interest trust' (see page 83) but is not affected by the 'parental trust for children' rules (see below).

to the young person up to age 25. In that case, there will be an IHT exit charge for payments out of the trust after age 18 under the rules described on page 90 for 18-to-25 trusts.

Parental trusts for children

Tax avoidance rules apply where a parent – but not any other person – sets up a trust that benefits their own children or could do so. The rules affect the Income Tax, but not CGT or IHT, treatment of the trust and apply to income from parental gifts to any type of trust: bare trust, interest-in-possession trust or discretionary trust. But these tax-avoidance rules specifically do not affect either a disabled person's trust or a bereaved minor's trust set up by a parent for their child.

Page 83 described the way that trust income may be taxed as yours if you set up a trust from which you or your spouse or civil partner can benefit (called settlor-interested trusts). Since April 2006, similar rules apply if you set up a trust from which, although neither you nor your spouse or civil partner can benefit, your dependent children can. A dependent child is your child or step-child who is under age 18 and unmarried.

If your child can benefit either directly or indirectly from the trust, then you will normally be responsible for any tax due on income paid out to the child, used for the benefit of the child, or which the child is entitled to receive. In practice, the trustees will work out the tax, hand it over to the HMRC and notify you of the amount. You must then declare this income and tax paid on your tax return and may have extra tax to pay or may be able to claim a refund. There is an exception: the rules described on page 86 apply, so that, if income from all your gifts to the child comes to less than £100 a year, it will count as the child's income rather than yours.

{ If your child can benefit from the trust, you will normally be responsible for tax. }

To claim special tax treatment for a disabled person's trust or bereaved minor's trust, complete form VPE1, which you can download from www.hmrc.gov.uk/trusts/vpe1.rtf or request from the tax office that normally deals with the trust concerned. Any solicitor you are using can help you obtain and complete the form.

INVESTMENTS FOR CHILDREN

The purpose of your gift and the amount will be big factors in determining the types of investments you choose for a child.

The investments you choose to give a child depend largely on the purpose of the investment, the amount involved and whether you want to invest on a regular basis or as a single lump sum, how long you want to invest, the amount of risk you are comfortable taking, and how the investment is taxed.

> The most suitable choices for medium- to long-term goals are usually share-based investments.

THE PURPOSE OF YOUR GIFT

The table below suggests some suitable investments depending on the purpose you have in mind. The list includes Child Trust Funds (CTF) accounts even though this scheme has stopped for children born from 1 January 2011 onwards. However, existing schemes for children born between 2002 and 2010 continue as normal. This includes being able to switch from one provider and/or type of account to another. For details of CTFs, see pages 98–100.

Investments for children	
AIM OF THE GIFT	**SUITABLE INVESTMENTS**
Teach the child money-management skills	Bank or building society account Cash ISA (if child is age 16 or over)
Encourage the child to learn how to save	Bank or building society account Cash ISA (if child is age 16 or over)
Build up a nest-egg	Junior ISA Child Trust Fund (CTF) NS&I children's bonus bonds NS&I premium bonds Friendly society tax-efficient plan Unit trusts and OEICs Investment trusts
Build up a pension	Stakeholder Pension

Short-term aims

To encourage money-management skills or the savings habit, cash gifts direct to the child are likely to be best. These can be paid into a bank or building society account. Many providers offer accounts specifically for children with free gifts, regular magazines, and so on. It is important that the child has ready access to the account, so check out banks and building societies that have branches near the child's home.

Long-term aims

Building up a nest-egg for a child is normally a medium- to long-term aim (five to ten years or more). The most suitable choices for medium- to long-term goals are usually share-based investments. In the past, share-based investments have tended to produce higher returns than bank and building society accounts. But share-based investments involve capital risk – in other words, the value of the investment can go down as well as up. If you are not comfortable with this risk, stick to the safer investments such as cash-based Child Trust Fund (CTFs) (if your child has a CTF – see page 98), savings accounts or NS&I children's bonus bonds.

A middling-risk option would be a stakeholder CTF. Another medium-risk option would be a friendly society tax-efficient plan (sometimes marketed as 'baby

bonds') invested on a with-profits basis. However, government rules limit the maximum investment in these plans to £25 per month or £270 per year per person. With such a small amount, any flat-rate charges can eat heavily into the investment, so check the impact of charges carefully before you invest.

This leaves a share-based CTF or unit and investment trusts as the main choices for long-term growth. A child can't hold unit and investment trusts direct, however you can make the investment in your name but 'designated' for the child. This is normally enough to ensure that a bare trust is created, though to be sure you could write to your tax office stating your intention that the investment be treated as belonging to the child.

A further option available from autumn 2011 is Junior ISAs. These will be open to all children under age 18 who do not have a CTF. They will be offered by banks, building societies, credit unions, friendly societies and other providers. Just like 'grown-up' ISAs, there will be two versions: cash and stocks-and-shares. The interest on cash Junior ISAs will be completely tax-free. The return from stocks-and-shares ISAs will be tax-free apart from 10 per cent tax on

---

 Capital risk The risk of losing some or all of the money you invest because the value of the investment can fall as well as rise

---

 If you are not sure which investments to choose, get advice from an independent financial adviser (IFA) – see page Useful Addresses on pages 214–17.

dividends. Unlike CTFs, there will be no payment from the Government and it will be up to you to decide whether or not to open a Junior ISA for your child. At the time of writing, further details were yet to be announced, including the yearly investment limit and any rules about being able to transfer from one ISA to another. However, unlike CTFs, there is no stakeholder version and, in general, the deal your child gets will depend on the specific charges, terms and conditions set by the provider, so you will need to shop around and compare, just as you do with 'grown-up' ISAs. Check the HMRC website for further details as they become available.

Finally, if you are thinking very long term indeed, you can pay up to £2,880 a year into a Personal Pension scheme for a child. This limit applies per recipient, so if you want to make gifts to several children you could pay in up to £2,880 a year for each of them. The child will not usually be able to take any proceeds from the scheme until he or she has reached at least age 55.

LOWER RISK INVESTMENTS IN DETAIL

With these investments, there is little or no risk of losing the amount originally invested, but over the long term the return tends to be lower than for higher-risk investments.

Bank and building society children's accounts

- **Description/suitable for** Accounts especially for children, usually offering introductory gifts, magazines, and so on. Useful as a way of teaching children how to manage money and getting them into the savings habit.
- **Return and charges** Interest, usually variable, on the amount invested. No explicit charges.
- **How long you invest for** Usually these are instant access accounts.
- **Minimum and maximum investment** Usually from £1. Usually no upper limit.
- **Tax** Interest usually paid with Income Tax at the savings rate already deducted. Children can usually reclaim this or arrange to be paid gross interest. But watch out if this is a gift from a parent (see page 86).

To compare various Personal Pensions on the market, use the comparison tables at www.moneyadviceservice/tables or call 0300 500 5000.

Children and Income Tax

Children are taxpayers in their own right and have a yearly tax-free Income Tax personal allowance (£7,745 in 2011–12). Most children have incomes well short of this allowance and so are non-taxpayers. Some types of income, such as that from bank and building society accounts, is paid with tax at the basic rate already deducted. If your child is a non-taxpayer, you can arrange for this interest to be paid 'gross' – in other words, without tax deducted – by completing form R85. You can get this form from the bank or building society concerned or download it from the HMRC website, www.hmrc. gov.uk. If your child has already received interest with tax deducted, you can reclaim the tax by using form R40 available from the HMRC website or the HMRC Orderline 0845 9000 404. You can go back up to four years after the end of the tax year in which the income was received to claim back tax. For example, provided you claim by 5 April 2012, you can claim back tax as far back as the 2007–8 tax year.

Cash CTF

- **Description/suitable for**
  Scheme for children born between 1 September 2002 and 31 December 2010. The Government provided vouchers (£250 at birth topped up to £500 for children in low-income families and a top-up for some children at age seven). These have been invested in the CTF and must be left untouched until the child reaches 18. Parents, friends and anyone else can add to the fund. At 18, the young person can use the fund in any way they choose. Parents choose how to invest the fund by opting for the cash version described here, a stakeholder CTF (see opposite) or a share-based CTF (see page 100). They can switch provider and/or type of CTF at any time. Although the CTF scheme ceased for children born after 31 December 2010, existing CTF accounts for children who were eligible are allowed to continue. There are no more government payments, but parents, family and friends can carry on paying in their gifts within the annual limit (see below).

- **Return and charges** Interest is added. Usually variable. Lump sum paid out at age 18. No explicit charges. May be charges or loss of bonus on switching.
- **How long you invest for** Until age 18.
- **Minimum and maximum investment** Minimum is the Government vouchers. Parents and others can add up to £1,200 a year in total.
- **Tax** Interest is tax-free.
- **How to invest** Contact the provider, which may be a bank or building society. For a full list of providers, see the foot of this page.

 For full information about CTF accounts, including a list of providers, visit the Government website at www.childtrustfund.gov.uk/ or call the Child Trust Fund Helpline 0845 302 1470.

There is either very low or no capital risk with the investments in this section. NS&I products are ultimately backed by the Government, so there is no risk. Banks and building societies must belong to the Financial Services Compensation Scheme, which covers savings up to £85,000 in the event of a bank or society going bust.

Cash ISAs

- **Description/suitable for** Savings account that pays tax-free interest. Many are instant access accounts. Must be aged at least 16. (However, the Government has proposed that new 'junior ISAs' be introduced from autumn 2011 for younger children.)
- **Return and charges** Interest on the amount invested. This is often variable, but occasionally fixed. Interest rates may be tiered with higher rates paid on larger balances. No explicit charges.
- **How long** you invest for For instant access accounts there is no set period. For other types of accounts, check the conditions.
- **Minimum and maximum investment** Often from £1. Maximum investment is set each year by the tax rules (£5,340 in 2011–12).
- **Tax** Tax-free interest.
- **How to invest** Contact provider, which may be a bank, building society or NS&I. You cannot hold an ISA on behalf of someone else (such as a child).

NS&I children's bonus bonds

- **Description/suitable for** Bonds that can be bought by anyone aged 16 and over for someone aged 16 or less. Useful as a way of giving a small nest-egg to a child.
- **Return and charges** Fixed return made up of interest and bonus added at end of term. Fixed return means the child would miss out if competing interest rates rose. No explicit charges.
- **How long you invest for** Five-year term. The child can have the money back early, but then loses interest. At the end of five years, you can reinvest for a new fixed return over five years, provided the child is still under age 16. Bonds must be cashed by age 21.
- **Minimum and maximum investment** From £25 up to £3,000 per issue per child.
- **Tax** Interest is tax-free.
- **How to invest** NS&I or through post offices.

NS&I premium bonds

- **Description/suitable for** Bonds that give you the chance to win prizes by, in effect, gambling with the interest you would otherwise have earned.
- **Return and charges** Prizes ranging from £25 up to £1 million. Random prize draw is held every month. Each £1 invested counts as a separate

---

 For information about NS&I products, visit its website at www.nsandi.com.

bond and has a chance to win. If winnings are not reinvested, or winnings are small, your capital is vulnerable to inflation risk. No explicit charges.

- **How long you invest for** There is no set period.
- **Minimum and maximum investment** £100 up to £30,000 including reinvested prizes.
- **Tax** Prizes are tax-free.
- **How to invest** NS&I or through post offices. Bonds can be bought on behalf of children by parents and grandparents.

HIGHER RISK INVESTMENTS IN DETAIL

The value of these investments can fall as well as rise, but they tend to give better returns over the long term than safer investments.

Stakeholder CTF

- **Description/suitable for** Scheme generally as for cash CTFs (see left). To use the name 'stakeholder', this type of CTF must meet various conditions concerning, for example, the way it is invested and charges.
- **Return and charges** Pay-out and options at 18 as for cash CTF. Charges must come to no more than 1.5 per cent a year of the value of investments in the fund. There must be no charge for switching into or out of a stakeholder CTF.

- **Risk** Medium risk. Many stakeholder CTFs work basically like unit trusts (see page 101). A stakeholder CTF must be invested in a range of assets, including stock-market investments. The aim is to balance a reasonable chance of long-term growth with a controlled level of capital risk. The fund must also be 'lifestyled', which means that, from age 13 onwards, the fund shifts out of stock market investments and into safer deposits in order to lock in gains and protect against the effects of any sharp fall in the stock market as the child approaches age 18.
- **How long you invest for** Until age 18.
- **Minimum and maximum investment** As for cash CTFs (see opposite). A stakeholder CTF must accept amounts as low as £10.
- **Tax** There is no tax for the investor to pay. Investments in the underlying fund build up largely tax-free but dividends from shares and similar income has had tax at 10 per cent deducted and this cannot be reclaimed.
- **How to invest** Through direct contact with providers, which are mainly banks, friendly societies and fund managers or through an IFA. However, all CTF providers must offer the option of a stakeholder CTF, so banks and building societies offering cash CTFs will also offer access to a stakeholder CTF – and sometimes this is from another provider.

Share-based CTF

- **Description/suitable for** As for cash CTFs (see page 98).
- **Return and charges** Pay-out and options at 18 as for cash CTF. Usually an up-front charge (up to 5 per cent or so of the amount invested) and an annual management charge (generally from 0.5 up to 1.5 per cent a year of the value of the fund). Other charges are deducted direct from the fund. Often charges for switching between funds.
- **Risk** Medium to high risk. Many work basically like unit trusts (see opposite).
- **How long you invest for** Until age 18.
- **Minimum and maximum investment** As for cash CTFs (see page 98). But minimum varies from one provider to another, for example, £10 to £100 for regular sums and £10 to £500 as one-off amounts.
- **Tax** As for stakeholder CTFs (see page 99).
- **How to invest** Through direct contact with providers who are mainly friendly societies, fund managers and stockbrokers or through an IFA.

Friendly society tax-efficient plans

- **Description/suitable for** Friendly societies are similar to insurance companies and generally offer similar types of product. But friendly societies are able to offer small savings plans that give a largely tax-free return (in contrast to most insurance policies where the insurance company has already paid tax on the return from the underlying investments). Useful as a way of building up a small nest-egg. Some of these plans are specifically marketed as investments for children.
- **Return and charges** The plan usually pays out a lump sum after a set number of years, for example ten. Usually, there is an administration fee when you invest. If the plan is invested on a unit-linked basis (similar to a unit trust), there is also usually an initial charge (up to, say, 5 per cent) and an annual management charge (for example, 1.5 per cent a year of the value of the investment fund) with other costs charged direct to the fund. If the plan is invested on a with-profits basis (see page 102), charges influence the level of bonuses.
- **Risk** Capital risk varies depending on the underlying investments.
- **How long you invest for** Usually you must invest for at least ten years. If you cash in your investment early, surrender charges reduce the amount you get back – perhaps to even less than you had invested.

 For a full list of providers, visit the CTF website: www.childtrustfund.gov.uk.

- **Minimum and maximum investment** Minimum varies from one society to another. Maximum set by tax rules at £25 a month or £270 a year.
- **Tax** There is no tax for the investor to pay and the investments in the underlying fund build up largely tax-free, but dividends from shares and similar income has had tax at 10 per cent deducted and this cannot be reclaimed.
- **How to invest** Through direct contact with friendly societies or via an IFA.

Share-based unit trusts and open-ended investment companies (OEICS)

- **Description/suitable for** You buy 'units' in a unit trust (or shares in an OEIC) which give you a stake in an investment fund. The fund is a ready-made portfolio of many different shares. You can choose funds that aim to produce income and/or growth.
- **Return and charges** The return takes the form of income distributions usually paid/credited every six months and/or, if you sell your units for more than you paid, a capital gain. You can choose growth funds that pay low or no distributions. There is usually an up-front charge (up to 5 per cent or so of the amount you invest) and an annual management charge (usually around 1 to 1.5 per cent a year of the value of your investment).

Other charges are deducted direct from the investment fund.
- **Risk** The price of the units can fall as well as rise, so you are exposed to capital risk.
- **How long you invest for** No set period but because the value of the investment fund can fall as well as rise you should normally aim to invest for the long term (more than five years).
- **Minimum and maximum investment** Varies from, say, £500 or more as a lump sum and £50 per month for regular savings. No maximum.
- **Tax** Distributions are paid with tax at 10 per cent already deducted. Non-taxpayers, such as most children, cannot reclaim this tax. Capital gains are taxable, the child is likely to have unused allowance in which case there will be no tax to pay. Watch out if gift from a parent (see page 86).
- **How to invest** You can go to the provider direct, but you'll often pay less in charges if you go to a discount broker or fund supermarket. You can also invest through most IFAs and many stockbrokers.

The price of the units can fall as well as rise.

Personal Pension schemes

- **Description/suitable for** A way of saving for retirement. Anyone – even a child – can have a scheme. Other people can invest in your scheme on your behalf. Money invested early in life has a long time to grow so makes a particularly valuable contribution towards retirement savings.
- **Return and charges** Your money can be invested either on a unit-linked basis (similar to unit trusts) or a with-profits basis (see box, below).
- **Risk** Capital risk varies depending on the underlying investments.
- **How long you invest for** Until at least age 55.
- **Minimum and maximum investment** From, say, £20, whether this is a regular contribution or a lump sum up to £2,880 a year (unless the child

Investment trusts

These give you a stake in an investment fund and so are an alternative to investing in unit trusts or OEICs, but work in a different way. You invest by buying the shares of the investment trust company.

has earnings, in which case more can be invested).
- **Tax** The Government adds basic-rate tax relief to the contributions (even for a non-taxpayer). Gains and most of the income from investing the contributions are tax-free. But income from shares and similar investments has had tax at 10 per cent deducted and this cannot be reclaimed. Part of the proceeds can be drawn as a tax-free lump sum; the rest must be taken as taxable pension.
- **How to invest** Through direct contact with pension providers or via an IFA.

With-profits investments

Your savings grow through the addition of yearly bonuses which, once added, can't usually be taken back. The size of bonuses depends largely on the growth of an underlying investment fund, which is typically invested in shares, bonds, property and cash. Bonuses are smoothed by keeping back in reserve some growth from good years to top up your return in poor years. An extra 'terminal' bonus is also added when the policy matures. You are not totally protected from large stock market swings because, if you cash in your policy early and investment returns have been poor, the provider can deduct a charge (called a 'market value reduction' or MVR).

SUMMARY

This chapter has considered a variety of ways to invest for a child, thinking about the purpose of your gifts, their structure (outright or in trust) and the types of savings and investment products you might use. Parents need to be particularly careful when making gifts to their own children and step-children to avoid any income produced by the gifts being taxed as income of the parent.

GIVING TO CHARITY

An aim of the Coalition Government is to create a cultural shift so that giving to charity becomes a social norm. If supporting good causes is already part of your financial planning, arranging your gifts efficiently can boost the amount your chosen charities receive and save you and your heirs tax as well.

A CULTURE OF GIVING

Just as wealth taxes are shaped by the political climate, so too are attitudes towards charitable giving. Reducing the size of the State goes hand-in-hand with encouraging giving to the voluntary sector.

WHAT'S IN THIS CHAPTER?

Governments generally encourage giving to charity, so in the UK there are a variety of schemes that either boost the amount you give to good causes or directly give you tax relief on your donations. This chapter covers:

- The political context for giving (see right).
- The Gift Aid and Payroll Giving schemes (page 106).
- Donations in the form of shares or property (page 115).
- Leaving money to charity in your will (page 117).
- A selection of schemes and products to help you make the most of the tax reliefs (page 118).

{ The Coalition Government aims to create a step change in giving. }

THE POLITICAL CONTEXT

There are two main schemes that offer tax breaks to encourage charitable giving: Gift Aid introduced in 1990 and Payroll Giving, which, though less popular, is the slightly older scheme having started up in 1987. Both schemes were introduced by a Conservative government. Although Labour governments extended the range of potential recipients to include community amateur sports groups and introduced tax breaks for gifts of shares and property to charities, the climate for giving has been little changed for more than two decades. The Coalition Government, driven by the need for austerity and an underlying Conservative ideology to reduce the size of the State, aims to create a step change in the UK public's approach to giving.

In December 2010, the Coalition Government published a paper (the 'Giving Green Paper') to discuss ideas around giving as part of its push to create a 'Big Society'. The paper invited debate on giving to charities and other good causes in the form money, assets, time, knowledge and skills. It stressed that giving should remain voluntary, but, drawing on the current fashion for behavioural science, sought to explore ways in which government could encourage a cultural shift. It set out five elements to achieve this shift (employing the acronym 'GIVES'):

- **Great opportunities.** This involves making giving painless and affordable. It includes ideas, such as 'Round Pound', by which you would round up most direct debit and similar payments to the nearest pound with the extra pence going to charity. Other ideas are the option to give to charity automatically every time you use a cash machine and having the opportunity to donate whenever you interact with the Government to, say, file a tax return, apply for a driving licence or renew your passport. Increasing opportunities for giving also involves harnessing new technology to make giving online easier. There are already a number of online schemes available and some of these are described on page 120.
- **Information.** The internet and other initiatives can be used to help you find out about opportunities for giving, especially volunteering your time.
- **Visibility.** The idea here is that there should be more openness around giving and volunteering, so that participating is seen as a social norm. If you see your family, friends and neighbours giving, you are more likely to feel that you should do the same. The discussion paper

suggests that, for cash donations, giving around 1 per cent of income to charity could become the norm, though some experts favour a proportion as high as 10 per cent.

- **Exchange.** The discussion paper emphasises that giving is not a 'one-way street' and that people who give feel good about themselves and also gain in more tangible benefits, such as opportunities to make new friends and gain new skills. Other initiatives could involve gaining credits for volunteering that you could trade in when you need help from others.
- **Support.** This element focuses on what government can do to help communities, charities and social enterprises to expand, including taking over responsibilities from the State. Ideas focus on, for example, removing red tape and encouraging businesses to get involved.

The remainder of this chapter focuses on the schemes that already exist to promote giving cash and assets to charity by offering tax savings, but you should be aware that new initiatives are likely to emerge as the Big Society debate unfolds.

Who gives to charity?

In 2009–10, over half (56 per cent) the UK adult population gave to charity in a typical month, with an average donation of £12 a month. Nearly half (47 per cent) of the total amount donated came from just 8 per cent of the population, who typically gave over £100 a month.

Source: HM Government, *Giving Green Paper*, December 2010.

 To find out which sports clubs qualify as 'community amateur sports clubs' and so can receive your Gift Aid and Payroll Giving donations, visit the HMRC website at www.hmrc.gov.uk/casc/clubs.htm.

CASH DONATIONS TO CHARITY

By arranging your donations to charity tax-efficiently, you benefit the charity as well as yourself.

GIFT AID

Gift Aid is a scheme to encourage you to make donations to charity by giving you tax relief on the amount you donate. You can get tax relief up to your highest rate on money you give to charity or a community amateur sports club through the Gift Aid scheme. You can make gifts of any amount this way.

The amount you give is treated as having had tax relief at the basic rate (20 per cent in 2011–12) already deducted. The charity then claims the tax relief from the HMRC and adds it to your gift. If you pay tax at the higher or additional rate, you can claim extra tax relief, which is given either through an adjustment to your pay-as-you-earn (PAYE) tax code or through the self-assessment system. The extra relief is given by 'grossing up' your net donation. For example, suppose you donate £100. This is treated as a net donation and you find its grossed-up value by adding back tax at the basic rate, in this case £25, since £25 is 20 per cent of the gross donation of £125. You can work out the grossed-up donation using the following sum: net donation ÷ (1 – tax rate). In this example: £100 ÷ (1 – 20%) = £125. The amount of your income taxed at the basic rate is increased by the gross contribution. In this example, that means an extra £125 of income is taxed at just the basic, rather than the higher or additional rate, giving you the extra tax relief due. See the case study, Naveed, opposite.

The charity claims tax relief at the basic rate from HMRC to add to your net donation. In the example above, the charity would receive £100 from your donation and claim £25 tax relief from HMRC, meaning that the charity would get £125 in total. (However, some special rules applied in the three tax years 2008–9, 2009–10 and 2010–11. In 2008–9, the basic rate of Income Tax was cut from 22 per cent to 20 per cent. For a transitional period of three years, although you still grossed up your donation at the new 20 per cent rate, the charity could claim tax relief at the old 22 per cent rate. So a £100 net donation would mean the charity got £128.21 in total,

See page 112 for how Gift Aid can boost donations of clothes and possessions to charity shops.

since £28.21 is 22 per cent of £128.21.)

To use the Gift Aid scheme, you simply need to give the charity concerned a Gift Aid declaration saying that you are a UK taxpayer and giving your name and address. The declaration does not have to be in any particular form and can be given by phone, as well as in person or by internet, email or fax. If you are a higher or additional rate taxpayer, you should ask for a record of your donation and the Gift Aid declaration to back up your claim for extra relief.

A Gift Aid declaration can apply to a single gift or can be indefinite and cover your current and future donations to that charity until you cancel the declaration. Make sure you cancel any continuing declarations if you become a non-taxpayer (see page 112).

In Budget 2011, the Government announced that from April 2013, Gift Aid can apply to small donations up to £10 without any written declaration. This means that some charities will be able to claim the Government addition on money you put in, say, collecting tins.

Gift Aid and tax allowances

If you're aged 65 or over, you qualify for a higher age-related personal allowance (often called 'age allowance') – see the table on page 109. And, if you are a married man and you or your wife were born before 6 April 1935, you can qualify for Married Couple's Allowance, which includes an age-related addition. However, if your 'total income' exceeds a given limit (£24,000 in 2011–12), your age-related allowances are reduced until they reach a basic amount. The rate of reduction is £1 for every £2 by which total income exceeds the limit.

Whatever your age, if your income exceeds £100,000, you start to lose the basic amount of personal allowance. Once again, you lose it at a rate of £1 of allowance for every £2 of total income above the threshold. This carries on until the whole personal allowance is lost, which, in 2011–12, happens when your income reaches £114,950.

'Total income' is basically your income from most sources, excluding tax-free income (for example, from Individual Savings Accounts (ISAs) or National Savings & Investments Certificates) less certain expenses that qualify for tax relief. Gift Aid donations are one such expense.

If you are in the income bracket where you are losing (or have just lost) either age allowance – see the table, opposite – or your basic amount of personal allowance, making donations by Gift Aid is especially tax-efficient. In addition to the charity claiming back relief on your gift, you will get an increase in your allowance that will reduce your tax bill. See the case study, Stan, left.

Gift Aid and tax credits

Working Tax Credit (WTC) and Child Tax Credit (CTC) are state benefits that are integrated with the tax system in the sense that the amount of credit you can get depends broadly on your income for tax purposes. If you are a couple, credits are based on your joint income.

Gift Aid donations are deducted from your income in assessing how much you qualify for in tax credits.

Case Study **STAN**

Stan is 76 and a widower. In 2011–12, Stan has an income from his state and occupational pensions of £28,000.

In 2011–12, the full age-related personal allowance for someone of Stan's age is £10,090. But, this is reduced by £1 for each £2 by which 'total income' exceeds £24,000, until the allowance matches the £7,475 basic amount. An income of £28,000 is £4,000 above the threshold, so Stan's age allowance is reduced to £10,090 – (£4,000 ÷ 2) = £8,090. Stan's tax bill comes to (£19,910 × 20%) = £3,982.

But then Stan decides to give £1,000 to the Royal Naval Benevolent Trust. The grossed-up donation is £1,000 ÷ (1 – 20%) = £1,250 and the charity is able to claim the £250 basic-rate relief from the Revenue.

Stan's grossed-up donation of £1,250 is deducted from his 'total income', reducing it to £28,000 – £1,250 = £26,750. This is £26,750 – £24,000 = £2,750 more than the £24,000 threshold at which age allowance starts to be lost. Therefore, Stan's age allowance is now £10,090 – (£2,750 ÷ 2) = £8,715. As a result, Stan's tax bill falls to (£19,285 × 20%) = £3,857.

The gross donation of £1,250 has reduced Stan's tax bill by £3,982 – £3,857 = £125, which is 10 per cent of the gross donation. Adding this to the 20 per cent relief claimed by the charity, Stan has, in effect, had total tax relief of 30 per cent on the gross donation of £1,250.

Age allowance and the income limit at which it is lost in 2011–12

AGE YOU REACH DURING THE TAX YEAR	IF YOU ARE MARRIED, AGE YOUR WIFE REACHES DURING THE TAX YEAR	MAXIMUM PERSONAL ALLOWANCE	MAXIMUM MARRIED COUPLE'S ALLOWANCE	INCOME LIMIT AT WHICH ALL AGE-RELATED ALLOWANCES LOST [1]
If you are a single person or a married woman [2]				
Under 65	Not applicable	£7,475	Not applicable	Not applicable
65 to 74	Not applicable	£9,940	Not applicable	£28,930
75 or over	Not applicable	£10,090	Not applicable	£29,230
If you are a married man [2]				
Under 65	Under 76	£7,475	Not applicable	Not applicable
	76 or over	£7,475	£7,295	£32,990
65 to 74	Under 76	£9,940	Not applicable	£28,930
	76 or over	£9,940	£7,295	£37,920
75	Under 76	£10,090	Not applicable	£29,230
	76 or over	£10,090	£7,295	£38,220
76 or over	Any age	£10,090	£7,295	£38,220

[1] You start to lose age allowance at a rate of £1 for every £2 of income over £24,000 in 2011–12.

[2] If you were married before 5 December 2005, the age-related part of the married couple's allowance is initially awarded to the husband and reduced in accordance with his income. For couples married on or after 5 December 2005 and for civil partners, the age-related part is awarded to the spouse or partner with the highest income – if this applies to you, in this table for 'married woman' read 'the person with the lower income' and for 'married man' read 'the person with the higher income'.

WTC is designed to help people who work but have only a low income. Households with no children would be unlikely to qualify if their income exceeds around £13,000 (single person) or £17,800 (couple) in 2011–12.

Households with children can qualify for CTC and, if they are in work, WTCs too. They can continue to be entitled to credits up to much higher levels of income than childless people. In 2011–12 you can get at least some CTC if your income is up to £41,300.

The tax credit system works by, first, assessing how much your household would receive if it had no income. This amount is made up of elements that vary according to your household circumstances – the main elements are shown in the table, overleaf. Next, your household's income is compared with an income threshold (see table overleaf). If your income exceeds the relevant threshold, you lose 41p of tax credits for every £1 of excess income. Since Gift Aid donations reduce your income for tax credit purposes, making

PLANNING POINT

Gift Aid donations can be especially tax efficient if you are getting age allowance or tax credits or you are losing personal allowance because your income is over £100,000. As well as tax relief on the donation, your tax allowance or tax credits may also increase.

For details of the tax credit rules and to check current rates, visit the HMRC website at www.hmrc.gov.uk/taxcredits.

GIVING TO CHARITY

Main features of the tax credit system in 2011–12

FEATURE	DESCRIPTION [1]	MAXIMUM AMOUNT £ A YEAR
Working Tax Credit (WTC) – main elements		
Basic	For every household	£1,920
Couple or lone parent	For two-person households or single parents	£1,950
30-hour	For households where at least one person works full-time	£790
Childcare	Covers a proportion of eligible childcare costs so parents can work	70% Maximum eligible costs: £175 a week for one child and £300 a week for more
Child Tax Credit (CTC) – main elements		
Family element	Single amount for a household with children	£545
Child element	Amount per child	£2,555
Income thresholds		
First threshold	Used where household qualifies for WTC (with or without CTC)	£6,420
First threshold – CTC only	Used where household qualifies for CTC other than just family element (and no WTC)	£15,860
Second threshold [2]	Applies to the family element	£40,000
Other features		
Taper	Rate at which tax credits reduced where income exceeds the relevant threshold	41%

[1] Tax credit rules are complex and the description here gives only a very broad outline.
[2] In 2012–13, this threshold is abolished and the family element will no longer be treated separately from the other tax credit elements.

Case Study ANDREA AND BOB

Andrea and Bob have one child, aged three months, and an income of £41,000. Bob works full-time and Andrea is currently at home looking after the baby. Their tax credit award for 2011–12 is worked out as follows:

- If they had no income, they would get the basic element of £1,920, the couple element of £1,950 and the 30-hour element of £790, a child element of £2,555 and the family element of £545.

- Apart from the family element, the elements would come to £7,215. But the household income is £41,000 – £6,420 = £34,580 above the first income threshold. This means their tax credits are reduced by 41% × £34,580 = £14,178. Since that is more than the total of the elements, their entitlement is reduced to £0.

- In 2011–12, the family element is treated separately. Income is compared against the second threshold of £40,000. Since their

income is £1,000 above the second threshold, they lose 41% × £1,000 = £410, reducing the family element to £545 – £410 = £135.

In other words, the family qualify for tax credits of £135 for the year. But the picture changes if Bob gives £400 to charity through the Gift Aid scheme. The grossed-up donation of £400 ÷ (1 – 20%) = £500 is deducted from his income. This means that, for tax credits, the household income is now £40,500. This is £500 above the second threshold and so the family element is reduced to £545 – (41% × £500) = £340. Andrea and Bob's income is still too high to qualify for any other tax credit elements. However, the family element is now £340 = £135 = £205 higher. This is equivalent to 41 per cent of the grossed-up Gift Aid donation. Adding this to the 20 per cent relief claimed by the charity, Bob and Andrea effectively get 61 per cent tax relief on the donation.

a donation not only saves tax, but can also increase your tax credits, boosting the effective tax saving. The case study, Andrea and Bob, opposite, gives an example of how this can work.

The tax credit system has been cut back in 2011–12 and is due to be reduced further from April 2012. This means fewer people are likely to qualify for tax credits and so be able to benefit from the impact of making Gift Aid donations. On the other hand, if you are still eligible for tax credits, the effective tax saving from making Gift Aid donations has, in many cases, increased. Tax credits are due to be abolished and replaced by a new state benefit for people of working age on low incomes probably from 2013 onwards.

Carrying back Gift Aid donations

For Gift Aid donations made on or after 6 April 2003, you can elect to have the gift treated for tax purposes (but not for tax credits) as if it had been paid in the previous tax year.

Your election must be made to HMRC in writing on or before the date on which you deliver your tax return for the year to which the donation is being carried back. There is space on the tax return to make this election.

For example, suppose you make a donation during 2011–12 that you want to carry back to the 2010–11 tax year. Your tax return for 2010–11 must be filed no later than 31 January 2012. This means you have until 31 January 2012 to both pay the donation and file your return. You cannot carry back the donation if you make it after 31 January 2012. If you

file your return early – say, by 31 October 2011 – you cannot carry back a donation made after that date.

To use the carry back election, you must have either income or capital gains in the earlier year on which you have paid tax.

Using the election affects only the tax relief you get and not the amount that can be reclaimed by the charity or sports club. It still claims back relief based on the basic tax rate for the year in which the donation was actually paid.

Carrying back a donation means you can claim any higher or additional rate tax relief more quickly and might save you tax in the following situations:

- You are a non-taxpayer or starting-rate taxpayer this tax year but paid tax at the basic, higher or additional rate last year.
- You are a basic-rate taxpayer this year but paid tax at the higher or additional rate last year.
- Your income last tax year was in the range where you were losing age or personal allowances.

Case Study JESS

In June 2011, Jess gives £250 to the Red Cross. After claiming tax relief, the Red Cross receives £312.50. Jess is a basic-rate taxpayer in 2011–12, so in the normal way there would be no further tax relief to come. But Jess was a higher-rate taxpayer in the previous tax year (2011–12). In January 2012, she is completing her 2010–11 tax return and elects to use the carry back rule so that her June 2011 donation is treated as if it had been paid in 2010–11. This means Jess qualifies for higher-rate tax relief of £62.50, which is given as a reduction in her tax bill for 2010–11.

Carrying back a Gift Aid donation does not affect a claim for tax credits because for this purpose the donation continues to be deductible for the year the donation was paid, not the year to which it was carried back.

Donating a tax rebate to charity

In the past, you have been able to use your tax return to elect that you donate all or part of a tax rebate to charity, opting for Gift Aid if you want. In Budget 2011, the Government announced that this arrangement has not been widely used and is being scrapped.

You will no longer be able to donate a tax rebate in this way, starting with the tax return for 2011–12 (that you receive in April 2012). And it will affect rebates for earlier tax years, where the refund is paid on or after 6 April 2012.

Of course, there is nothing stopping you from receiving your tax rebate and choosing to donate it to charity anyway – and via Gift Aid if that is right for you. You will simply need to make the arrangements yourself.

Gift Aid if you pay little or no tax

Do not use Gift Aid if you are a non-taxpayer or will have only a very low Income Tax and/or CGT bill for the year in which you pay the donation (or the year to which you elect to carry it back).

If you are a non-taxpayer, the charity will still claim the relief from HMRC. But HMRC will then ask you for tax equal to the relief given. Similarly, if your tax bill for the year is less than the amount of tax relief that you are treated as having deducted from your donation, the charity will still claim full tax relief on the donation, but HMRC will ask you for tax equal to the excess relief given.

'Retail Gift Aid'

Gift Aid only applies to gifts of money, not things. But there is a way you can use the Gift Aid scheme when you donate goods to a charity shop, if the shop operates 'retail Gift Aid'. In effect, the shop acts as your agent to sell your unwanted goods and you then freely choose to donate the proceeds of the sale to the charity using Gift Aid.

There are a couple of potential tax traps to note. Since the charity is acting purely as your agent, the goods remain yours until they are sold. Therefore, you are selling an asset and normal CGT rules apply. Most small

Case Study SHIMAILA

Shimaila is 68. She has an income of £10,000 a year from her state pension, a small widow's pension, a small amount of savings and pension credit. Tax on her income is expected to be just £12 in 2011–12. In September 2011, Shimaila decides to give £200 to The Friends of Verrington Hospital, a local charity supporting the hospital where her late sister was nursed through her final illness. If Shimaila makes the donation through Gift Aid, she will be treated as having deducted tax relief from the gift of £50 (20 per cent of the grossed-up gift of £250). This is £50 – £12 = £38 more than her expected tax bill for the year, so she can expect her tax office to adjust her bill to collect the extra £38. To avoid this, Shimaila makes the gift without using the Gift Aid scheme.

items that you would sell through a charity shop will be covered by the exemptions that apply to chattels (see Chapter 2) or fall within your yearly tax-free limit (see Chapter 3). However, if you were selling a valuable item, there could be CGT to pay and it would normally then be more tax efficient simply to give the item to the charity.

If you regularly sell items through charity shops – for example, jewellery or cards that you make – rather than running into CGT, you could find that HMRC treats you as if you are running a business and seeks to charge Income Tax on the profits that you make and, if your turnover were high enough, you might have to register for VAT. However, a business operating as a sole trader or partnership can still use the Gift Aid scheme to donate part or all of its profits to the charity.

Other points to note about Gift Aid

Your gift will not qualify for Gift Aid if you (or someone connected with you, such as a family member) in return get some benefit as a result of the gift and the benefit exceeds the limits shown in the table, below.

But you can ignore the following benefits:

- The right to free or reduced-price entry to properties preserved for the public benefit, where maintaining such properties is the main or sole purpose of the charity and the opportunity to benefit is publicly available.
- The right to free or reduced-price entry to observe wildlife, where the conservation of such wildlife is the sole or main purpose of the charity and the opportunity to benefit is publicly available.

Case Study JUNE

June is not a regular churchgoer but likes to go to a service from time to time. Last Sunday, she noticed a pile of envelopes as she entered the church with 'Gift Aid' printed across the top. The steward explained that, provided she was a taxpayer, instead of just putting cash direct on the collection plate, she could first put her offering in one of these envelopes, filling in the form on the front. That way the church could claim back tax relief on whatever she gave. June put £3 in the envelope. The church can claim back 75p in tax relief, bringing the total offering to £3.75 at a cost to Mary of just £3. Multiplied across its whole congregation, Gift Aid is a valuable source of extra funds for the church.

Maximum benefit for Gift Aid

SIZE OF YOUR GIFT	MAXIMUM BENEFIT ALLOWED	EXAMPLE
up to £100	25% of the value of the gift	You give £50, any benefit must be worth no more than £50 × 25% = £12.50
Over £100 up to £1,000	£25	You give £500. The maximum benefit is £25
Over £1,000	5% up to a maxiumum value of £2,500	You give £1,500. Any benefit must be worth no more than £1,500 × 5% = £75

Limits from 2011–12 onwards. The limits shown apply to the total of your gifts in the same tax year to the same charity.

PAYROLL GIVING SCHEMES

Payroll Giving (also called 'Payroll Deduction') is a method of making regular gifts to charity out of your salary. It is open only to employees and only to those whose employer operates a Payroll Giving scheme. You can give any amount using this scheme.

The scheme works like this. Your employer sets up an arrangement with an agency approved by the HMRC (in fact, a few employers have set up their own agencies).

You then tell your employer how much you want to give each payday and to which charity or charities. The employer deducts the specified amount from your pay and hands it over to the agency, which arranges for the money to be transferred to the charities you picked. The agency may make a charge – for example, 5 per cent of the donations it handles – to cover its own running costs, but sometimes there is no charge or your employer might separately cover any administration costs.

Your donation is deducted from your pay before tax (but not National Insurance) is worked out, so you automatically get full Income Tax relief. Payroll Giving is popular with charities because they receive the whole (gross) donation direct from you, thereby avoiding any paperwork and delay involved in claiming tax relief from HMRC as they have to with Gift Aid.

If your employer operates a Payroll Giving scheme, he or she can provide you with details and an application form. You do not have to keep up your donations for any minimum period of time. You stop making them whenever you like simply by informing your employer of your wishes.

Payroll Giving cannot be used in combination with any of the other tax-advantageous ways of giving to charity. So, for example, you cannot claim Gift Aid relief on donations made through a Payroll Giving scheme. HMRC rules do not allow Payroll Giving to be used to pay subscriptions entitling you, for example, to membership benefits from a charity.

Case Study MARY

Mary earns £1,030 a month, before tax, working in the local supermarket. The supermarket operates a Payroll Giving scheme through which Mary gives £10 a month each to Age UK and Barnardo's. Normally, Mary would pay £81.42 a month in Income Tax (during the 2011–12 tax year), but after deducting the Payroll Giving from her pay, the tax bill is reduced to £77.42 a month. In other words, Mary gets tax relief of £4 a month, which reduces the cost to her of the £20 she gives to charity to just £16.

 One of the largest agencies running Payroll Giving schemes is the Charities Aid Foundation (CAF) – www.cafonline.org – which operates a scheme called Give As You Earn (GAYE).

OTHER DONATIONS

You do not have to donate cash to charities. You could instead give something you own: for example, land, premises, a car, furniture or investments such as shares.

Normally you might have to pay CGT and even IHT when you give something away. But gifts to charities and community amateur sports clubs, are generally completely free of these particular taxes.

For the exemption from IHT to apply, you must relinquish all your rights to whatever it is that you are giving. For example, there might well be a tax bill if you gave the freehold of your home to a charity but continued to live there. For more details about the way CGT and IHT work, see Chapter 3.

In addition to the CGT and IHT reliefs described above, gifts of some types of assets to charities – but not community amateur sports clubs – can also qualify for Income Tax relief. This applies to gifts of shares and similar investments and also gifts of land or buildings.

▪ PLANNING POINT ▪

Giving shares, unit trusts, land or property direct to charity, rather than selling them first and giving cash, can be very tax-efficient where you would stand to make a gain on the assets if they were sold. If the assets are standing at a loss, it can be more efficient to sell them first and give cash using the Gift Aid scheme.

GIFTS OF SHARES OR SIMILAR INVESTMENTS

You can claim Income Tax relief when you give any of these investments to a charity:

- Shares or securities listed on a recognised stock exchange.
- Unlisted shares or securities dealt on a recognised stock exchange (including the Alternative Investment Market).
- Units in an authorised unit trust.
- Shares in an open-ended investment company (OEIC).
- An interest in an offshore investment fund.

You can claim the market value of the shares or units you give (plus any costs of disposal you incur) as a deduction from your income. This means you get Income Tax relief up to your top rate. If you receive anything for the shares or units – either cash or a benefit in kind – this is deducted from the amount you can claim.

This relief is available not only for gifts to charities but also to the National Heritage Memorial Fund, the Historic Buildings and

Monuments Commission for England, the British Museum and the Natural History Museum.

Note that you can only claim this Income Tax relief against your income and not against any capital gains you make on other sales or gifts. This means that giving shares or units will not be tax-efficient if you do not have enough income against which to set the relief.

GIFTS OF LAND OR BUILDINGS

Income Tax relief is available on a gift of land or buildings to charity – but not community amateur sports clubs – made on or after 6 April 2002. Giving land or buildings works in much the same way as giving shares (see above), so you can claim the market value of the property plus any disposal costs less anything you receive in exchange.

The property must be in the UK but can be either freehold or leasehold. You must completely give up your ownership rights and, if you own the property jointly with other people, you must surrender your rights to the charity.

In general, relief is withdrawn if, within five years of 31 January following the tax year in which you give the property away, you acquire any interest or right in the property. There are two exceptions: first, if you acquire the interest through the death of someone; and second, if you pay the full going rate for the interest or right – for example, if you live in the property but pay the full market rent.

To claim the relief, you must have a certificate from the charity concerned describing the property, the date it was given and stating that the charity has accepted the gift.

Case Study HARRY

Harry, who is a higher-rate taxpayer, wants to make a substantial donation to the Arthritis Research Campaign (ARC). He is considering funding his donation by selling some of his Tesco plc shares.

Harry could sell the shares for £2,500, of which £1,000 would be taxable. He has already used up his CGT allowance for the year (see page 43), so he would have to pay tax of 28% × £1,000 = £280. This would leave £2,500 – £280 = £2,220 to give to ARC. The gift would qualify for Gift Aid (see page 106), so ARC would claim back basic-rate tax relief on the £2,220 and Harry would get higher-rate relief on the gift. This would mean ARC received £2,775 in total at an overall cost to Harry of £2,220 + £280 – £555 = £1,945.

Instead, Harry could give the shares direct to ARC. There is no CGT to pay on gifts to charity. And Harry can claim Income Tax relief on the market value of the gift, which is £2,500. This means Harry gets Income Tax relief of 40% × £2,500 = £1,000. The charity sells the shares to realise the full £2,500. In this way the charity gets £2,500 at a cost to Harry of £2,500 – £1,000 = £1,500. Therefore, giving the shares direct is the better option.

OTHER WAYS OF GIVING

I n addition to tax incentives already described, there are several other arrangements you can use to ensure that both you and the charity get the most from your gifts.

CHARITABLE BEQUESTS

If you leave money or assets to charity in your will, your estate pays no IHT on the gift. (Your estate is all your possessions less any debts at the time of death.)

In Budget 2011, the Government announced that, for deaths on or after 6 April 2012, where at least one-tenth of the estate is left to charity, the IHT rate on the remainder will be reduced from the normal 40 per cent to 36 per cent. At the time of writing, the details had yet to be announced, but the Government said the benefit of the reduction would go to the charity, not your remaining heirs.

A bequest to charity can also save IHT in a further way, because the value of your estate is reduced by the amount of your gift to charity. This can mean less IHT on the estate as a whole. Bear in mind, though, that making a bequest to charity cuts down the amount of the estate left for your heirs to inherit, so you should not use this as a tax-saving method unless you intend to make philanthropic gifts anyway.

All gifts from your estate when you die – whether to charity or to other organisations or to people – are free of CGT.

Some charities offer you help in making your will – for example, paying the cost – in the hope that you will leave something to the charity. For the will to be legally watertight, it is essential that there can be no question of the charity having brought undue influence to bear on you. If it was thought that a charity had pressurised you into leaving it a bequest, your will could be challenged by other beneficiaries and, in the end, your gift to the charity might not be made after all. To avoid any problems of this sort, you should ensure that:

- You have written details of the arrangement by which the charity is helping you to make your will and the procedures to be followed.
- You do not proceed if the charity's help is conditional on your making it a bequest.

A solicitor can help you to insert an appropriate clause in your will to leave a bequest to charity. See also the *Which? Essential Guide* to *Wills & Probate*.

- The solicitor you use takes instructions from you alone and not the charity.
- No details of your will are disclosed to the charity without your consent.
- You do not proceed if you feel in any way pressurised to include the charity in your will.

CAF CHARITY ACCOUNT

The Charities Aid Foundation (CAF) is a charity whose aim is to promote charities generally and give them support and assistance. One of the services it runs is the CAF Charity Account. This is like a bank account with the sole purpose of making gifts to charity. The advantages of the Charity Account are that the money you give is increased by tax relief and you have a convenient, flexible way of giving to a wide range of charities. CAF makes a charge for running the account. It works as follows.

You pay money into your Charity Account using the tax-efficient means already discussed: Gift Aid (see page 106), Payroll Giving (see page 114) or gifts of shares and similar investments (see page 115). Because CAF is itself a charity, it is able to claim tax relief on the money you pay in using Gift Aid and it adds this to your account. With Payroll Giving, you qualify for tax relief directly as normal. With gifts of shares, your gift is free of CGT and you can claim Income Tax relief. CAF sells the shares and then credits the proceeds to your account.

CAF sets minimum limits on the amount you can pay into the account of £100 as a lump sum or £10 a month if you pay in regularly. In 2010, CAF makes a deduction from the amount going into your account (your donations plus any tax relief paid in). For annual amounts up to £17,000, the deduction is 4 per cent, made up of a 0.75 per cent fee for running the account, a 2.25 per cent donation to CAF and a 1 per cent donation to the National Council for Voluntary Organisations (NCVO). On annual payments of £17,001–£92,500 into the account, the only deduction is the 1 per cent donation to NCVO. On larger donations, there is no deduction. If you pay into the account using Payroll Giving, your employer might agree to pay the charges. The money in the account does not earn interest. You can make donations to any charity, whether registered or not. When you want to make a donation to charity from your account, you can do this in several ways:

- Online transfer over the internet where you carry out a variety of transactions including making donations.
- By phone using a plastic 'Charitycard'.
- By post using a Charity Account chequebook.
- By standing order, if you want to make regular donations to a particular charity.

 For details of the Charities Aid Foundation (CAF) Charity Account or to find out about setting up a trust through CAF, see www.cafonline.org.

Note that you do not get any further tax relief when you make the donation, because it has already had the benefit of tax relief when you first paid the money into the Charity Account.

The normal rules that apply to Gift Aid and Payroll Giving apply when you are paying into the CAF Charity Account. For example, the CAF Charity Account is not suitable if you pay little or no tax and would receive a bill from HMRC for the tax relief paid over to CAF by Gift Aid (see page 112).

GIFTS FROM TRUSTS

A trust is a special legal arrangement where money, shares or other property are held for the benefit of others (see Chapter 4). Trustees have the duty of seeing that the property in the trust and any income and gains from it (which together make up the 'trust fund') are used as set out in the trust deed and rules. With a 'discretionary trust', the trustees are given the power to decide how the trust fund is used

(within any constraints imposed by the trust rules).

Special tax rules apply to trusts (as described in Chapter 4), but gifts to charity from a discretionary trust can be very tax-efficient. The charity will be able to reclaim all the Income Tax – usually at 50 per cent (in 2011–12) rather than just the basic rate – that the trust has paid on the income it gives. If the trust makes a gift to charity of capital, there will be no CGT or IHT to pay.

DONATION CARDS (AFFINITY CARDS)

A number of charities and credit card companies have joined forces to issue donation cards (also called 'affinity cards'). These are normal credit cards but the card issuer promises to make donations to charity (or sometimes non-charitable groups, like football clubs) when you first take out the card and each time you use it. The donations are fairly small, for example, £10 when you take out the card and 5p each time you buy something using the card.

If you use a credit card anyway, a donation card is a way in which indirectly you can give to charity, but check that the card terms and conditions are competitive. If not, you would probably do better taking

> **!** If you do not normally use a credit card, be wary of taking out a donation card. Do not risk putting yourself in a situation where you run up debts that you cannot afford.

out a card that offers a better deal and using the money you save in interest or earn in cashback to make your own donations direct to charity using one of the tax-efficient schemes outlined in this chapter.

INTERNET SEARCHING AND SHOPPING

Although internet search engines are free for the searcher to use, they do generate revenue typically from an advertising fee paid by firms each time a user clicks on their link from the search results. A few organisations, such as goodsearch.com in the USA and everyclick.com in the UK, are offering search engines where part (usually, half) of the revenues generated are paid over to a charity of your choice. These organisations also donate to charity if you shop at online stores run by participating businesses. You can support as many charities as you like, but only one at a time.

The attraction of schemes like these – sometimes dubbed 'web-use giving' or 'wugging' – is that, in effect, you are donating to charity at no extra cost to yourself. In the past, there was some inconvenience in remembering to search or shop using the wugging site, but recently everyclick has launched an 'app' (application or small downloadable program) to kick in your wugging automatically whenever you search or shop online. In its Giving Green Paper (see page 104), the Government has expressed interest in seeing greater use of schemes like this.

SUMMARY

This chapter has looked at a range of ways to give tax efficiently to charity mainly during your lifetime, but also by leaving bequests in your well. The Charities Aid Foundation (CAF) operates some useful schemes that help you make flexible, low-cost use of these opportunities.

Tax-efficient schemes, particularly Gift Aid and Payroll Giving, can help you to give more and give more regularly, but typically involve some planning on your part. There are also opportunities to donate regular, small sums to charity with a minimum of conscious effort by signing up to affinity cards and web-use giving schemes that then make donations automatically as you go about your daily life.

{ The attraction of 'wugging' is that you are donating to charity at no extra cost }

INHERITANCE PLANNING

Planning ahead for what happens after your death can help to ensure that your survivors are financially secure, your wealth is passed on to the people you choose and any tax bill is kept to a minimum. You might also want to consider steps to guard against the costs of long-term care ruining your inheritance plans.

WHY PLAN FOR INHERITANCE?

This chapter draws together a number of points already discussed and the strategies we will be looking at in the remaining chapters to show how you can plan your giving through inheritance more precisely and tax-efficiently.

WHAT'S IN THIS CHAPTER?

Now that you have covered the basics of how the key taxes affecting gifts work and the alternatives to making outright gifts. You can draw these together to form the basis of your inheritance plan. This chapter looks at:

- Strategies for passing on wealth tax-efficiently in your will (page 125).
- Making lifetime gifts as a strategy for reducing the size of the estate you leave (page 130).
- How to use life assurance to deal with potential or expected tax bills or as part of a scheme for making gifts (page 133).
- How you may be able to use pension schemes for inheritance (page 136).
- Tax rules and other potential problems to watch out for that could upset your planning (page 138).

THE PURPOSE OF PLANNING

There are two main aims to planning inheritance:

- To make sure that your estate is divided as you had wished.
- To minimise the amount of tax to be paid on the estate.

Clearly, the two aims are interlinked since lower Inheritance Tax (IHT) means more of your estate can be left to your family and friends. Strategies to meet either or both aims are summarised in this chapter and looked at in more detail in the chapters that follow.

The particular inheritance planning strategies you adopt will depend largely on your personal intentions and circumstances. Many can be applied simply and with a minimum of paperwork. Others are not so straightforward and may hide potential pitfalls that you should take into account, so it is crucial to get advice if your plans are at all complicated.

Many more complex tax saving schemes aim to minimise tax on your estate at death by taking valuable assets out of your estate while still enabling you to use the assets during your lifetime without triggering the gift-with-reservation rules (see Chapter 4). The scope for this type of planning has been severely reduced by the introduction of the Pre-Owned Assets Tax (see Chapter 4) and the Government's threat to introduce further 'retroactive' measures to counter successful tax avoidance schemes (see Chapter 1). Broadly, you would appear to be safe using tax-saving opportunities that are specifically allowed in the tax legislation (for example, making tax-free gifts, using your tax-free limit). But if you contemplate anything more complex, you should get professional advice and be aware that any tax savings could disappear if the scheme becomes the target of a change in tax law.

Case Study GODFREY

Godfrey dies on 1 January 2012 leaving an estate of £300,000. You saw in Chapter 3 (page 56) how his death affected tax on some of the gifts he made in the years before his death. Here you can see how the most recent of those gifts affect the tax on his estate. Tax on the estate depends on the size of the estate and the taxable gifts within the last seven years. This means gifts he made in 2002 and 2004 (more than seven years ago) can be ignored. Godfrey made the following gifts during the last seven years of his life (assume the annual tax-free exemption has already been used up each year):

1 January 2002	Taxable gift	£129,000 to a discretionary trust
1 January 2004	Taxable gift	£70,000 to a discretionary trust
1 February 2005	Taxable gift	£68,000 to a discretionary trust
1 June 2007	PET	£80,000 to his nephew, John

The PET (potentially exempt transfer) was initially treated as a tax-free gift when it was made, but on Godfrey's death it is reassessed as a taxable gift. Therefore, the estate counts as a final gift of £300,000 in a running total of £68,000 + £80,000 + £300,000 = £448,000. The earlier gifts use up £148,000 of the £325,000 tax-free limit. £177,000 of the estate uses up the remaining part of the tax-free limit, leaving £123,000 of the estate to be taxed at 40 per cent – i.e. 40% × £123,000 = £49,200.

What happens to your estate if you don't plan?

If you die without a will, the law dictates who inherits your estate. The law favours husbands, wives, civil partners and children. However, other people – such as an unmarried partner – do not have any automatic rights to inherit. For more information on this subject, see Chapter 8 on pages 145–52.

What happens to IHT if you don't plan?

Your estate

Your estate is treated as the last gift you make

All or part, e.g. gifts to your spouse, might be tax-free

| Tax-free part | Taxable part |

Any taxable part of your estate is added to any other taxable gifts and potentially exempt transfers (PETs) you have made during the seven years up to the time of death

7 years	
6 years	GIFT A
5 years	
4 years	GIFT B
3 years	
2 years	
1 year	YOUR ESTATE

You have a tax-free limit

──── Tax-free limit (the nil-rate band) ────

Taxable gifts and PETs over the last seven years use up the limit in the order the gifts were made

| GIFT A | GIFT B | YOUR ESTATE | |

──── Tax-free limit (the nil-rate band) ────

If the taxable estate falls within the limit, no tax is due

| GIFT A | GIFT B | YOUR ESTATE | |

──── Tax-free limit (the nil-rate band) ────

If part or all of your taxable estate falls above the limit, tax is due

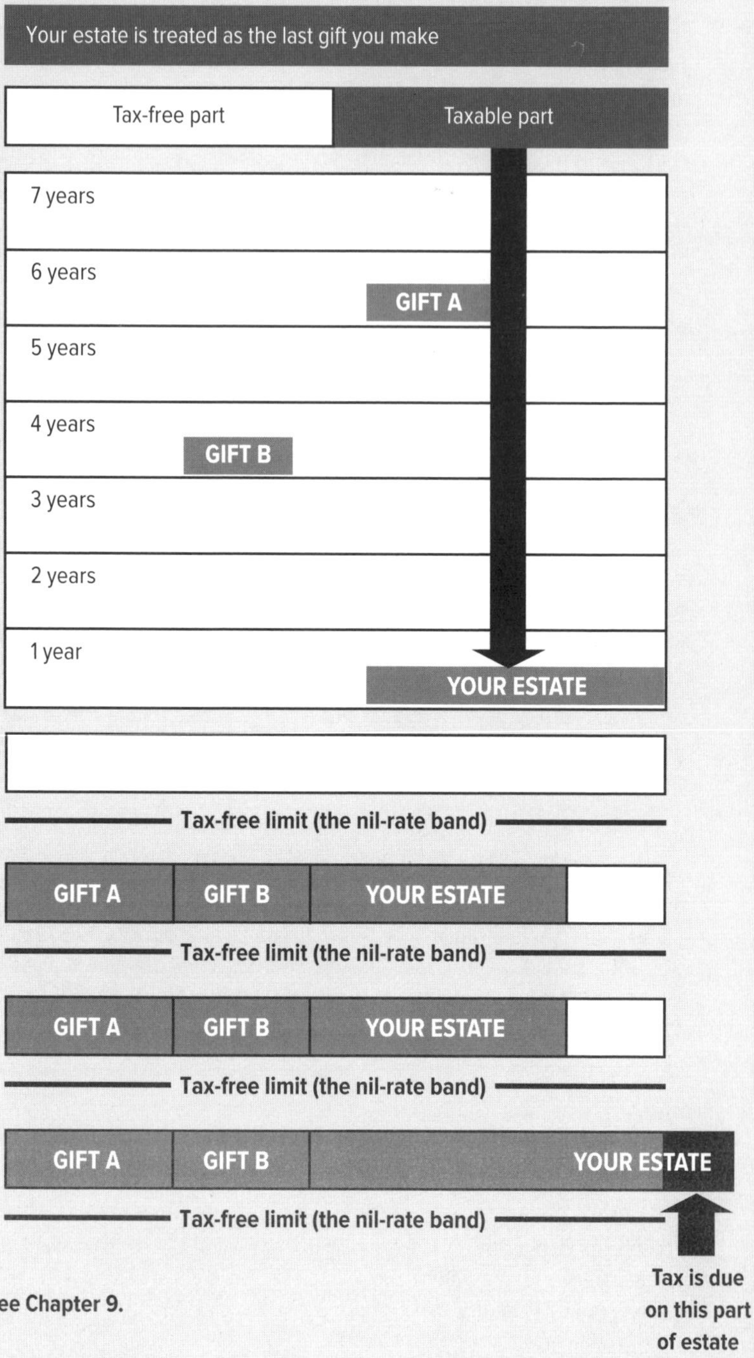

| GIFT A | GIFT B | | YOUR ESTATE |

──── Tax-free limit (the nil-rate band) ────

Tax is due on this part of estate

For more information, see Chapter 9.

124

PLANNING STRATEGIES

Here is a summary of the most commonly used strategies for inheritance planning.

GIFTS WHEN YOU DIE

By using your will, you can arrange to make tax-free gifts on death and to use your tax-free limit.

Make tax-free gifts in your will

Some gifts you make on death are always free of IHT, for example, bequests to charity and whatever you leave to your husband, wife or civil partner (provided they are UK-domiciled – otherwise there is a limit of £55,000).

In addition to these and other gifts that are always tax-free, whether made on death or during your lifetime (see Chapter 2), there are a few gifts that are specifically tax-free on death only:

- Lump sum from a pension scheme, provided the trustees had discretion to decide who would receive it (though in practice they generally follow any nomination made by you). The lump sum bypasses your estate altogether and goes straight from the scheme to the recipient.
- Similarly the proceeds of a life insurance policy that was written in trust for the recipient. The proceeds bypass the estate, going straight from the life insurance company to the recipient. See page 136 for more about pensions.

- The whole estate if the person died from a wound, accident or disease acquired or exacerbated while on active service against an enemy. To claim this exemption, the personal representatives need a certificate from the Ministry of Defence.
- Up to £10,000 received by the deceased as an ex-gratia payment to the survivors (or spouses of survivors) who were prisoners of war held by the Japanese during the Second World War.
- Amounts received by the victim (or his or her spouse) from specified schemes that provide compensation to people (such as Holocaust victims) for wrongs suffered during the Second World War.

Extra benefit for charities

The Government has announced that in 2012–13, where at least one-tenth of the estate is left to charity, the remaining IHT will be reduced to 36 per cent. The tax saved will go to the charity (see page 117).

Use your tax-free limit

Try to make use of your tax-free limit. Normally, this is £325,000 in 2011–12 (and frozen at this level until 2014–15). This means you can, for example, leave £325,000 of assets to an unmarried partner or children without any IHT being due (assuming lifetime gifts have not used any of the tax-free limit).

Bequests to a spouse or civil partner are usually completely tax-free, so do not use any of the tax-free limit. HMRC statistics show that, typically, four-fifths of the value of the estates of married men is left to their wives. Seven-tenths of the value of wives' estates is left to their husbands. In the past, this often meant that the tax-free limit of the first of a couple to die was wasted. However, under rules that came into effect in October 2007, any unused allowance of the first to die is no longer lost but can be 'inherited' by the surviving spouse or civil partner. This means that married couples and civil partners typically share a tax-free limit up to £650,000 at 2011–12 rates and can decide to use up to half on the first death, holding back the remainder to use on the second death.

Transferring the tax-free limit between spouses and civil partners is an option where the second death occurs on or after 9 October 2007. The earlier death can have happened at any time and the ability to inherit the deceased's tax-free limit is not lost, even if the surviving spouse or civil partner remarries or enters a new civil partnership.

It is the job of the people who sort out the estate of the second person to claim the inherited tax-free limit and they must do this within 24 months of the end of the month in which the second death occurred. To make the claim, they will need paperwork from the first death to show the proportion of the tax-free limit that was unused. They will also need to know the tax-free limit for the year in which the first person died. The case study, John and Pam, opposite, shows the basics of how the transfer works.

If a person is widowed more than once, they can inherit any unused tax-free limit from all the spouses or civil partners who died before them, but the maximum total tax-free limit that can be inherited is 100 per cent. This means the biggest tax-free limit the surviving spouse could have is capped at twice the current limit, in other words £650,000 in 2011–12.

The combination of tax-free giving between spouse or civil partners plus the ability to pass on the nil-rate band is extremely useful. For example, it enables a husband, wife or civil partner to leave their share of the family home to the surviving spouse or civil partner, ensuring the survivor has a secure home. But the home can eventually be passed on to children without necessarily incurring a high IHT bill. The position is more difficult for unmarried partners. They can use their tax-free limits but do not benefit from tax-free giving to each other – see the case study, Sam and Harriet, opposite.

Case Study **JOHN AND PAM**

Pam was widowed in March 1995. Her husband, John, left £15,000 to each of their two children and the remainder of his estate to Pam. When Pam died in December 2010, her estate, including the family home, was worth £570,000.

At the time of John's death, the tax-free limit was £150,000 (see page 49). He used £30,000 of this limit on the bequests to the children, leaving £120,000/£150,000 = 80% of the limit unused.

Luckily, Pam held on to a copy of John's will and the probate paperwork from sorting out his estate, so her executors (the people sorting out her will) were able to apply for John's unused tax-free limit to be transferred to Pam. When Pam died, the tax-free limit was £325,000 and to this was added a further 80% × £325,000 = £260,000 tax-free limit inherited from John. In total, then, Pam was able to leave £585,000 (including any taxable lifetime gifts in the seven years before death) before any IHT was due. In fact, she had made no lifetime gifts and so the estate of £570,000 was completely covered by the tax-free limit, with no IHT to pay at all.

Case Study **SAM AND HARRIET**

In August 2007, Sam died leaving his whole estate of £250,000 to his partner, Harriet. The bulk of his estate was his share of the home they shared. Since the couple were not married, his bequest to Harriet was not tax-free. But, at that time, the tax-free limit was £285,000, so there was no IHT to pay on Sam's estate.

Harriet died in July 2012. Her whole estate, valued at £570,000, was left to their only child, Phyllis. The first £325,000 of Harriet's estate was tax-free, but IHT of 40% × £245,000 = £98,000 was payable on the rest. So Phyllis inherited £472,000 once the tax was paid.

Be aware of how gifts are taxed

If IHT is due on your estate, the tax does not usually fall evenly across all your heirs. Chapter 9 describes in detail how gifts you leave in your will are taxed in different ways. Briefly, there are three types of gift:

- **Tax-free gifts,** such as bequests to your husband or wife. None of the IHT on the estate may be paid from these gifts.

 If you do not have paperwork relating to the earlier death of a spouse or civil partner, the court service (see Useful contacts) may be able to provide copies. See page 49 tax-free limits back to 1986 and www.hmrc.gov.uk/rates/iht-thresholds.htm for earlier years.

- **Gifts that bear their own tax.** A proportionate amount of the tax on the estate is deducted from each of these gifts before the remainder is paid to the recipient.
- **Free-of-tax gifts.** Although these are taxable gifts, tax on them is paid out of the residue of the estate, not the free-of-tax gifts themselves.

There are two important points that you should bear in mind when planning gifts under your will. First, a gift that bears its own tax will normally be smaller than a gift of the same size which is free-of-tax. Second, if you leave a lot of free-of-tax gifts, the residue of your estate may be reduced to a trivial amount (or nothing at all).

Consider will trusts: an interest-in-possession trust

A trust set up under your will is deemed to start on the date of death. There are several situations in which setting up a trust in your will can be particularly useful.

▌PLANNING POINT ▌

An interest-in-possession trust can be useful for IHT planning if assets are being passed to subsequent generations. This is because a reversionary interest does not count as part of a person's estate and so there is no IHT liability if it is transferred to someone else. For example, if your children held the reversionary interest in a trust, they could easily transfer this interest to their own children if they wished to do so, without incurring any IHT liability.

The first is where you want to give some of your assets to the next generation but your wife, husband or civil partner will carry on needing the income from, or use of, those assets. One way around this is to leave the assets in trust, giving, say, your spouse an interest in possession during his or her lifetime, with your children (or perhaps their children) holding the reversionary interest (see page 76).

But note that, while this ensures that your assets are used largely as you would wish, it does not have any IHT advantage over making an outright gift if, under the tax rules for trusts (see Chapter 5), the trust counts as an 'immediate post-death interest (IPDI) trust'. This means that, although it generally qualifies for favourable IHT treatment (see page 82), the person with an interest in possession is treated as if they own the underlying trust assets. They are then treated as if they give the assets away when the interest ends. So, if the trust ends on that person's death, the trust assets count as part of that person's estate, and there could be a large inheritance bill at the time of this second death.

There are two ways you could avoid this problem. First, you could instead set up a discretionary trust (see opposite). Second, you could set up an interest-in-possession trust in your will that does not meet all the conditions necessary for it to qualify as an IPDI trust (get advice from your solicitor on how to do this). In both cases, the gift in your will is taxable and so can use up all or part of your tax-free limit, and the trust assets will not count as part of your spouse's or civil partner's estate so will not contribute towards a tax bill on their death.

Consider will trusts: a discretionary trust

Under IHT law, you can use your will to set up a discretionary trust. This can be tax-efficient provided the transfer of assets into the trust is covered by your tax-free limit at the time of death (or one of the other exemptions).

For example, you could leave an amount up to your tax-free limit to a discretionary trust with both your spouse and your children named as beneficiaries. The trustees would have discretion over how the trust property and any income from it were used. You could informally, prior to death, make known to the trustees your hope that the assets could be largely preserved to be handed down to your children, but the trustees would not be bound to follow your wishes.

A discretionary will trust does not work so well where the main asset in your estate is your family home. Leaving part of your home to the trust and part to your partner means that your partner does not have free use of the family home. A solution might be to set up an IOU discretionary will trust. Under this arrangement, your partner buys the trust's share of the house but, assuming he or she does not have ready cash to pay the purchase price, instead gives the trust an IOU. This means the trust is lending money to your spouse or civil partner. The whole home passes to your partner who can use it freely during their lifetime (and move home if they choose). On your partner's death, the trust calls in the loan, which usually would be repaid by selling the home. For this plan to work efficiently, it is very important

that the wording of the trust is precise and essential that you get professional advice. A simpler option may be to set up an interest-in-possession trust in your will, provided it does not count as an IPDI trust (see opposite).

Another way to use a discretionary will trust is as a device for devolving decisions to others who can make them in the light of the actual circumstances at the time of your death. Provided the property in a discretionary will trust is distributed within two years of your death, the gifts from the trust can be treated for IHT purposes as if they had been bequests under your will. This can be particularly useful if, say, you want to leave a bequest to a grown-up child but you are unsure that they would sensibly manage a large sum of money or you are fearful that their unsuitable partner might misappropriate the bequest. By setting up a discretionary trust, you can leave it to trustees – who, needless to say, should be familiar with your misgivings and people you trust completely – to make decisions in the light of circumstances at the time.

USING LIFETIME GIFTS

One way to reduce the IHT payable on your death is to reduce the size of your estate by making gifts during your lifetime. However, before going down this road, you must consider your own financial needs.

Any IHT payable on your estate is a problem for your heirs, not you. IHT on your estate reduces the amount by which others benefit from what you leave, but does not affect you in your lifetime. It is not worth jeopardising your financial security in order to reduce the IHT bill of your heirs.

Assuming that you can afford to make a number of gifts during your lifetime, you will obviously want to ensure that they do not themselves give rise to a large tax bill. Chapter 2 lists the gifts that you can make during your lifetime that are tax-free.

It is not enough to look only at the IHT position of lifetime gifts. You must also consider the Capital Gains Tax (CGT) position (see Chapters 2 and 3). Taking the two taxes together, the 'best' gifts to make will tend to be the following:

- Cash gifts (always free of CGT) that qualify for an IHT exemption.
- Cash gifts that count as PETs (see page 55) for IHT purposes.
- Business assets that qualify for hold-over relief from CGT (see page 59) and count as PETs for IHT or qualify for business property relief.
- Other gifts that are exempt from IHT or that count as PETs and for which the CGT bill is relatively small due to unused CGT allowance (see Chapter 3).

 Any IHT payable on your estate is a problem for your heirs, not you.

 For guidance on business property relief, see the HMRC website at www.hmrc.gov.uk/inheritancetax/pass-money-property/business-relief.htm.

Make tax-free lifetime gifts

Of particular importance for IHT purposes is your yearly tax-free exemption (see page 33), which lets you give away up to £3,000 each year without incurring any IHT liability. If you choose cash gifts, there will be no CGT either.

Another very useful gift that is free of IHT is normal expenditure out of income – this can be particularly handy when used in conjunction with an insurance policy (see page 133).

For tax purposes alone, it is not generally worth making, in your lifetime, a gift that would, in any case, be tax-free on your death – for example, a gift to charity. A safer course would be to retain the assets in case you need to draw on them and make the desired gift in your will.

Case Study **SAMIR**

Samir has a good income boosted by the return from a substantial portfolio of investments. From this income, he gives each of his three children £5,000 every Christmas. He has been doing this for a number of years and has kept meticulous records of the gifts, so there should be no problem convincing HMRC that these are normal expenditure out of his income. The gifts mount up, so that over a period of ten years, Samir will have given away £150,000 in total, completely free of IHT.

Give assets whose value will rise

If your aim is to reduce the value of your estate by the time you die, then it makes sense to give away assets whose value you expect to increase. In that way the increase will accrue to the recipient of the gift and will be outside your estate.

Make loans

One way to 'freeze' the value of part of your estate is to make an interest-free loan to someone and leave him or her to keep the proceeds from investing the loan. A condition of the loan would normally be that it is repayable on demand. From your point of view, this is more secure than making an outright gift and can be a useful arrangement if you are unsure whether or not you will need the money back at some time in the future.

Of course, there is little point demanding repayment of a loan if the borrower simply does not have the money available to repay you. An even more secure route would be to make the loan indirectly by giving it to a discretionary trust and naming the intended recipient as a potential beneficiary under the trust.

Consider lifetime gifts to a trust

The holy grail of all inheritance planning is to be able to give assets away tax-efficiently but still have access to them if later you find you need them after all. In general this is not possible because of the gift-with-reservation rules (see Chapter 4).

However, although you cannot be a beneficiary or potential beneficiary of a trust you set up without the assets you put into it counting as a gift with reservation, your husband, wife or civil partner can benefit. The fact of their being a beneficiary of the trust does not trigger the gift-with-reservation rules, provided that you yourself in no way benefit from your spouse's (or civil partner's) interest in the trust.

A further exception to the gift-with-reservation rules is that if you retain a reversionary interest (see page 76) in a trust to which you have given assets, the gift does not count as one with reservation.

But bear in mind:

- Whatever type of trust you use, the gift will almost certainly count as a taxable gift for IHT. There will be no immediate tax bill provided the gift is within your tax-free limit (£325,000 in 2011–12), but you'll need to survive seven years to ensure that the gift has no effect on tax on your estate, and
- The fact of your husband, wife or civil partner benefiting from the trust makes it a 'settlor-interested trust' (see page 83) for the purpose of the Income Tax rules. This will tend to make this type of arrangement unattractive.

> If you inherit money or assets that are surplus to your needs, you might consider 'generation skipping'.

Generation skipping

If you yourself inherit money or assets that are surplus to your needs, you might consider passing them on straight away to your children or grandchildren – this is a practice known as 'generation-skipping'. The transfer can often be made tax-efficiently through a 'deed of variation' (see page 208) or possibly a 'disclaimer' (see page 207).

Case Study ELAINE

When Elaine's mother died, she left an estate worth £280,000 to her daughter, made up of a property, cash, unit trusts and other investments. But Elaine, by then aged 58, was already well settled with her own home and a good income from her career as an academic. Elaine thought it over for a year or so and then decided she would rather that her grandchildren had the inheritance to use later towards their education.

Elaine could just have given the money and investments to the grandchildren, in which case the gift would be a PET for IHT purposes and she would have had a CGT bill of around £12,000 on the gift of the non-cash assets.

Instead, Elaine chose to have a deed of variation drawn up so that the gifts to the grandchildren were treated, for both IHT and CGT purposes, as if they had been made by Elaine's mother in her will. Elaine decided to get a solicitor to draw up the deed and this cost her about £600, but she saved £12,000 CGT. In addition, because there was no PET from Elaine to her grandchildren, there are no tax implications if Elaine dies within seven years.

USING LIFE INSURANCE

There are three straightforward ways in which life insurance can be a useful inheritance planning tool:

- Covering the potential tax bill on a PET.
- Making a gift that builds up outside your estate.
- Covering an expected tax bill on your estate.

These are discussed in turn below. All rely on making use of two factors:

- **Tax-free gifts.** Taking out insurance for the benefit of someone else means that the premiums count as gifts. You can ensure that there is no possibility of IHT on these premiums if you make sure they count as tax-free gifts. The most commonly used exemptions are to make the premiums as normal expenditure out of your income (see page 30) or to ensure that they fall within your yearly tax-free exemption of £3,000 (see page 33).
- **Trust status.** If the proceeds of an insurance policy are payable to you, the payout will be added to your estate when you die, which will increase the size of your estate and will cause delay before your beneficiaries have access to the payout. Therefore, it is important that the policy proceeds are paid direct to the intended beneficiary. You make sure this happens by 'writing' the insurance policy 'in trust', which means that the policy is held in

trust for the benefit of whomever you name and the proceeds are the property of that person rather than of you or your estate. Insurance companies will generally write a policy in trust for you at no extra charge (since they are able, in most cases, to use standard documents). It is also possible to transfer an insurance policy into trust after it has been set up. But, in either case, see the box, 'Life insurance and trusts', overleaf.

The cost of insurance increases with the likelihood of the insurance company having to pay out. So, if you are in poor health or very old, buying life insurance may be very expensive.

Potentially Exempt Transfers (PETs) and insurance

If you make a gift that counts as a PET, you may want to be absolutely sure that any IHT bill that subsequently arises could be paid. (Similarly, you might want to ensure that any extra tax on a chargeable gift arising on death could be paid.) One way of ensuring this would be to take out a '**term insurance**' policy.

Term insurance pays out if you die within a specified time – in this case, seven years; should you survive the specified period, it pays out nothing. Since the liability for IHT on a PET decreases as the years go by, the cover you need can also reduce – in other words, you want 'reducing term insurance'.

Transferring a life insurance policy into trust either when it is set up or later can trigger IHT bills at the time and on the 10-year anniversaries of the trust (see Chapter 4). However, there is usually no problem with life insurance that pays out only on death (term insurance and some types of whole-of-life insurance) because it typically has a low value for IHT purposes. There is also no IHT problem in holding a life policy through a bare trust (see page 76) since these do not come within the IHT rules that apply to most other trusts. Where a life insurance policy can build up a surrender value (endowment policies and most whole-of-life policies), there could be IHT complications and you are strongly advised to get advice from an independent financial adviser (see Useful contacts).

It is also important to consider who pays the premiums for life insurance and whether the policy is a single-life or joint-life policy, in order to avoid falling foul of the income-tax settlor-interested trust rules (see page 83) and the IHT gift-with-reservation rules (see page 64). Again, seek help from an independent financial adviser.

In some circumstances, it may be simpler to take out a 'life-of-another insurance policy' rather than insurance on your own life. For example, a wife could take out, and pay the premiums for, a policy to pay out to her on the death of her husband without the need for any trust arrangement. This would be an alternative to the husband taking out a policy on his own life under trust to pay out to his wife on his death. You must stand to lose financially from someone's death to be allowed to take out a policy on their life (called having an 'insurable interest'). Legally, you are assumed to have an unlimited interest in your own life and in the life of your spouse or civil partner. If the death of someone else – for example, within seven years of giving you something – would create an IHT bill for you, your insurable interest is the amount of tax you would have to pay.

PET insurance could be purchased by either the person making the gift or the person receiving it. If the giver buys the insurance it should be written in trust to pay out to the recipient in the event of the giver's death. The premiums the giver pays for the insurance count as a gift from the giver to the recipient but can be tax-free gifts if, say, they come within the giver's £3,000 annual allowance or count as normal expenditure out of income. If the insurance is purchased by the recipient, the insurance is not a gift so there is no IHT implication.

Reducing the size of your estate

You could use life insurance to build up a gift that does not count as part of your estate. For example, you might use the full £3,000 yearly tax-free exemption to pay the premiums for an investment-type life insurance policy (such as an endowment or whole-life policy) that will pay out to the recipient either:

- After a specified period, in which case, you need an **endowment policy**, or
- When you die, in which case, you need a **whole-life policy**.

In choosing this strategy, you will need to weigh it against alternative strategies: for example, setting up a trust that could invest in a wider range of assets. The 'up-front' costs of setting up your own trust will be higher but the ongoing costs might work out to be less than for a life insurance policy. If you have relatively small sums to give, the insurance route would be more appropriate.

You can use Personal Pension schemes in a similar way by making regular contributions to a scheme for someone else (see page 102). The charges for 'stakeholder' schemes are capped at 1.5 per cent of the amount in the pension fund for the first ten years and 1 per cent thereafter.

Paying IHT when you die

You could take out a whole-of-life policy to provide a lump sum to meet an expected IHT bill on your estate.

In essence, this is no different from using insurance as a way of making a gift on death, as already discussed, but the factors to consider are slightly different: you could save in your own investment fund (either within your estate or within a trust) to meet a potential IHT bill but it would take time to build up the full amount needed. If you died in the meantime, your investment would be insufficient to cover the tax. Taking out a whole-of-life insurance policy removes that risk because (provided you have bought the appropriate level of cover) it would pay out the full amount needed whether you die sooner or later.

If you have made a PET and die within seven years, the PET will use up some of the tax-free limit available at the time of death. This could cause extra tax to be due on the estate. Therefore, in addition to a whole-life policy to cover the main tax on the estate, it may be worth taking out a

> **?**
>
> **Decreasing term insurance** Type of term insurance where the sum to be paid out on death decreases as the policy term progresses.
>
> **Endowment policy** Type of life insurance policy that runs for a specified term (often at least ten years). It pays out if you die within the term, but also pays out a cash sum at the end of the term. The amount it pays out will usually depend on the performance of an underlying fund of investments.
>
> **Level term insurance policy** Type of term insurance where the sum to be paid out on death stays at the same level throughout the policy term.
>
> **Term insurance policy** Type of life insurance that provides protection only and no investment. It pays out a pre-set sum if you die within a specified term but nothing if you survive.
>
> **Whole-of-life policy** Type of insurance that runs until the date you die. Because eventual death is a certainty, the policy must inevitably pay out at some time and often the policy is structured so that it builds up a cash value. The value is usually linked to an underlying fund of investments and tends to increase the longer you have the policy. Some whole-of-life policies just payout on death with no earlier cash-in value.

seven-year level term insurance policy to cover the extra tax bill on the estate if you die within seven years of making a PET. This is quite separate from a reducing term insurance policy to cover possible tax on the PET itself (see page 133).

PENSION SCHEMES AND INHERITANCE PLANNING

For many people, savings built up in a pension scheme are the largest single asset they own. While they are intended to finance income in retirement, it would be useful if they could be available to pass on to survivors too. In 2006, the rules surrounding pension schemes were radically changed. In the case of death after age 75, a combination of IHT and pension scheme taxes meant any remaining pension fund passed on to survivors could suffer tax at up to 82 per cent. This made pension schemes uneconomic as a route for inheritance planning.

However, the Coalition Government has changed the tax rules applying to pension schemes from April 2011 onwards. As a result, it is now feasible to pass on unused savings in pension schemes. This section outlines the measures as set out in a draft Finance Bill published in December 2010. At the time of writing, Parliament had yet to approve these changes. To understand the changes, you first need to know that there are two types of pension scheme to be aware of:

- **Defined benefit.** This type of scheme is offered by some employers and you are promised a pension worked out according to a set formula. Usually the pension is a fraction of your pay for each year you have been in the scheme.

Quite separately, defined benefit schemes usually offer tax-free lump sum life insurance if you die before retirement and pensions for your partner and/or children on death before or after retirement. You will be asked to complete an 'expression of wish' form to say who you would like to benefit from any lump sum life cover and pensions

- **Defined contribution.** This type of scheme is typically offered by smaller employers and is always the type you get if you take out your own Personal Pension scheme. You pay in contributions – and your employer, if you have one, may contribute as well. These contributions are invested to build up a pension fund. At retirement, you use the fund to provide your pension. There are two main ways of doing this. You can buy a lifetime annuity, which means giving up your pension fund and in return getting an income for the rest of your life. Alternatively, you can leave your pension fund invested and regularly cash in part of it to provide yourself with income – this is called a drawdown pension.

The new rules particularly affect defined contribution pension schemes. From April 2011, if you die before you start to draw your pension and you are under age 75, the savings that have built up in your scheme can be paid out to your survivors tax-free. In all other cases, any lump sum paid from your scheme on death is subject to a single deduction of tax at 55 per cent. IHT will no longer apply. As now, alternatively savings left in pension schemes can be used to provide a pension for a surviving partner and/or children.

It is only possible to have money left in your pension scheme on death if you either die before starting your pension or, if later, you have opted for a drawdown pension. However, drawdown pensions are in general a more risky way of providing your pension than buying an annuity. As a result, it is likely that only people with six-figure pension schemes or a secure income from other sources will be able to consider pension schemes as a possible route for IHT planning as well as retirement income.

GIFTS FROM THE DEATHBED

If, say, you are seriously ill and do not expect to live for long, you might make a gift in contemplation of your death – known as a *donatio mortis causa*. Such a gift does not take effect until your death and it lapses completely if you do not die after all (or if the recipient dies before you).

In this situation, should your intention be to make an outright gift to someone that is not conditional on your dying, it would be wise to set down your intention in writing – in, say, a signed letter to the recipient – to safeguard against the gift being mistakenly treated as a *donatio mortis causa* (and thus being treated as part of your estate if you survive).

A further point to watch out for is that a gift that is made by cheque is not made until the cheque has

Defined benefit scheme Pension scheme that promises you a set level of pension. Offered mainly by larger employers.

Defined contribution scheme Pension scheme where your savings build up a fund for use at retirement to provide a pension.

Drawdown pension The practice of leaving your pension fund invested and periodically cashing in small parts of it to provide yourself with retirement income. Unless you have a substantial secure income from other sources (from April 2011 onwards), tax rules restrict the pension you can draw to prevent you running down the pension fund too fast.

Lifetime annuity Special type of investment where you hand over a lump sum (such as your pension fund) and, in return, get an income for life. Because the income carries on however long you live, lifetime annuities are a sort of insurance against living longer than expected.

been cleared against the giver's account. If death takes place before then, the gift would become invalid.

> A gift that is made by cheque is not made until the cheque has been cleared.

ANTI-AVOIDANCE RULES

Complicated tax planning will not necessarily save you tax. In an ideal world, you would be able to make tax-efficient lifetime gifts to reduce the eventual tax on death but in the meantime continue either to have the use of the assets you give away or to get an income from them.

The tax authorities do not recognise the kind of arrangements outlined above as genuine gifts. As described in Chapter 4, if you give something away but continue to benefit from it, you fall foul of the IHT gift-with-reservation rules. These work by continuing to include the value of the gift as part of your estate either until you cease to benefit or until you die, whichever happens first.

A variety of complicated schemes have been marketed that aim to exploit legitimate loopholes in the legislation that let you both reduce the size of your estate and continue to receive an income from the gifted assets. Many are now caught by the POAT (see Chapter 4) and HMRC has made clear its intention to attack and close down new tax-planning schemes if it deems they are unfairly exploiting loopholes in the law (see Chapter 1).

Complex schemes have traditionally been the preserve of the seriously rich, but they have become attractive to many more people in recent years because of the dramatic rise in house values during the 20 years or so to 2008. Chapter 10 outlines the strategies – albeit limited – that might help you to avoid or reduce IHT on your estate if your home is your main asset and it is taking you above the IHT tax-free limit.

Do bear in mind, though, that IHT on your estate becomes payable only at your death. If that is likely to be many years ahead, circumstances might have changed – for example, you may find that substantial wealth you had planned to leave gets whittled away in care home fees in later life. Or falling house prices might mean that a home that just tips into the IHT bracket now slips out again in future. So think carefully before committing yourself to any complex or inflexible IHT planning.

 If you are attracted to complicated tax planning, always get professional advice, for example, from a member of the Society of Trust and Estate Practitioners (STEP).

USING LONG-TERM CARE PLANS

Needing long-term care in later life can quickly eat away any wealth that you have built up. Long-term care plans can limit the damage.

If you need care in later life, it could be very expensive. On average, a care home easily costs around £400 to £500 a week (up to £26,000 a year) but you could pay substantially more than this.

HELP FROM THE STATE

If your capital comes to less than £23,250 (England and Northern Ireland), £23,500 (Scotland) or £22,500 (Wales) in 2011–12 and your income is low, the State will pay some or all of the costs for you if you need to move into a care home. If your capital is greater than this, you will have to pay the whole lot out of your own pocket until your capital has been run down to this level.

If your husband, wife or other dependant would be left at home, the value of your house should not be included in the assessment of how much capital you own. But, if you had been living alone, your home would normally count as part of your capital and might have to be sold to cover the care fees.

A long-term care plan can help you protect at least part of your capital.

How a long-term care plan could help

There are two types of long-term care plan you can consider:

- **Long-term care insurance.** You buy this in advance and it pays out a regular sum towards the cost of care if required in future. Long-term care insurance is not well developed in the UK and there are very few policies available.
- **Immediate care plan.** You buy this at the time you need care with a single lump sum. The lump sum buys an annuity that pays out an income for the rest of your life. Provided the income is paid direct to the care provider, it is tax-free.

Long-term care plans are costly and buying them makes a large dent in your assets. But you can view this as damage-limitation, because you are swapping the uncertainty of large expenses for an indefinite period for a known cost.

SUMMARY

This chapter has considered a wide range of ways you can plan ahead for inheritance by making use of tax-free bequests, reducing your estate through lifetime gifts, passing on the growth of your estate by using loans and life insurance, and possibly using pension schemes. If, nonetheless, IHT seems inevitable, you can use life insurance to cover the bill. But, whatever plans you make, it is important to bear in mind that the future is uncertain and can throw up unexpected twists and turns, so you should be wary of committing to inflexible planning, especially if it could threaten your own financial security. Remember that, ultimately, IHT on your estate is a problem for your heirs rather than you.

For a more detailed look at long-term care plans, see *Care Options in Retirement*, available from Which? Books.

MAKING A WILL

Fewer than half of UK adults have made a will. Without one, it's unlikely the wealth you leave will be passed on in the way you had hoped and you could unnecessarily be leaving a handsome legacy to HMRC.

WHY YOUR WILL MATTERS

Nّone of us likes to think about death, but failing to write a will can leave a mass of problems for your survivors.

WHAT'S IN THIS CHAPTER?

Central to any plan to ensure your family's security or to save tax is making a will. This is the only sure way to exercise control over how your wealth is passed on and to whom. Yet, according to the Office of Fair Trading, fewer than half (47 per cent) of UK adults have made a will. This chapter looks at:

- What happens if you do not make a will (page 145).
- Different ways to hold assets jointly with other people and how this affects the way the assets are passed on (page 154).
- What's involved in making your will (page 156).

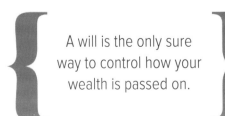

A will is the only sure way to control how your wealth is passed on.

WHAT ARE THE PROBLEMS?

A will is a legal document that says how your possessions (your estate) are to be dealt with when you die. Even if your estate is small and your intentions regarding it extremely simple, you should still make a will. If you do not, a number of problems can arise, for example:

- Your survivors may waste time trying to find out whether or not you did write a will; it may take them a long time to trace all your possessions; and they may have to spend time and money tracing relatives.
- If there is no will, it may take longer and cost more to 'prove' the estate (an administrative process that has to be completed before your estate can be 'distributed' – that is, handed on – to your heirs).
- Without a will, your next of kin (often a wife, husband or civil partner) will usually be appointed to sort out your affairs. At the time of bereavement, he or she might prefer not to take on this role and you may, in any case,

have friends or relatives who would be more suited to the task.

- The law will dictate how your estate is passed on and this may not coincide with your wishes.
- The law may require that various trusts are set up. The terms of these trusts may be overly restrictive and, especially where small sums are involved, unnecessarily large expenses may be incurred.
- Your heirs may have to pay IHT (or more tax) than would have been the case had you used your will to pass on your possessions tax-efficiently (see Chapter 9).

Apart from avoiding these problems and ensuring that your possessions are given away as you would choose, a will can be used for other purposes too: you can appoint guardians to care for young children; and you can express your preferences about funeral arrangements and any wishes about the use of your body for medical purposes after death.

Don't put off making a will for now, thinking that you will sort it out when you get older. First, this leaves the people around you now vulnerable should you die young. Second, to write a valid will, you must be of sound mind. As you age, there is an increased risk of developing mental health conditions that might prevent you from being able to draw up a will later. Sometimes, thinking

Administrators The name given to your personal representatives if you have not made a will. They will distribute your estate in accordance with the law.

Beneficiary A person or organisation left something under a will.

Executors The name given to your personal representatives if you have made a will. They will try to ensure that the instructions in your will are carried out.

Personal representative The person, people or organisation that sees that your estate is distributed following your death.

Power of attorney A legal arrangement that appoints someone (called your 'attorney') to take over your affairs for you. There are different types of power of attorney, but commonly they are designed to let someone take over in the event that you develop a mental condition that prevents you from making your own decisions any more.

Testator/testatrix The man or woman whose will it is. You must be aged 18 or over (and of sound mind) to make a valid will.

MAKING A WILL

To find out more about mental capacity and powers of attorney, see the free guide *Help with Managing your Money – if you or someone you care for lacks mental capacity* from www.moneyadviceservice.org.uk.

- Although most people living as unmarried couples realise their partner will not automatically inherit from them, only 23 per cent have made a will.

- Over half of married people incorrectly believe their husband or wife would inherit everything even without a will. The figure is higher still (71 per cent) for civil partners.

- Nearly two-thirds of parents have not made a will, so are missing a straightforward way to ensure that their children are financially provided for and guardians appointed.

ahead, people draw up a **power of attorney** so that someone else can take over managing their affairs if they lose the mental ability to do this for themselves. But be aware that, although an attorney can take over many financial and other matters, he or she is not permitted to write a will for the person for whom they are acting.

Scotland and Northern Ireland

The rules relating to wills and intestacy in Scotland and Northern Ireland differ in a number of respects from the rules for England and Wales. The rules described in the bulk of this chapter apply to England and Wales. For the differences in Scotland and Northern Ireland, see pages 151–3.

{ Even if your estate is small and your intentions simple, you should still make a will. }

DYING WITHOUT A WILL

If you die without making a will ('intestate'), the law dictates how your estate will be passed on.

The law aims, in the first instance, to protect your immediate family – husband, wife, civil partner and children. People who are not formally part of your family – for example, an unmarried partner – have no automatic rights under the intestacy laws (though they might still have a claim against your estate – see page 163).

Giving priority to your spouse and children might coincide with your wishes but, even if it did, the intestacy rules still might not result in your estate being used as you had expected or would have wished.

The intestacy laws assume that all your possessions could be sold by your personal representative to convert your whole estate into cash, which would then be distributed according to the rules described on pages 146–53. In practice, the possessions would not necessarily be sold and could be passed on intact, but problems can arise where there is a large possession – for example, the family home – if it needs to be split between two or more beneficiaries.

A welcome measure under the intestacy rules is that where part or all of your estate would pass to your spouse or civil partner, this will only happen if he or she survives you by at least 28 days. This 'survivorship provision' (which is also a common device used in wills) makes sure that, in cases where you and your spouse or civil partner die within a short time of one another (for example, as a result of a road traffic accident), the relatives of each of you benefit from your respective estates rather than everything going to the relatives of the second to die.

A person under 18 (12 in Scotland) cannot make a valid will, so the estate of a child who dies – including any assets held under a bare trust for the child – will always be subject to the intestacy rules.

When you make a will, it should cover all your assets. But, if you fail to say how part of your estate is to be used, that part will be subject to the intestacy rules, even though the rest of your estate is disposed of in accordance with the will. This is called 'partial intestacy'.

Joint assets

The intestacy rules do not apply to joint assets where you hold them under a 'joint tenancy' (see page 154) with one or more other owners. Your share of such assets would pass automatically to the surviving co-owner(s).

WHAT THE INTESTACY RULES SAY

Without a will, the law decides who will inherit from you and gives preference to your husband, wife, civil partner and children.

If you are survived by a spouse or civil partner and no children

Your husband, wife or civil partner is entitled to all your personal chattels (meaning your personal possessions, such as clothes, furniture, jewellery and private cars). If your estate is valued at £450,000 or less, your husband, wife or civil partner also inherits the whole estate.

If your estate is valued at more than £450,000, your spouse or civil partner gets the whole lot, provided you had no living parents or brothers or sisters at the time of your death. If you are survived by parents, brothers or sisters, your spouse or civil partner is entitled to a fixed sum of £450,000 (plus interest at a set rate from the date of death until the date the payment is made) plus half of whatever remains. The remainder goes to your parents or, if they are dead, to your brothers and sisters. If a brother or sister has died, their children (if any) inherit in their place.

Who inherits if you leave a spouse/civil partner and no children

START

Is your estate worth more than £450,000? — **no** → Your husband, wife or civil partner inherits the whole estate

yes ↓

Do you have parents? — **yes** → Your husband, wife or civil partner gets £450,000 (with interest) plus half the remaining estate. Your parents inherit the rest

no ↓

Do you have brothers and/or sisters? — **yes** → Your husband, wife or civil partner gets £450,000 (with interest) plus half the remaining estate. Your brothers and sisters (or their children[1]) inherit the rest

— **no** → Your husband, wife or civil partner inherits the whole estate

[1] If a brother or sister has died, their children (if any) inherit in their place.

If you are survived by children but no husband, wife or civil partner

If you leave children, but no husband, wife or civil partner, the inheritance position is simple: your children share your estate equally.

If you are survived by a husband, wife or civil partner and children

If, as well as children, you are survived by a husband, wife or civil partner, he or she is entitled to all your chattels. And, if your estate is valued at £250,000 or less, he or she also inherits the whole of that.

If your estate is valued at more than £250,000, your husband, wife or civil partner receives a fixed sum of £250,000 (plus interest at a set rate from the date of death until the date payment is made) and a life interest in half of the remaining estate. A life interest gives him or her the right to the income from that part of the estate (or use of it in the case of, say, a house) but he or she cannot touch the capital. (However, the husband, wife or civil partner can decide to take an appropriately calculated lump sum from the estate in place of a life interest – if you are in this situation, ask whoever is administering the estate to work out how much lump

sum you would get before you make your decision.)

The rest of the estate passes to your children to be shared equally between them. If any child of yours has died, their children (if any) inherit in their place. They also become entitled to the capital that had been subject to the life interest when your husband, wife or civil partner dies. Children can inherit capital outright only once they reach the age of 18, so they can only have income from it up to that age.

 **Children** For the purpose of the intestacy rules, 'children' includes offspring from your most recent marriage, any previous marriages, adopted and illegitimate children. But it does not include stepchildren, so even if you are married and regardless of whether you have always treated your partner's children from an earlier relationship as your own, your stepchildren will not inherit from you unless you make a will.

> { Stepchildren will not inherit from you unless you make a will. }

 For more information about the intestacy rules in England and Wales, visit the Government's courts website at www.hmcourts-service.gov.uk.

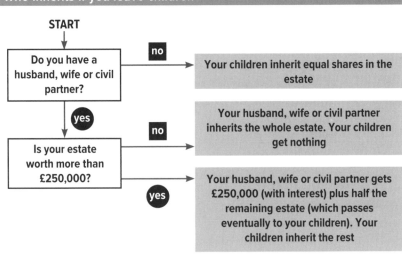

Who inherits if you leave children

START

Do you have a husband, wife or civil partner? — **no** → Your children inherit equal shares in the estate

yes

Is your estate worth more than £250,000? — **no** → Your husband, wife or civil partner inherits the whole estate. Your children get nothing

yes → Your husband, wife or civil partner gets £250,000 (with interest) plus half the remaining estate (which passes eventually to your children). Your children inherit the rest

Case Study **ALAN**

Alan died leaving an estate valued at £450,000. Of this amount £400,000 represented his half-share in the family home (which he and his wife, Julia, owned as tenants in common – see page 154). However, he had made no will. Under the intestacy rules Julia and his only child inherited the estate in the following shares:

Julia's share

Capital: fixed sum	£250,000
plus interest	£3,090
Total capital	£253,090

Remaining estate

£450,000 – £253,090 = £196,910

| So Julia also gets income/use from half of £196,910 i.e. | £98,455 |

Child's share

| Capital now | £98,455 |
| Capital to be set aside for future (Julia has life interest) | £98,455 |

Unfortunately, Julia's outright inheritance of £253,090 and interest in a further £98,455 come to less than the value of the family home. In order to comply with the intestacy rules requiring capital of £196,910 in total to be set aside for the child, part of the family home must be held in trust for the child.

If you are survived by no near-relatives

If you leave no husband, wife or civil partner and no children, the intestacy rules rank your heirs in the order in which they will inherit your estate (see the chart, below).

If you have no relatives who are eligible to inherit, your estate passes to the Crown in *bona vacantia* (which literally means 'unclaimed goods'). The Crown may make ex gratia payments if your dependants or distant relatives make an application to it. It is important to realise that such claimants have no right to receive anything – payments are at the discretion of the Crown. Applicants who are most likely to succeed include the following:

- Someone who had a long, close association with you: for example, an unmarried partner or someone who lived with you as a child.
- Someone whom you clearly intended to benefit under a will that was invalid for some reason.

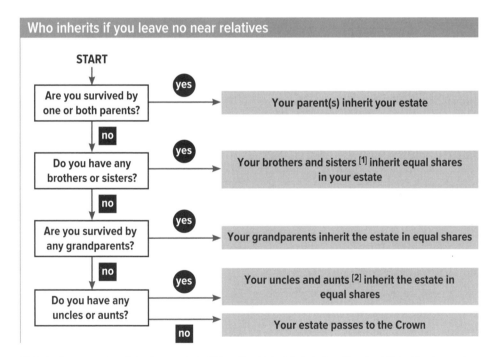

Who inherits if you leave no near relatives

START

Are you survived by one or both parents? — **yes** → Your parent(s) inherit your estate

no

Do you have any brothers or sisters? — **yes** → Your brothers and sisters [1] inherit equal shares in your estate

no

Are you survived by any grandparents? — **yes** → Your grandparents inherit the estate in equal shares

no

Do you have any uncles or aunts? — **yes** → Your uncles and aunts [2] inherit the estate in equal shares

no → Your estate passes to the Crown

[1] If a brother or sister has died before you, their children (if any) inherit in their place. Note that full-blood brothers and sisters inherit in preference to half-brothers and half-sisters. For example, if your nearest relatives were one brother and one half-sister, your brother would inherit, but not your half-sister. But if you died and your nearest relative was just one half-sister, she would inherit rather than any grandparents or more distant relatives.

[2] If any uncle or aunt has died before you, their children (if any) inherit in their place. If you have no full uncles or aunts, any half-uncles or half-aunts will share the estate instead.

PROBLEMS CAUSED BY INTESTACY

The main problems of intestacy arise where you are survived by a partner (either married or not) and/or you have children. Unless you make a will, you cannot be certain that they will be adequately provided for in the event of your death.

Unmarried couples

If you are not married to your partner, he or she has no automatic right of inheritance in the event of your death. However, they will be able to claim a share of your estate under the Inheritance (Provision for Family and Dependants) Act 1975 if they lived with you as husband, wife or civil partner throughout the two years prior to your death. If that condition does not apply but if they can show that they were being partly or wholly maintained by you when you were alive, they may still be able to claim support from your estate.

In either case, a claim must usually be made within six months of permission being granted to distribute the estate. It will then be considered by the courts, which is generally a lengthy and often costly procedure.

Married or in a civil partnership

If you are married or in a civil partnership, there is a tendency to assume that your husband, wife or civil partner will automatically inherit everything. The foregoing sections have shown that this is by no means certain.

Even if you are happy for your husband, wife or civil partner and children to share your assets, the practical application of the intestacy rules may be very distressing to your survivors. Where the estate must be shared between your spouse or civil partner and children, or shared with other relatives, your husband, wife or civil partner has the right to claim the family home as part or all of his or her inheritance (provided he or she lived there with you prior to your death). If the home is worth more than the amount he or she is entitled to inherit, your husband, wife or civil partner can 'buy' the excess from the estate. But if they don't have sufficient resources to do this, the home may have to be sold so that the cash raised can be split as required by the intestacy provisions.

Children

Minors cannot inherit directly under the intestacy laws, so any assets passing to children under 18 years of age (and unmarried) must be held in trust. This will be

> If you are not married to your partner, he or she has no automatic right of inheritance.

a 'bereaved minor's trust' for the purpose of Inheritance Tax (IHT) (see page 92).

The trustees will be required to invest the assets in accordance with the Trustee Act 2000, assuming the law of England and Wales applies. This places a number of duties and constraints on the trustees, in particular regarding the way the trust assets are invested. Fortunately, the Act gives the trustees very wide investment powers. But they may be required to obtain professional advice, which could be unduly costly if only a relatively small sum is involved. In Scotland and Northern Ireland, the more restrictive investment rules of the Trustee Investments Act 1961 apply. This could mean an unduly high proportion of the trust fund being held as deposits, gilts and other bonds, and the trustees will be required to get investment advice unless they stick to a narrow range of investments largely made up of National Savings & Investments products.

Assets continue to be held in trust until the child reaches age 18, at which point he or she takes over direct ownership of the assets. This might be earlier than you would have wished. In a will, you could require assets to be held in trust until a later age (though the trust may then have to pay IHT – see Chapter 5).

TAX AND INTESTACY

Although intestacy might mean your estate is not passed on as you would have wished, it does in fact impose a certain amount of tax-efficiency. This is because the rules require a share of your estate above the fixed amounts to be passed to people other than your husband, wife or civil partner, so using up some or all of your IHT-free limit.

INTESTACY IN SCOTLAND

The law in Scotland works differently for those who die without making a will, as follows. The amounts stated have applied since 1 June 2005:

- **If you were married with no children.** Your husband or wife has 'prior rights' to the family home (provided it is in Scotland) up to a value of £300,000, furniture and household effects up to £24,000 and a cash sum up to £75,000. He or she also has 'legal rights' to half the remaining 'moveable estate' (i.e. excluding land and buildings). See below for the remaining estate.

 See page 49 for the IHT limits for recent years and up to 2014–15.

- **If you were married with children.** Your husband or wife has prior rights to the family home up to £300,000, furniture and effects up to £24,000 and a cash sum up to £42,000 plus legal rights to share one-third of the remaining moveable estate. The children also have legal rights to share one-third of the moveable estate between them. See below for the remaining estate.

- **If you had a civil partner and no children.** Your civil partner has legal rights to half your moveable estate.

- **If you had a civil partner and children.** Your civil partner has legal rights to one-third of your moveable estate. The children also have a legal right to share one-third of the moveable estate between them.

- **If you had children but no husband, wife or civil partner.** The children have legal rights to half the moveable estate.

- **The remaining estate.** Whatever remains after meeting the prior rights, the legal rights and, in the case of partial intestacy, bequests under a will is known as 'the dead's part' and is distributed in the following order of priority:
  – children
  – if there are both parents and brothers and sisters, half the remainder goes to the parents, half to the brothers and sisters
  – brothers and sisters, if there are no parents
  – parents, if there are no brothers and sisters
  – husband or wife
  – uncles and aunts (or, if they have died, their children)
  – grandparents
  – brothers and sisters of grandparents (or, if they have died, their children)
  – remoter ancestors, going back one generation at a time
  – the Crown.

Note that, as a general principle, full-blood brothers and sisters inherit in preference to half-blood siblings. For example, if you died leaving no children or parents and had a brother and half-sister, your brother would inherit the 'dead's part' and your half-sister would get nothing. But if you died leaving no children or parents and your only sibling was a half-sister, she would inherit the 'dead's part'.

> Your husband or wife has prior rights to the family home up to £300,000.

INTESTACY IN NORTHERN IRELAND

The law is also different in Northern Ireland for those who die without making a will:

- **If you were married or in a civil partnership with no children.** Your husband, wife or civil partner inherits all your personal effects plus the first £450,000 of your estate and half of any residue. The remainder passes to parent(s) or brother(s) and sister(s) if there are no parents still living. If there are no children, no parents and no brothers or sisters (or nephews or nieces), then your spouse inherits your whole estate.
- **If you were married or in a civil partnership with children.** Your husband, wife or civil partner inherits all your personal effects plus the first £250,000 of your estate plus half of any residue if there is one child, or one-third of the residue, if there are two or more children. The remainder of the estate passes to the child(ren) – in trust if they are aged under 18.

- **If you had children but no husband, wife or civil partner.** The estate is divided equally between the children.
- **If you had no children and no husband, wife or civil partner.** Your estate goes to your relatives, starting with parents but extending to very distant relatives if no closer ones survive you.

Note that, in contrast to England, Wales and Scotland, the law for Northern Ireland specifically requires half-blood brothers and sisters to be treated in the same way as full-blood siblings. So, for example, if you died and your nearest relatives were a brother and a half-sister, they would share your estate.

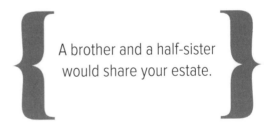

{ A brother and a half-sister would share your estate. }

JOINTLY OWNED ASSETS

How you own assets affects inheritance both under intestacy and if you make a will.

You may well have property, bank accounts, savings accounts and investments that are jointly held by you and someone else, typically your husband, wife, civil partner or unmarried partner.

In England, Wales and Northern Ireland, there are two ways of holding assets jointly: under a 'joint tenancy' or as 'tenants in common'. These are legal terms that can apply to any type of asset and not just to the way you share a home. Different arrangements apply in Scotland – see opposite.

Under a joint tenancy, you and your co-owner (or owners if there are more than two of you) own the whole asset, you have identical interests in it, and you cannot sell or give away the asset without the agreement of the other person. In the event of one of you dying, the other automatically becomes the sole owner of the asset (though the deceased person's share still counts as part of his or her estate). This automatic passing on of your share of the asset overrides the intestacy rules or any contrary instructions in a will.

Under a tenancy in common, you and your co-owner(s) have the right to enjoy or use the whole asset, but you each have your own distinct share in the asset and the shares need not be equal. On your death, your share of the asset does not automatically

pass to your co-owner and you can leave it to anyone you choose. If you have not specified who is to inherit your share, it is passed on according to the intestacy rules. It is important to think how you own shared assets. Joint tenancy has the advantage of automatically giving your spouse, partner or other co-owner some financial security. They retain the assets you jointly own and continue to have access to them without any break after your death. But tenancy in common allows more flexible inheritance planning because you can leave your share of assets to someone other than your co-owner. This will not necessarily save IHT, but can help you to pass assets on the way you wish.

CHANGING THE WAY YOU SHARE OWNERSHIP

Some solicitors advise that you need a formal, signed and witnessed deed in order to switch from a joint tenancy to a tenancy in common. In fact, that is not the case. The law simply requires that one joint owner gives the other notice in writing. The notice does not have to be in any particular form – a letter would do – nor do you have to use any particular words. But your intention must be clear. To make matters doubly clear, you might consider drawing up a joint statement that you both sign.

Switching from a tenancy in common to a joint tenancy does require a formal deed, which a solicitor can draw up for you.

JOINT ASSETS IN SCOTLAND

In Scotland, jointly owned assets are nearly always held as tenants in common – i.e. with each person owning a distinct share of the asset. However, if the owners have agreed on it, there can be a 'survivorship destination clause' written into the ownership documents. Like joint tenancy in the rest of Britain, the survivorship destination clause ensures that the share of a co-owner who dies automatically passes to the remaining owner(s) – even if the will stipulates that something different should happen. Note that the clause can only be cancelled with the consent of all the owners and it requires a formal deed which can be drawn up by a solicitor.

SHARED OWNERSHIP AND OTHER TAXES

For Income Tax and Capital Gains Tax (CGT) purposes, you are taxed on your share of any income or gain in proportion to the way you share the investment or other asset with other people.

But there are special rules for husbands, wives and civil partners. For Income Tax, HMRC will first assume that any assets you hold jointly are held under a joint tenancy. This means that you will each be treated as receiving half of any income from the asset. If you want the income to be treated differently, you need to send your tax office a completed form 17 (from www.hmrc.gov.uk or your usual tax office or local tax enquiry centre) setting out how the income is to be shared between you.

The way the income is split for tax purposes must reflect your actual shares in the asset. You cannot just choose the most convenient income split if it does not match the real shares and you cannot choose one split for Income Tax purposes and another for CGT.

Joint bank and building society accounts are almost always held as joint tenants, so can only ever be held on a 50/50 basis, but of course there's nothing to stop you transferring cash to your husband, wife or civil partner so they can pay into an account in their own name. If, exceptionally, you do hold an account as tenants in common, you must send HMRC proof of this arrangement at the time you submit form 17.

In the case of other assets, such as shares and unit trusts, say, you do not need to send in proof with form 17 but, if requested to do so, you should be prepared to provide some proof. This might be, say, copies of application forms or documents that you signed when you first acquired the asset.

MAKING A WILL

You could draw up your own will but usually it is better to get professional help, which need not be expensive.

In many people's minds, making a will is inextricably linked with using a solicitor but this need not be so. Provided your personal circumstances are straightforward and you understand what you are doing, there is no reason why you should not write your own will. The main advantage of writing your own will is, of course, the saving in solicitors' fees. But a simple will, for example involving only personal (no business) assets in the UK, with everything left to your husband, wife or civil partner, need not cost much even if you do go to a professional.

If your affairs are more complex, you should be wary of the DIY route. A will, to fulfil its purpose, must record your intentions clearly and unambiguously and should include contingency plans to cover the possibility, for example, of a beneficiary dying before you. There are also various pitfalls to be avoided – some that would invalidate the will and leave your estate subject to the intestacy laws and others that would not invalidate the will but would interfere with the intentions expressed in it. For example, a valid will must be signed by two or more witnesses, who may not also be beneficiaries (or the husbands, wives or civil partners of beneficiaries) under the will. So, if you are leaving anything to your husband, wife or civil partner, say, do not ask him or her to be a witness – the will would be valid but your spouse or civil partner would not be allowed to inherit under it.

If your affairs are complicated – for example, you run your own business, you have been divorced or you have stepchildren – or you do not feel confident about your knowledge of the law relating to wills, you would be wise to employ a professional rather than trying to draw up a will yourself. Lawyers claim to make more money from sorting out defective DIY wills than from writing wills themselves.

{ Lawyers claim to make more money sorting out defective wills than from writing wills themselves. }

 For more information on making a will, see the *Which? Essential Guide to Wills & Probate*.

WHERE TO GET A WILL

Solicitors are the best choice for most people and are not necessarily expensive.

Solicitors

The traditional source of help drawing up a will is a solicitor. Most high-street firms can draw up a simple will – leaving, say, everything to your husband, wife or civil partner. The cost of a simple will typically starts around £75. If you and your spouse or civil partner draw up similar wills at the same time (often called 'reciprocal wills', 'mirror wills' or 'back-to-back wills'), you might get a special rate of, say, £120 the pair.

But prices vary greatly. So be prepared to shop around. If your affairs are complicated, the charge will depend on the time the solicitor needs to devote to your case and so you should expect to pay more. Always check the expected price before going ahead.

> ! Solicitors must belong to a professional body – one of the Law Societies – that lays down strict rules of business conduct backed up by disciplinary procedures and ensures that you have access to the Legal Ombudsman if things go wrong.

{ Prices vary greatly. So be prepared to shop around. }

Will-writing firms

Will-writing services are an alternative to a solicitor. These are often small firms working under a franchise or as agents of a larger company. Most work by gathering the necessary details from you and feeding these into a computer which produces your will.

At present, there is no requirement for will-writers to be regulated. Unlike solicitors, people running or working for will-writing firms are not required

 Which? Legal Service offers an online will-writing service with full telephone support. Charges are £89 for a single will and £149 for mirror wills. For more information, go to www.whichlegalservice.co.uk/our-services/make-a-will.

MAKING A WILL

to have any legal training or formal qualifications or abide by any set professional standards. However, some belong voluntarily to trade bodies that do impose requirements on their members. For example, the Institute of Professional Willwriters (IPW) and its sister body, the Institute of Scottish Professional Willwriters operate as self-regulating bodies for their members and aim to set rigorous professional standards. Members must pass an entrance exam or hold an equivalent legal qualification, participate on an annual basis in a programme of continuous professional development to update their skills and maintain at least £2 million of professional indemnity insurance and comply with the IPW's code of business practice, which has been approved by the Office of Fair Trading, a government department with responsibility for trading standards.

Will-writers do not have to belong to the IPW or any other trade body, so you need to check carefully before you do business with a will-writer that you are satisfied with the person's or firm's skills, integrity and arrangements should anything go wrong. In the past, problems have arisen with some of these firms, for example, a case where a large number of wills contained a flaw. There are also concerns that unregulated firms could pressurise you to take up additional services, such as will storage, overcharge for such services, and produce unsuitable or even fraudulent wills. But relatively few (7 per cent) consumers seeking a will go to a will-writer and there is a lack of evidence to suggest whether problems are persistent or widespread.

Therefore, in autumn 2010, the Legal Services Board, a body set up by statute with overall responsibility for regulation of legal services, commissioned its consumer panel to gather evidence to feed into a review on whether will-writing firms should in future become regulated.

Will-writers generally charge a flat fee for wills and tend to be a bit cheaper than solicitors. Not surprisingly, the wills tend to have a standardised format – if your affairs are complex, a solicitor will normally be the better choice.

Other will-writing services

A third source of will-writing is banks, building societies and life insurance companies. These offer a will-preparation service but some insist that you agree to them also acting as executors of the will (which is not generally a good idea – see page 160).

You have an interview with the bank, society or company either at their offices or in your home. The interviewer you meet is not usually the person who actually draws up the will. If a bank or building society writes the will and you have a complaint, you can go to the Financial Ombudsman Service (FOS). The FOS does not cover insurance companies drafting wills.

Many charities also offer will-writing services. It is essential that you make sure that the solicitor or other will-writer is acting for you alone and that you do not feel under any pressure to make a bequest to the charity in your will.

Finally, there are a growing number of online will-writing services that guide you through an online questionnaire to construct a will. Which? itself offers such a service and sets high standards by using initial questions to check whether an online will would be suitable, providing phone support from solicitors and full checking of your online will by solicitors before it is sent to you.

> Give your executors a sealed copy of the will.

OTHER RELATED SERVICES

In addition to writing your will, a solicitor or other will-writing service might offer extras, such as storing your will, drawing up a 'living will' (also called an 'advance directive') or severing a joint tenancy to create a tenancy in common (see page 154). Do not feel pressurised into taking up any of these services unless you want to.

Will storage

Most important is that your executors will be able to find your will and can be confident that it is your most recent will. If you are known to have a family solicitor, storing your will with the firm could be a good idea. You do not necessarily have to pay anything for this – some firms will store your will free of charge (because they hope to be employed later in executing your will). If you do not have an ongoing relationship with a solicitor, that might not be the best place to store your will. Other options include a bank safe-deposit box or a safe or strong box at home. Whatever you decide, it is a good idea to give your executors a sealed copy of the will.

Living will

This typically sets out in advance your wishes regarding healthcare – especially refusal of medical treatment – if you become incapacitated by a terminal illness or degenerative disease. In general, medical practitioners are required to give whatever treatment they deem necessary but a patient has the right to refuse treatment. Clearly an unconscious patient cannot do this but refusal can still be effective even if it was given in advance of becoming unconscious. There has been much debate about the legal status in the UK of living wills, but it seems that, provided the document states your intentions clearly and reflects your

 To find a solicitor, contact the relevant Law Society for details of its members. See Useful Addresses on pages 214–17.

informed decision, a living will is likely to be legally binding. A good place to store a living will would be with your medical records.

Severance of joint tenancy

As discussed on page 154, if you want to transfer ownership of something – such as your home – from a joint tenancy to a tenancy in common, you do not need a formal deed drawn up by a solicitor. If you do not feel confident about getting the detail right, however, you might prefer a solicitor to draw up a notice for you.

APPOINTING EXECUTORS

You have a choice when it comes to deciding who will sort out your affairs for you in accordance with your will: you can appoint a professional as your executor – e.g. a solicitor or your bank – or you can appoint friends or relatives. In general, professionals often charge more and if problems arise, such as long delays, the beneficiaries can do little because they do not themselves have a contract with the executor, so have little access to information and limited power to challenge the executor's actions. If, instead, you appoint relatives or friends, they always have the option of employing a solicitor direct if they need help.

You can choose anyone you like to act as executor (provided they are aged 18 or over or 16 or over in Scotland when they apply for probate) and it is common to appoint the main beneficiary. Normally, you should appoint at least two executors, just in case one dies before you or refuses to act. Make sure you ask the people concerned whether they would be willing to take on the role.

Bear in mind that being an executor is a demanding task. Your executors will need to locate your will and personal papers, track all your assets and establish their value, establish what gifts you have made during the last seven years, deal with debts and funeral expenses, trace and contact beneficiaries, handle paperwork, deliver an account to HMRC and ensure any tax is paid. As tax will depend not just on the estate you leave but also on gifts made within the seven years up to death, your executors will be expected actively to try to trace gifts. This may mean trawling through old bank and building society statements and making enquiries among family members. Make sure you choose someone who has the time, energy and confidence to deal with officials and form-filling.

You can make your executors' lives easier if you lodge a record of your assets, their location and any gifts you have made along with your will or personal papers.

> Being an executor is a demanding task. Choose someone who has time, energy and confidence.

REVIEWING YOUR WILL

You should not view making a will as a task once done to be forgotten. As your circumstances alter, so your will needs to be updated.

In some situations – for example, if you marry, remarry or form a civil partnership – any will made before the marriage or civil partnership will automatically be invalidated (unless it was a will made specifically in contemplation of the marriage or civil partnership). All bequests and references to your ex-husband, ex-wife or ex-civil partner are automatically revoked by divorce or the dissolution of a civil partnership and the appointment of your 'ex' as guardian of any children will be revoked, unless you have made clear that this is still your intention. In other respects, the rest of your will stands.

The same is not true of separation – the whole will including bequests to your spouse or civil partner is still valid; in that situation, you should review the terms of your will.

Other circumstances in which you might want to revise your will are the birth or adoption of a child or if you decide that you would like to leave a legacy to a charity. It is wise to read through your will every couple of years, say, as a matter of course, to check that it reflects your current wishes.

If you do decide to alter a will – even slightly – it is better to draw up a new will containing the revisions than to add an amendment (a 'codicil'). The trouble with codicils is that they can easily become detached from the will and lost.

Beware of stapling, clipping or pinning anything other than a codicil to a will. It is quite likely that any other note or document would be detached before the will was sent for probate and the marks left on the will might then raise doubts about whether there had been a codicil attached that has become lost. Enquiries into the non-existent codicil could delay proceedings.

A new will should always start with a clause revoking any previous wills; this automatically invalidates any earlier wills. Interestingly, if a will is not automatically revoked – by, say, a later will or marriage – the law requires that you physically destroy your will if it is to be revoked. Simply putting a cross through it and scribbling 'cancelled' or 'revoked' across it is not enough.

MAKING A WILL

As your circumstances alter, so your will needs to be updated.

See www.willaid.org.uk/ if you would like to make a will and, instead of paying a solicitor, donate the fee to charity. The Will Aid scheme runs in November each year.

MAKING GIFTS IN YOUR WILL

In your will, you can give away anything you own. There are different types of gift. The distinction between them is important both for tax reasons (see Chapter 9) and because of the order in which they can be redirected to meet expenses and settle debts that you leave at the time of your death. The main types of gift are described as follows.

Specific gift

This can be a named or identifiable possession, such as a piece of furniture, an item of jewellery or a particular car. It may be a specific possession that you own at the time you write the will. If you later sell the item the beneficiary who was to have received it will get nothing after all.

Alternatively, you might leave a more general type of specific gift. This would be the gift of a possession but not restricted to a specific item that you own at the time of drawing up the will. For example, you might give away 'the car I own at the time of my death', which would take into account the possibility that you might change your car from time to time.

A specific gift might be even more widely defined: for example, simply 'a car'. In this latter case, the executors of your will would have a duty to make sure that the beneficiary received a car – either one that you owned at the time of death or, if you had none, one bought specifically to fulfil the terms of the will – or, alternatively, the

trustees would have to pay over an equivalent sum of money.

Legacies

A 'pecuniary legacy' is a particular type of specific gift that is a straightforward gift of money: for example, '£1,000 to my niece, Claire'.

A 'demonstrative legacy' can be either a general gift or a pecuniary legacy, which is to be paid from a specific fund: for example, 'a violin to be paid for out of my account with Barclays Bank' or '£1,000 from my account with the Nationwide'. If there was not enough money in the account, the shortfall would have to be met by using other assets in the estate.

On the whole, it is best to keep bequests of particular items or demonstrative gifts to a minimum. Particularly where your will is made a long time before death, there can be many changes to your possessions and the accounts and investments you hold.

Your personal representative(s) have wide powers (called the power of appropriation) to use any part of your estate to satisfy legacies. For example, if you leave £1,000 to your niece, the executors could give, say, shares worth £1,000 rather than selling the shares and giving her the proceeds from the sale.

An unmarried partner's claim can only be for reasonable maintenance.

Residuary gift (the 'residue')

A will that assigned every part of your estate as a particular gift or legacy would be out of date almost immediately, because the value of your estate fluctuates even in the course of your daily transactions and will alter more widely during the course of time. Therefore, it is usual to leave whatever remains of your estate, after all your debts, expenses and various gifts, as listed above, have been paid, as a 'residuary gift' or 'residue'.

You may intend your residue to be a substantial gift or it may be a small amount with, say, the bulk of your estate given away through pecuniary gifts.

To meet debts and expenses, any intestate part of your estate will be used up first, followed by the residue.

GIFTS YOU DO NOT MAKE

By omission, your will can also express your intention not to leave anything (or only very little) to people who might have expected to inherit from you. However, if these people were dependent on you (or you had a partner who had lived with you for at least two years as husband, wife or civil partner without necessarily being dependent), they have the right to make a claim through the courts under the Inheritance (Provision for Family and Dependants) Act 1975 for reasonable provision out of your estate. If you have not made a will, dependants who do not benefit under the intestacy can also make a claim under this Act.

The main people who are entitled to make such a claim are as follows:

- Your husband, wife or civil partner
- A former husband, wife or civil partner, provided he or she has not remarried (and is not precluded from making a claim under the divorce or dissolution settlement)
- A child of yours (whether legitimate, illegitimate or adopted)
- A child of your family (i.e. a stepchild or foster child)
- An unmarried partner.

An application under the Act must usually be made within six months of the personal representatives being given permission to dispose of the estate, though the court can extend this time limit. The court decides whether or not the applicant is entitled to financial support from the estate and, if it decides in favour of the applicant, it can order the payment of either a lump sum or income (or both). However, in the case of an unmarried partner, a claim can only be for reasonable maintenance not a general share of the late partner's estate (even if some of the deceased's possessions had been informally considered to be shared assets).

You might seek to anticipate and thwart such a claim by giving away as much of your estate as possible but this strategy will not work. The court has the power to revoke such gifts in order to ensure that enough funds are available to meet the needs of your surviving dependants.

You can include in your will a statement setting out your reasons for excluding your dependants and the court will take this into account. It would be worth seeking advice from a solicitor about the most effective wording to use.

In Scotland, you cannot disinherit your husband, wife, civil partner or children, who can claim their 'legal rights' to part of your estate.

SUMMARY

This chapter has looked at why making a will – and keeping it up to date – is so important. Without a will, your wealth may be passed on in unexpected ways, failing to provide for the people nearest and dearest to you and benefiting others who do not need your support. A will is especially important if you have dependent children, not just to ensure they are financially provided for, but also to avoid the cost and administrative burden of trusts being set up unnecessarily. Writing a will is not a difficult task, but needs to be done well. Usually a solicitor will be the best choice, especially if your family circumstances or affairs are at all complex.

{ In Scotland, you cannot disinherit your husband, wife, civil partner or children. }

TAX AT THE TIME OF DEATH

Although you might be most concerned with the total amount of tax due on your whole estate, it's important to bear in mind how the tax bill will be distributed among your heirs.

TAXES TRIGGERED BY DEATH

When you die, you are deemed to make a final gift of all your possessions just before death. The good news is that there is no Capital Gains Tax (CGT) on your estate, but there might be IHT on both the estate and any gifts in the seven years before death.

WHAT'S IN THIS CHAPTER?

However well you have planned, there may still be some Inheritance Tax (IHT) to pay after you are gone. This chapter considers:

- How IHT may bite on gifts you made earlier and on what you leave at death (page 167).
- How any tax is apportioned between different bequests, so you can plan for this in your will (page 169).
- Special rules that may apply if you are passing on a business (page 177).
- The administration involved in reporting and paying the tax (page 179).

{ Whatever you give away on death is completely free of CGT. }

NO CGT

Whatever you give away on death is completely free of CGT. For CGT purposes, your heirs take over your possessions at their value on the date of death. This completely wipes out even very substantial gains that may have built up during your lifetime.

Any gifts with reservation during your lifetime (see Chapter 4) are still treated as part of your estate for IHT so might cause IHT to be payable. But gifts with reservation are *not* part of your estate for CGT purposes so do not benefit from the wiping out of gains. From the CGT point of view, the gift is valid from the date in your lifetime when you originally gave it away, so any increase in its value since then has built up in the hands of the recipient (and could be taxable when they dispose of the asset). In a way, this means that tax may be levied twice on the same gain in the form of IHT on your estate and CGT in the recipient's hands.

TAX ON GIFTS MADE BEFORE DEATH

Chapter 3 looked at the immediate tax position of gifts made during your lifetime. With Potentially Exempt Transfers (PETs) there is no IHT to pay at the time of the gift but, if you die within seven years, the gift may become taxable. The effective rate of tax ranges from 8 per cent up to 40 per cent, depending on the time that has elapsed since you originally made the gift (see page 56).

Similarly, a chargeable transfer – on which IHT may have been paid at the time of the gift at the lower lifetime rate of 20 per cent – is reassessed and there may be further tax to pay if you die within seven years of making the gift (see page 48).

The reassessment of these earlier gifts and payment of any tax on them is entirely separate from the calculation of tax on your estate. However, if you made PETs within seven years of dying, the fact that they have been re-assessed as taxable gifts will increase your running total up to the time of death and that could create or increase an IHT bill on your estate (see the case study overleaf). Moreover, there is no taper relief (see page 56) on any extra tax payable on the estate due to the reassessment of PETs. This is a constant source of confusion but taper relief can apply only to tax on the reassessed PETs themselves; taper relief has no impact whatsoever on extra tax on the estate.

■ PLANNING POINT

If your husband, wife or civil partner is terminally ill, this is naturally a distressing time for the family and inheritance planning is unlikely to be foremost in your thoughts. However, it does present a tax-planning opportunity that you and your partner might wish to consider if your partner is looking at putting his or her affairs in order. If you own assets whose value has increased over the time you have owned them and would trigger a big CGT bill if you sold them, consider giving them to your partner. Gifts between husbands, wives and civil partners do not trigger an immediate tax bill (see Chapter 2) and on their death, any capital gains would become tax-free. If your partner leaves the assets to you in his or her will, you would reacquire them at their higher, present value. However, your partner would be free to leave the assets to anyone else. Your gift would not be genuine (and would not work for CGT-planning purposes) if it was conditional on it being given back to you in your partner's will.

> There is no taper relief on any extra tax payable on the estate due to PETs.

See page 49 for tax-free limits for earlier years and the years up to 2014–15.

TAX ON YOUR ESTATE

On your death, IHT is due on the value of your estate plus your running total of gifts made in the seven years before death if they come to more than the tax-free limit. The tax-free limit for 2011–12 is £325,000. This may seem a large sum, but the £325,000 limit can soon be swallowed up, especially if you own your own home. Your estate is made up of:

- The value of all your possessions at the time of death, including your home, car, personal belongings, cash and investments.
- Plus any gifts with reservation (see Chapter 4) that you made and any assets that you elected to be treated as if they were gifts with reservation in order to escape the Pre-Owned Assets Tax (POAT) (see page 72).
- Plus the proceeds of any insurance policies, which are paid to your estate.
- Less your debts.
- Less reasonable funeral expenses (say, around £2,500 but could be more).

This total is called your 'free estate' and it is the amount that is available for giving away. For the purpose of calculating any IHT, you can deduct from the free estate any gifts made in your will that count as tax-free gifts (see page 125). But you must add all the PETs and other taxable gifts that you made in the seven years before death to find the relevant running total. If the running total comes to more than the tax-free limit, IHT at a rate of 40 per cent is payable.

Case Study PRAVEEN

In addition to using his £3,000 a year tax-free limit, Praveen made the following gifts in his lifetime:

- 30 May 2007   £20,000 to a grandchild (a PET)
- 21 November 2010   £100,000 to a discretionary trust (a taxable gift)

On 16 August 2011, Praveen died. He leaves an estate of £300,000. You might think his estate is fully covered by the tax-free limit (£325,000 in 2011–12) and no IHT would be due. But the estate is not looked at in isolation. It is considered as the last gift Praveen made in a running total of gifts over the seven years. The PET in May 2007, now reassessed as a taxable gift, uses up £20,000 of the limit. The gift to the discretionary trust in November 2010 uses a further £100,000. This leaves only £205,000 of the limit to set against the estate, on which tax of £38,000 is due.

Praveen's tax-free limit £325,000			
PET £20,000	Gift to trust £100,000	First £205,000 of estate	Remaining £95,000 of estate

IHT = 40% × £95,000
= £38,000

GIFTS IN YOUR WILL

I f tax is due on your estate, who pays it depends on the types of gift that you leave.

If the value of your estate plus taxable gifts in the seven years before death comes to less than the tax-free limit, making gifts under your will is fairly straightforward. Assuming that the estate is sufficiently large (after paying off debts and expenses), the recipients will receive the amounts that you specify in your will.

However, if there is IHT due on the estate, matters are not always so simple. To work out how much the recipients will actually receive, you need to know how tax will be allocated between the various gifts.

DIFFERENT TYPES OF GIFT

For IHT purposes, there are three types of gift that you can leave in a will:

- **Tax-free gifts** (see Chapter 2). There is no tax at all on these.
- **Gifts that bear their own tax.** With these, the amount you give is treated as a gross gift out of which the recipient must pay any tax due.
- **Free-of-tax gifts** (not to be confused with tax-free gifts). The recipient gets the amount you specify and any tax due is paid out of the residue of the estate.

In general, a specific gift under your will is automatically treated as a free-of-tax gift unless it is tax-free or you have explicitly stated that the gift should bear its own tax. But, to avoid confusion, it is a good idea to state for every gift whether it is 'free-of-tax' or 'to bear its own tax'. Whatever is left of your estate after deducting specific gifts is called the residue, which can be tax-free or taxable. Any taxable part bears its own tax.

The fun starts when you try to calculate how much tax will be deducted from each gift and the residue. The calculations vary depending on the mix of gifts. The following sections describe the main possibilities. If you find the calculations that follow daunting, do not despair – you can always ask your solicitor or accountant to work them out. The important point to grasp is that tax can affect seemingly similar gifts in different ways.

■ PLANNING POINT ■

Beware of specifying that a gift of a thing – for example, a piece of jewellery, furniture, painting or other heirloom – should bear its own tax, unless you are confident that the recipient has other resources from which to pay the tax. Otherwise, the gift you have made may need to be sold in order to pay the tax due.

HOW DIFFERENT GIFTS ARE TAXED

How your bequests are taxed might seem unimportant but just a few seemingly trivial words in your will can have a big impact on the amount each of your heirs inherits.

{ Just a few seemingly trivial words in your will can have a big impact. }

If all your gifts are tax-free

This is the simplest case. As with lifetime gifts, some gifts from your estate are free of IHT, in particular: gifts of any amount to your husband or wife, gifts to charities, gifts of national heritage property, gifts to political parties and gifts to housing associations (see Chapter 2).

For example, you might make a gift to charity and leave the residue to your husband or wife. Since both types of gift are tax-free, there is no IHT at all.

If all your specific gifts bear their own tax

The amount of tax on each gift is in proportion to the values of chargeable gifts. This is done by working out the tax due on the whole of the chargeable estate and then

---

Case Study **SIOBHAN**

When Siobhan dies in October 2011, she leaves an estate made up as follows:

Cottage	£65,000
Personal possessions	£21,500
Cash in bank	£496
Investments	£331,204
Gross value of estate	£418,200
less various small debts	£500
less funeral expenses, administration costs, etc.	£2,700
Net value of 'free estate'	£415,000

Siobhan had made no gifts during the previous seven years. Since the value of the estate exceeds the tax-free limit, you might expect IHT to have been payable. In fact, it was not, because Siobhan used the whole of the 'free estate' to make tax-free gifts. She left a legacy of £100,000 to charity and the residue to her husband. (Note that, since Siobhan did not use any of her tax-free limit, her husband can inherit this in full – see page 126.)

expressing this as a percentage of the chargeable estate – this gives you an 'effective' IHT rate. The effective rate is then applied to each gift that is to bear its own tax to find out the amount of tax due on the gift. It is the recipients who pay the tax.

If all your specific gifts are free of tax

The main complication in this situation is that, when the estate pays the tax due (out of the residue), it is deemed to be making a gift of the tax as well. To take account of this, all the free-of-tax gifts must be 'grossed up', which simply means that you find the total that equals the amount of the actual gifts plus the tax on them. The tax is then deducted from the residue.

If you leave free-of-tax and other taxable gifts

This is the most complex situation and is illustrated in the case study, Alec, overleaf. Problems arise because the free-of-tax gifts must be grossed up by the IHT rate. The snag is that we do not know what IHT rate to use. The correct rate will depend on the amount of tax due on the whole chargeable estate which is made up of the gifts bearing their own tax as well as the free-of-tax gifts. But we cannot work out tax on the whole estate until we know the grossed-up value of the free-of-tax gifts. As you can see, we are in a circular trap.

The way out of the trap is to use a process called 'iteration'. Using iteration, you start with an estimate of the IHT rate – initially the death rate of 40 per cent – and repeat the

---

Case Study JIM

Jim dies in July 2011 leaving an estate of £575,000. He makes two specific gifts bearing their own tax: £175,000 to his friend Ben and £180,000 to his cousin Gerald. He leaves the residue to his wife. Jim made no PETs or chargeable transfers in the seven years before he died. The tax position is worked out as follows:

Tax position of the estate

Value of free estate	£575,000
less tax-free gifts (i.e. residue to his wife)	£220,000
Chargeable part of estate (£150,000 + £180,000)	£355,000
less tax-free limit	£325,000
	£30,000
Tax on £30,000 @ 40%	£12,000
Effective tax rate ([£12,000 ÷ £355,000] × 100)	3.380%

Who gets what

Tax on Ben's gift of £175,000 @ 3.380%	£5,915
Net amount Ben receives	£169,085
Tax on Gerald's gift of £180,000 @ 3.380%	£6,084
Net amount Gerald receives	£173,916
Amount left to wife	£220,000

Alec also dies in July 2011 leaving an estate of £575,000. He makes two specific gifts that are free of tax: £175,000 to his friend Douglas and £180,000 to his friend Annette. He leaves the residue to his wife. Alec made no PETs or chargeable transfers in the seven years before he died. The tax position is worked out as follows:

Step 1: Grossing up the gifts

Add together all free-of-tax gifts (£175,000 + £180,000)	£355,000
less tax-free limit	£325,000
	£30,000
gross up £30,000 at the 40% tax rate (i.e. divide by 1 − 0.4 = 0.6)	£50,000
The grossed-up value of the gifts is £50,000 + £325,000	£375,000

Step 2: Tax position of the estate

Value of estate	£575,000
less tax-free part of the estate (£575,000 − £375,000)	£200,000
Chargeable estate	£375,000
less tax-free limit	£325,000
	£50,000
Tax on £50,000 @ 40%	£20,000

Step 3: Who gets what

Net amount Douglas receives	£175,000
Net amount Annette receives	£180,000
Amount left to wife (£575,000 − £175,000 − £180,000 − £20,000)	£200,000

calculation, each time using an improved estimate. You would have to go through the calculation several times to find the absolutely correct rate. But this involves a lot of work for only a small increase in the amount of tax collected and the tax authorities are happy to lose a bit of tax for the sake of making the calculations simpler. So, in practice, the tax authorities let you stop after two rounds by which stage the rate you are using is not perfect but ensures most of the tax due is collected.

You will need to do the same sort of calculation if, in addition to leaving free-of-tax gifts, you also divide the residue so that part is tax-free and part is taxable – this would be the position, for example, if you divided the residue between your children and your husband or wife. The taxable part of the residue is treated as if it is a gross gift bearing its own tax, so it does not need to be grossed up. See the case study on page 174.

Leaving a mixture of gifts makes the sums complex. The examples on pages 171–4 show you how the sums work.

Case Study ALEC

Suppose, in the example opposite, of his estate worth £575,000, Alec left £175,000 free of tax to Douglas and £180,000 free of tax to Annette, as before, but also left a gift of £10,000 to bear its own tax to his daughter Judy. He leaves the residue to his wife. The tax position is as follows:

ROUND 1

Step 1: Grossing up the gifts

Add together all free-of-tax gifts (£175,000 + £180,000)	£355,000
less tax-free limit	£325,000
	£30,000
gross up at the 40% tax rate (i.e. divide by 1 − 0.4 = 0.6)	£50,000
The grossed-up value of the gifts is £50,000 + £325,000	£375,000

Step 2: Tax position of the estate

Value of estate	£575,000
less tax-free part of estate (£575,000 − £375,000 − £10,000)	£190,000
Chargeable estate	£385,000
less tax-free limit	£325,000
	£60,000
Tax on £60,000 @ 40%	£24,000
Notional rate of IHT ([£24,000 ÷ £385,000] × 100)	6.234%

ROUND 2

Step 1: Re-grossing up the gifts using a better estimate

Total free-of-tax gifts	£355,000
gross up at the notional IHT rate (i.e. divide by [1 − 0.06234] = 0.9377)	
Re-grossed-up value of free-of-tax gifts	£378,602

Step 2: Revised tax position of the estate

Value of estate	£575,000
less tax-free part of estate (£575,000 − £378,602 − £10,000)	£186,398
New total for chargeable estate	£388,602
less tax-free limit	£325,000
	£63,602
Tax @ 40% on £63,602	£25,441
Final estate rate ([£25,441 ÷ £388,602] × 100)	6.547%

Step 3: Who gets what

Tax on Judy's gift @ 6.547%	£655
Net amount Judy receives	£9,345
Net amount Douglas receives	£175,000
Net amount Annette receives	£180,000
Tax to be deducted from residue (£25,441 − £655)	£24,786
Amount left to wife (£575,000 − £175,000 − £180,000 − £10,000 − £24,786)	£185,214

 See overleaf for an example where, in addition to a free-of-tax bequest, the residue is split between a tax-free and taxable gift.

Percy dies in October 2007 leaving an estate of £800,000. He makes a specific free-of-tax gift of £350,000 to his son, Harold, and leaves the residue equally to his wife and his daughter, Rose. Percy made no PETs or chargeable transfers in the seven years before he died. The tax position is worked out as follows:

ROUND 1
Step 1: Grossing up the gifts

Add together all free-of-tax gifts	£350,000
less tax-free limit	£325,000
	£25,000
gross up at 40% tax rate (i.e. divide by 1 – 0.4 = 0.6)	£41,667
The grossed-up value of the gift is £41,667 + £325,000	£366,667

Step 2: Tax position of the estate

Value of estate	£800,000
less tax-free part of the estate (£800,000 – £366,667 – [residue ÷ 2])	£216,667
Chargeable estate	£583,334
less tax-free limit	£325,000
	£258,334
Tax on £258,334 @ 40%	£103,334
Notional rate of IHT ([£103,334 ÷ £583,334] × 100)	17.714%

ROUND 2
Step 1: Re-grossing up the gifts

Free-of-tax gift	£350,000
gross up at the notional IHT rate (i.e. divide by [1 – 0.17714] = 0.8229)	
Re-grossed up value of free-of-tax gift	£425,325

Step 2: Revised tax position of the estate

Value of estate	£800,000
less tax-free part of estate (£800,000 – £425,325 — [residue ÷ 2])	£187,338
New total for chargeable estate	£612,663
less tax-free limit	£325,000
	£287,663
Tax @ 40% on £287,663	£115,065
Final estate rate ([£115,065 ÷ £612,663] × 100)	18.781%

Step 3: Who gets what

Harold receives	£350,000
Tax on Harold's legacy @ 18.781% of £425,325 (to be borne by estate)	£79,880
Residue (£800,000 – £350,000 – £79,880)	£370,120
Wife receives (1 ÷ 2 × £370,120)	£185,060
Tax on Rose's share of the residue @ 18.781% × £185,060	£34,756
Rose receives (£185,060 – £34,756)	£150,304

SUCCESSIVE CHARGES RELIEF

This relief is available to reduce a double tax charge where a beneficiary dies soon after inheriting.

If you left a substantial gift in your will to someone – for example, a son or daughter – who then died shortly after you, there could be two IHT bills on the same assets in a short space of time. To guard against this, a claim can be made for successive charges relief (previously known as quick-succession relief).

This relief is available where the person inheriting the assets dies within five years of the assets becoming part of that person's estate (even if the assets are then sold or given away before the recipient's death). The relief is deducted from the tax due on the estate of the second person to die, but at most the relief can reduce tax on the estate to zero. The relief is tapered: full relief is given if the recipient's death occurs within one year of the gift; a reduced rate applies if a longer time elapses (see the table, right).

Successive charges relief is also available where the original gift was a lifetime gift and the recipient dies within five years. However, the amount of tax due, if any, on the original gift will not be known until seven years have passed since the gift was made, so there may be a delay before the amount of any relief can be calculated.

For successive charges relief to be available, there must be IHT on both the earlier gift and your estate. For example, if the earlier gift was tax-free or was covered by the giver's tax-free limit, no tax would have been paid and so no relief can be claimed. This is the case even if the inclusion of the earlier gift in the estate of the second person to die is a major reason why IHT becomes due on the second death.

Successive charges relief

YEARS BETWEEN FIRST AND SECOND DEATH	TAX RELIEF ON SECOND DEATH AS A PERCENTAGE OF TAX APPLICABLE TO THE ORIGINAL GIFT [1]
Up to 1	100
More than 1 and up to 2	80
More than 2 and up to 3	60
More than 3 and up to 4	40
More than 4 and up to 5	20
More than 5	no tax relief

[1] The percentage is multiplied by the formula:

$$\frac{G \times T}{E}$$

where   G = the increase in value of the recipient's estate
E = the value of the earlier transfer or gift
T = the tax paid on the earlier transfer or gift

Sam's sister, Joan, died in May 2009, leaving him £50,000. Joan's whole estate was valued at £335,000. The tax-free limit then was £300,000 (see page 49) and so IHT of £14,000 was paid.

Sam dies in October 2011. He leaves an estate worth £505,000 to be shared by his two children. Tax on the estate would normally be 40% × (£505,000 – £325,000) = £72,000. But his personal representatives can claim successive charges relief in respect of the £50,000 he inherited. The inheritance was more than three but less than four years ago, so relief is due at 40 per cent. The relief equals:

$$\frac{\text{The increase in Sam's estate}}{\text{The value of Joan's estate}} \times \text{Tax on Joan's estate} \times 40\%$$

$$= \frac{£50,000}{£335,000} \times £14,000 \times 40\% = £836$$

The £836 relief is deducted from the IHT on Sam's estate, leaving a net IHT bill of £72,000 – £836 = £71,164

In February 2008 Ahmed gives his nephew, Jagdish, £30,000. The gift is a PET but Ahmed dies two years later. The PET is reassessed as a taxable gift and Jagdish pays £9,600 tax that then becomes due.

Tragically, Jagdish is killed in a car crash in November 2011. His estate of £450,000 passes to his partner. They were not married and IHT of £50,000 is charged on the estate. However, this is reduced by successive charges relief in respect of the gift from Ahmed. The gift was made more than three but less than four years before Jagdish's death so the successive charges relief percentage is 40 per cent. The relief is worked out as follows:

$$\frac{(£30,000 - £9,600)}{£30,000} \times £9,600 \times 40\% = £2,612$$

Tax on Jagdish's estate becomes £50,000 – £2,612 = £47,388.

For more guidance on successive charges relief, visit the HMRC website at www.hmrc.gov.uk/cto/customerguide/page13-2.htm.

PASSING ON YOUR BUSINESS

You may be able to arrange to pass on a business or farm without IHT taking a bite.

Handing on your business is a complex matter. There are many different ways of arranging the transfer, and which is appropriate for you will depend very much on your particular circumstances.

Business planning is outside the scope of this book and the aim of this section is just to draw to your attention to the fact that important reliefs against IHT may be available when you pass on a business.

BUSINESS PROPERTY RELIEF

If, on death, your business passes to someone else, your personal representatives may be able to claim 'business property relief' which will reduce the value of the transfer of the business for IHT purposes and thus reduce or eliminate any IHT otherwise payable. To be eligible, you must have been in business for at least two years. Only 'qualifying' business assets attract relief; these are assets that are either:

- Used wholly or mainly for the purpose of your business, or
- Are required for future use by the business.

Assuming you operate your business as a sole trader or as a partner in a partnership, business property relief will be given at the higher rate of 100 per cent – that is, it could completely eliminate an IHT charge.

Relief of 100 per cent is also available if you pass on a holding of shares in an unquoted company – which includes shares traded on the Alternative Investment Market (AIM).

A lower rate of business property relief – set at 50 per cent – is available to set against transfers of a controlling holding (i.e. 5 per cent or more) in a fully quoted company.

Business property relief is intended to take most handovers of family companies outside the IHT net. However, even 100 per cent relief will not necessarily entirely mitigate an IHT bill. In particular, you should note that, if the business property is subject to a binding contract for sale, relief will not normally be given. This might be the case where, say, a partnership has arranged that the surviving partners will buy out the share of a partner who dies; the deceased partner's share of the business would not qualify for relief in this situation. This sort of problem can be avoided with some advance planning – for example, by giving surviving partners the option but not the obligation to buy – so it is very important that you get advice from an accountant or other tax adviser at the time you draw up the partnership agreement.

Most types of business can qualify for business property relief. The only exception is businesses whose sole or main activity is dealing in stocks, shares, land or various other investments. Letting out property does not normally count as a business and so does not usually qualify for business property relief.

Any IHT due after business property relief has been given can be paid by interest-free instalments over a period of ten years.

Most types of business can qualify for relief.

AGRICULTURAL PROPERTY RELIEF

Agricultural property relief – which is similar to business property relief – is available when a farm is handed on. The relief, which is given automatically and does not have to be claimed, is given against the agricultural value of the land and buildings. The equipment and stock do not qualify for agricultural property relief but they may qualify for business property relief. Note that the agricultural value of the farm may be lower than the market value if, say, the land has development value – the excess will not qualify for agricultural property relief, though it may be eligible for business property relief.

To qualify for agricultural property relief, you must either have occupied the farm, or a share of it, for the purpose of farming for at least two years, or you must have owned the farm, or a share in it, for at least seven years. If you farmed the land yourself, relief is given at the higher rate of 100 per cent. If you let the land to someone else to farm, relief is restricted to the lower rate of 50 per cent.

As with business property relief, agricultural property relief is also not available if the farm is subject to a binding contract for sale (see above).

Any IHT due after relief has been given can be paid by interest-free instalments over a period of ten years.

 Passing on your business or farm is a complicated area with a lot at stake, so get advice from your accountant and a solicitor.

TELLING HMRC

W hen you die, your personal representatives will be responsible for sorting out your estate.

Before your personal representatives can distribute any of your assets to your heirs, they must obtain probate (in England, Wales or Northern Ireland) or confirmation (in Scotland), which is proof of their right to dispose of the assets. Probate or confirmation is granted only after any IHT due has been paid (or in some cases partly paid) or your representatives have shown that no tax is due.

THE FORMS YOUR PERSONAL REPRESENTATIVES NEED

If no IHT is due and the estate counts as an 'excepted estate', your representatives will normally deliver a simplified account of the assets in your estate to the Probate Registry on form IHT205 (England or Wales), the Probate and Matrimonial Office on form IHT205 (Northern Ireland) or Sheriff's Court on form C1 (Scotland) (for contact details, see below). The relevant form will be included in the pack your personal representatives are sent on contacting the relevant probate registry, office or court or they can download it from the HMRC website.

For deaths on or after 1 September 2006, an excepted estate is one where all the following conditions are met:

- The person who died had their permanent home in the UK.
- The estate involves either no trusts or only one trust.
- No more than £150,000 of the estate is trust property.

{ Probate or confirmation is granted only after any IHT due has been paid. }

 For form IHT205, go to www.hmrc.gov.uk/inheritancetax/iht-probate-forms/index.htm; for the Probate and Matrimonial Office, go to www.courtsni.gov.uk; or for the Sheriff's Court, go to www.scotcourts.gov.uk. For phone numbers and addresses, see Useful Addresses on pages 214–17.

- No more than £100,000 of the estate property is situated outside the UK.
- Any gifts in the seven years before death were of cash, chattels, quoted shares or securities, land or buildings and came to no more than £150,000. Gifts covered by the small gifts exemption, yearly tax-free limit, wedding gifts and normal expenditure out of income can be ignored but other tax-free gifts must be included.
- Any gifts of land and buildings within the seven years before death were outright gifts to another person (e.g. not gifts into a trust).
- The person who died had not made any gifts with reservation (see Chapter 4) or elected to have any transfers treated as if they had been gifts with reservation in order to escape the POAT (see page 72).

AND THE ESTATE IS EITHER
- **Small.** The gross value of the estate and gifts in the seven years before death does not exceed the IHT-free limit

OR
- **Exempt.** The gross value of the estate and gifts in the seven years before death does not exceed £1 million and the value of the estate, excluding amounts passing tax-free to a spouse, civil partner or charity, comes to no more than the standard tax-free limit (£325,000 in 2011–12).

The relevant tax-free limit is normally the amount for the year in which death occurs but is the amount for the previous tax year if the death occurred between 6 April and 5 August inclusive and the representatives apply for probate by 5 August.

Bear in mind that it may be possible to increase the tax-free limit for the estate of a widow or widower by claiming any unused tax-free limit from their husband's, wife's or civil partner's earlier death (see page 126).

If the estate is not an excepted estate or if IHT is due, the personal representatives must complete a detailed account on form IHT200, which they can obtain from the HMRC and which is sent to the relevant HMRC IHT office. The time limit for sending in form IHT200 is 12 months from the end of the month in which death occurred or, if later, within three months of the personal representatives starting to act.

{ The time limit for paying the tax is generally earlier than the time limit for delivering the IHT200 form. }

For detailed information about the personal representatives' role and how to complete the forms involved, see the *Which? Essential Guide* to *Wills & Probate*.

PAYING THE TAX

Your personal representatives have six months from the end of the month in which death occurred within which to pay any IHT due – less if they want to get probate/confirmation granted sooner than this. The time limit for paying the tax is generally earlier than the time limit for delivering the IHT200 form and your personal representatives may find initially they have to base the tax bill on an estimated account. Once the account is finalised, they pay any extra tax due or claim a refund of any overpayment. Interest is charged on tax paid late and added to refunds.

Having to pay the tax before the grant of probate/confirmation throws up another problem. The personal representatives will not necessarily have any ready cash with which to pay the bill. Although in general assets cannot be released to the representatives before probate/confirmation, there is an exception that allows some types of asset to be released early specifically to pay the IHT under a scheme whereby the money due is transferred direct to HMRC. These assets are: most National Savings & Investments products, gilts and, where banks and building societies have signed up to the scheme, money held in bank and building society accounts. If there are no such assets available or they fall short of the amount of tax due,

the personal representatives may need to take out a temporary loan to pay the tax.

Where tax is due in respect of land, buildings, shares that gave the deceased a controlling interest in a company (whether listed or unlisted) or certain unquoted shares, the personal representatives can apply to pay the tax in ten equal yearly instalments. Interest is charged on the amount outstanding.

HMRC can agree to accept heritage property in lieu of some or all of the IHT due. Eligible property includes pictures, prints, books, manuscripts, works of art and scientific objects, provided they are 'pre-eminent' for their national, scientific, historic or artistic interest. Buildings and land of outstanding scenic, historic or scientific interest and items associated with them are also eligible.

{ The personal representatives must complete a detailed account on form IHT200. }

HMRC used to publish a range of free guides about IHT. These have now all been withdrawn and instead you can find guidance on its website at www.hmrc. gov.uk/inheritancetax/index.htm. If you do not have access to the website, contact the Probate and Inheritance Tax Helpline on 0845 3020 900.

SUMMARY

In this chapter, you have seen that the way you leave bequests can have some surprising effects, once tax is taken into account and apportioned appropriately between your gifts. In particular, the residue can be whittled away if you leave a lot of gifts 'free-of-tax' and splitting the residue equally between a spouse or civil partner (a tax-free gift) and someone else (who does not qualify for tax-free gifts) means the two end up receiving quite different amounts. When deciding what to leave in your will and how to put your affairs in order, be aware of the work your executors will have to do.

Bequests can have some surprising effects, once tax is taken into account.

TAX AND YOUR HOME

IHT planning is especially tricky if most of your wealth is tied up in your home. You can't save tax by giving away your home in your lifetime if you still need to live there. But there are some other options you could consider, including sharing your home and equity release schemes.

10

BASIC PLANNING

In essence, your home is no different from any other asset. Many of the planning points in earlier chapters apply equally to your home.

WHAT'S IN THIS CHAPTER?

As you saw in Chapters 2 and 3, there are some special rules that eliminate or reduce any Capital Gains Tax (CGT) if you give away (or otherwise dispose of) your only or main home. By contrast, the Inheritance Tax (IHT) rules described in the previous chapters do not generally distinguish your home from any other assets that you might want to give away. But, for many people, the bulk of their wealth is tied up in their home. Moreover, there is clearly a problem in giving away an asset that you need in your lifetime and that cannot readily be divided between several people. This chapter looks at:

- The limited inheritance planning opportunities regarding your home (page 187).
- How to ensure a secure home for your survivors (page 190).
- Whether equity release can be considered a solution (page 192).

WHO OWNS WHAT?

If you own your home jointly with someone else, it is important to think about how you own it. As discussed in Chapter 8, there are two forms of joint ownership (in England, Wales and Northern Ireland): joint tenancy and tenants in common.

If you own your own home as a joint tenant with someone else, you each have equal shares in the home and have identical rights to enjoy the whole home. On death, the share of the owner who dies passes automatically to the remaining co-owner(s). This is very simple and convenient and can be the best arrangement for married couples and other partners in stable relationships, especially if the value of their estates taken together is no more than the tax-free limit for IHT (£325,000 in 2011–12).

However, owning the home as tenants in common gives you greater flexibility. Tenants in common still have the right to enjoy the whole home but you each have distinct shares in the home which need not be equal and do not pass automatically to the other owner(s) on death. Instead, the share of the home is passed on in accordance with your will or, if you had not made a will, the rules of intestacy.

USING YOUR TAX-FREE LIMIT

Anything husbands and wives and civil partners leave to each other is normally a tax-free gift (see Chapter 2). As a result, prior to October 2007, when the first of a married couple or civil partners died, their tax-free limit was often wasted when everything was left to the surviving spouse or civil partner and there could be a substantial IHT bill when the survivor died. From October 2007, this changed. Now, any unused tax-free limit on the first death can be inherited by the survivor (see page 126). As a result, the survivor's tax-free limit can be up to double the standard amount (up to £650,000 in 2011–12). This has removed the need for married couples and civil partners to make elaborate arrangements in order to simultaneously protect their partner's right to the home and save IHT. The main planning required is now administrative:

- Keep paperwork relating to the first death where the people sorting out the estate on the second death can find it.
- Make sure the people who will sort out the estate know that they need to make a claim to inherit the unused tax-free limit.

Bequests between unmarried couples are not tax-free, so they are forced to use their tax-free limit when they leave things to each other. This means that, where the late partner's estate (plus taxable gifts within the previous seven years) comes to no more than the tax-free limit, the surviving partner can inherit the late partner's share of the home without any tax problem. But, where the estate comes to more, as you saw in Chapter 9, any tax due will be apportioned between all the taxable bequests – it is not possible to specify that the tax-free limit should be set against some selected taxable bequests but not others.

THE IMPORTANCE OF A WILL

Chapter 8 described the problems that can arise if you die intestate. These can be especially acute if your home is the main asset in your estate.

If you die without a will and you are survived by children or other relatives, your husband, wife or civil partner inherits outright only a certain part of your estate. He or she does have the right to opt to take his or her share of your estate in the form of the home rather than other assets. But what if that share of your estate is worth less than the home? The husband, wife or civil partner may well find that part of the home has to be put into trust for the benefit of young children, say, or that older offspring or more distant relatives insist on the sale of the home in order to release their own inheritance as cash.

The position of an unmarried partner is even worse. He or she may have no automatic right to share in your estate. However, if he or she has been your partner throughout the two years up to death or has been financially dependent on you, he or she can apply to the courts under the Inheritance (Provision for Family and Dependants) Act 1975 (see page 163). However, the claim can only be for reasonable maintenance.

There is no procedure for claiming a share of the home simply on the grounds that unmarried partners had always viewed it as their shared family home.

Therefore, if the home is jointly held as tenants in common, it is essential that you make a will specifying how your share of the home is to be passed on.

Case Study **CHRISTINE AND MARK**

Mark, 83, never made a will – 'tempting fate', he always said. Now, it is too late because he is suffering from dementia and has moved to a nursing home. (As you saw in Chapter 8, a person has to be of sound mind to write a valid will.) His wife, Christine, still lives in the family home, which is worth around £300,000 and is in Mark's name. Christine and Mark have one son, Geoff, who is married with children. Christine is worried about whether she will be able to stay in the family home if Mark dies.

Without a will, the intestacy rules (see Chapter 8) will determine how Mark's estate is passed on. Since Mark is both

married and has a child, Christine would inherit Mark's personal possessions, £250,000 of the estate outright plus a life interest in half the remainder. The rest would pass to Geoff. Since only the part going to Geoff would be taxable, there is unlikely to be any IHT on the estate.

It is likely that Christine's inheritance would be sufficient to ensure that the family home could stay in her hands during her lifetime. However, with part of the estate going direct to Geoff, she will have to consider whether she has enough assets and income to afford to stay on. Her future would look more secure if Mark had written a will.

 If the home is jointly held as tenants in common, it is essential that you make a will.

 For a reminder of the key distinctions between 'joint tenancy' and 'tenants in common', see pages 154–5.

YOUR HOME AS A LIFETIME GIFT

I t would be very tax-efficient if you could give away your home during your lifetime. Of course, the snag is: you also need somewhere to live.

YOUR ONLY OR MAIN HOME

If you expect your estate at death to exceed the tax-free limit, it would be convenient if you could give away your home now in your lifetime. Making a gift of your home to your children, say, would count as a Potentially Exempt Transfer (PET). There would be no IHT to pay at the time you made the gift and, provided you survived seven years, no IHT at all. But if you give away your home, where do you intend to live? If you mean to stay in the home, the gift will not work for IHT purposes, because it will count as a gift with reservation (see Chapter 4). There are a couple of ways around this problem, though neither is very satisfactory.

First, you could share the home with the people to whom you give it. Provided you all live together and you bear your full share of the running costs of the home, the gift should not count as one with reservation. But, if the recipients subsequently move out, the gift will become a gift with reservation – so make sure you do not fall out!

The second solution relies on the caveat that a gift is not a gift with reservation if you give full consideration in money or money's worth for the use you continue to make of the gift. For example, you could give away your house but pay the full market rent to live there under a tenancy agreement or licence. Or you could buy a lease at the full market rate which lets you live in it for some specified period – for example, long enough to cover your expected remaining years, plus a few extra years to be on the safe side. Alternatively, you might offer your services as, for example, a housekeeper or gardener, provided the value of your work was equivalent to the market rent for the property you continue to occupy.

Other promising ideas tend to fall foul of the rules governing associated operations (see Chapter 1) or the Pre-Owned Assets Tax (POAT) (see Chapter 4). Tax experts, from time to time, come up with other complicated schemes, but their legal status is often unclear and the Revenue is quick to lay a challenge.

The only satisfactory way of giving your home as a lifetime gift is if you genuinely do have somewhere else to live – for example, a retirement cottage or moving in with friends or relatives.

When considering gifts or other transactions in connection with your home, keep an eye on the Stamp Duty Land Tax (SDLT) position. SDLT is paid by the purchaser of a property and levied as a percentage of the amount paid (see the table, below). If you give away your home, or part of it, and receive nothing in return, the likelihood is that this is a genuine gift and there is no SDLT to pay. However, if you receive anything in return, this will be treated as a payment and SDLT may then apply. For example, the recipient taking over paying part of the mortgage would count as you receiving something in return for the gift. Bear in mind that if you pay SDLT

for the recipient, this will count as a gift for IHT purposes, but might be covered by one of the exemptions in Chapter 2. Check out any planned gift involving your home with a solicitor before you go ahead.

MORE THAN ONE HOME

Giving away a property is obviously more feasible if you have more than one home. But you need to take care that any continuing use you make of the property you have given away does not trigger the gift-with-reservation rules. The IHT legislation says that a gift with reservation occurs if the recipient of a gift does not enjoy the gifted assets 'virtually

SDLT rates 2011–12	
AMOUNT PAID (OR TREATED AS PAID)	**RATE [1]**
Up to £125,000	0%
Over £125,000 to £250,000	1% [2]
Over £250,000 to £500,000	3%
Over £500,000 to £1 million	4%
Over £1 million	5%

[1] Rate shown applies to total amount paid (not just the slice above the threshold). For example, SDLT on a £300,000 property would be 3% × £300,000 = £9,000.

[2] 0% for first-time buyers £250,000 between 25 March 2010 and 24 March 2012, inclusive.

 If you want to explore more complex ways to make a lifetime gift of your home, get professional advice from an accountant or other tax adviser.

to the entire exclusion of the donor and of any benefit to him'. These words are not defined but the Revenue has provided some guidance on benefits you might still enjoy without triggering the reservation rules – see box, below.

CHANGE OF PLAN

Suppose your circumstances change and you move back into a home you had previously given away? This could trigger the gift-with-reservation rules. However, if you become unable to maintain yourself because of old age, infirmity or some other reason and your moving back into your old home is a reasonable way for the recipient of the gift – who would have to be your relation or spouse – to provide care for you, the gift-with-reservation rule will not apply.

WATCH OUT FOR CGT

Giving away your home does not normally trigger a CGT bill, because any gain on your only or main home is generally exempt. In some situations, however, there could be a CGT bill. These arise where:

- You have lived away from home for a time.
- You have let out all or part of the home.
- Part of the home has been used exclusively for your work.
- The garden was greater than the normal size for a home of that type (usually taken to be greater than half a hectare).

If you give away a second home, CGT will normally be payable on the gift – see Chapter 3.

Benefits that should not trigger the gift-with-reservation rules

In relation to a home you have given away, they include:

- You stay in the home in the absence of the recipient for no more than two weeks a year.
- You go to stay in the home with the recipient but for no more than a month a year.
- You are invited to make social visits that do not include overnight stays, provided you visit the recipient no more often than you would have done if the gift had not been made.
- You stay temporarily with the recipient for a special reason, such as while you or the recipient is convalescing or your home is being redecorated.
- You visit the home in order to babysit or for some other domestic reason.

PROBLEMS IF YOU COHABIT

If you share a home with, say, an unmarried partner, a sibling or your adult children, IHT on death might force the sale of your home. Planning ahead can help to avoid problems.

A husband, wife or civil partner inherits tax-free from their partner, so there is no problem passing the family home to the survivor. But a bequest to an unmarried partner, a brother, sister, child, friend or carer is a taxable bequest. If your estate is worth more than your tax-free limit, IHT will bite into the amount you leave them. This can cause a problem if your major asset is your home and that person shares it with you, because the home may have to be sold to raise the money to pay the tax.

The problem can arise both where a valuable property is jointly owned and where only one of the cohabitees owns the property.

POSSIBLE SOLUTIONS

If you or your cohabitee might have to sell up to pay an IHT bill when one of you dies, there is only a limited range of options that you could consider.

Sisters challenge the law

Two sisters, Joyce and Sybil Burden, took a case to the European Court of Human Rights. The sisters, in their 80s, share and jointly own the family home which they inherited and where they have lived their whole lives. With rising house prices, the home was, at the time of the case, worth £875,000. Although they have left their share of the home to each other, the hefty tax bill that would be due on the first death means that the surviving sister would have to sell the home to pay the tax.

The sisters claimed that their rights under article 14 of the Convention on Human Rights, which outlaws discrimination, were being violated, since married cohabitees or civil partners would not pay tax or be forced to sell their home.

In December 2006, the court agreed that married couples and civil partners were treated differently, but said the UK government '*cannot be criticised for pursuing, through its tax system, policies designed to promote marriage; nor can it be criticised for making available the fiscal advantages attendant on marriage to committed homosexual couples*'. It concluded that the different treatment under UK law is reasonable and justified and the sisters lost the case

Create a joint ownership

If you are the sole owner of a property that you share with one or more other people and you would like them to be able to carry on living in the home, an answer might be to give a share in the home to the other cohabitee(s). Points to bear in mind are:

- The gift will normally be a PET, so to be effective in saving tax you need to survive seven years after making the gift (see Chapter 3).
- You must not benefit from the part of the home you give away. If you do, the PET will fail and instead you will have made a gift with reservation that stays in your estate (see Chapter 4). In practice this means you must pay at least your full share of the running costs of the home or pay a market rent to your co-owner(s).
- There will be no CGT on the gift, provided the home is your only or main residence.
- If even your remaining share of the home is above your tax-free limit, a problem may remain and you may want to consider insurance (see above right).
- Consider your own security should a co-owner die before you. Your security would be greatest if you owned the property as joint tenants (see page 154).

Take out whole-of-life insurance

Whether you are the sole owner of a property or own a valuable share, you could consider taking out whole-of-life insurance written in trust for your co-owner(s) to cover any IHT due on your death (see page 135). Other co-owners should consider doing the same to protect your security.

This solution is feasible if you are still reasonably young and fit. But if you are getting on in age and/or your health is poor, insurance could be prohibitively expensive.

Case Study BETH

Beth is the sole owner of a house worth about £380,000, which she shares with her adult daughter, Viv. Beth is retired and Viv is disabled. The family does not have much income and very few assets apart from the house. As it stands, if Beth dies, there would be an IHT bill of at least £22,000 to pay. Viv would then have to sell the home to pay the tax.

Beth decides to transfer a half share in the home to Viv. This reduces Beth's estate to around £190,000 which is now well within her tax-free limit (£325,000 in 2011–12) provided she survives seven years after making the gift so that it drops out of the running total of gifts up to the date of death. For the gift to work, it is essential that Beth does not benefit from the half of the home that she has given away, so she must pay at least half of all the costs associated with the home. Beth and Viv would be wise to keep records of how they split the bills, just in case they have to prove their case to HMRC at some time in the future.

 For help deciding on whether whole-of-life insurance would be a suitable and affordable option, consult an independent financial adviser (see Useful Addresses on pages 214–17).

EQUITY RELEASE SCHEMES

These schemes let you raise money from your home while you still live there and, in the process, also reduce the value of your estate. But there is a price to pay.

WHAT ARE EQUITY RELEASE SCHEMES?

Equity release schemes are a way of raising money from the capital you have tied up in your home. There are two main types of scheme:

- **Lifetime mortgage.** You take out a mortgage on your home. Usually this is a 'roll-up' loan which means you don't pay any interest on the mortgage during your lifetime. Instead, the interest is added to the outstanding loan, which is eventually repaid when you no longer need the home – usually on your death but possibly earlier if, say, you move permanently into long-term care.
- **Home reversion scheme.** You sell all or part of your home to a reversion company. You receive a lump sum now and retain the right to live in the home either rent-free or for a peppercorn amount for as long as you still need the home. The reversion company gets its money back from the sale of the home after you have died or, say, moved permanently into care.

In either case, schemes can be taken out for a single person or a couple. In the latter case, the right to remain in the home continues until the second of you dies or moves into care.

Equity release schemes were mainly designed to address the problems of older homeowners who are 'asset rich, cash poor' enabling them to raise extra income or cash from their home in order, say, to boost their income or pay for repairs to their home. But they have also been marketed as a way to mitigate IHT.

HOW AN EQUITY RELEASE SCHEME REDUCES IHT

An equity release scheme reduces the value of your estate and so any potential IHT bill in two ways:

- First (but not particularly helpfully), you do not get full value for the part of your home you mortgage or sell (see the case study, opposite). So you get an instant depreciation in the value of your estate.

- Second, and more positively, the money released is yours to do with as you will. Provided you don't keep it, it ceases to be part of your estate. You could spend the money. You could use it to make lifetime gifts. You could use it to buy an annuity to provide you with extra income for life. (The annuity ceases to be part of your estate at the time you die because the income stops on death.) But if you keep and invest the money raised, it will continue to be part of your estate, in which case the equity release scheme will not be particularly effective in saving IHT.

ARE EQUITY RELEASE SCHEMES VALUE FOR MONEY?

There is no easy answer to this question. It depends how much you value being able to have cash now either to spend or to give away while being able to remain in your home.

The only way to release the full value of the equity in your home is to sell it and move somewhere cheaper. There are sound reasons why an equity release scheme does not give you full value for the part of your home you give up.

In the case of a typical lifetime mortgage, you are not paying any interest during your lifetime. The unpaid interest is added to the outstanding loan, so you or your heirs will eventually have to pay back a lot more than just the original amount you borrowed. Because interest is then charged on the loan plus the interest already rolled up (a process called

---

Case Study **ROSEMARY**

Rosemary, aged 70, has an estate worth £580,000, but £460,000 of this is tied up in the value of her home. When she dies, Rosemary's whole estate will pass to her daughter, Claire. Based on today's values, there would be an IHT bill of 40% × (£580,000 – £325,000) = £102,000.

Rosemary has been thinking about taking out a home reversion scheme. The one she has in mind would give her a lump sum of £101,500 if she sold half her home. This would reduce her estate as follows:

- An immediate reduction of £230,000 (half of the home which is sold) less £101,500 (the lump sum raised) = £128,500. This represents the loss of value through using equity release and the charges for the scheme.
- Provided Rosemary spends or gives away the £101,500 raised, her estate will eventually be reduced by the full £230,000 (at today's values).

IHT on Rosemary's estate would be reduced to 40% × (£580,000 – £230,000 – £325,000) = £10,000. This is a tax saving of £92,000. But Rosemary has effectively lost £128,500 of her estate in order to make this tax saving.

 For a more detailed look at equity release schemes, see the *Which? Essential Guide: Finance Your Retirement*. See also www.which.co.uk for advice on equity release.

'compounding'), the outstanding loan increases at an alarming rate – see the table, below. You should always check that any lifetime mortgage has a 'no-negative-equity guarantee'. This means that the outstanding loan will never grow to more than the value of the home, so you and your heirs should never owe more than your home is worth.

With a home reversion scheme, the company buying your home or a share of it for cash today will normally have to wait many years until it gets its cash back. The company estimates how long that will be by looking at the average life expectancy of someone of your age and gender and then estimates how

Roll-up lifetime mortgage: an example

YEARS SINCE PLAN TAKEN OUT	RATE OF INTEREST (FIXED FOR DURATION OF PLAN)		
	5%	7%	9%
Initial loan	£50,000	£50,000	£50,000
1	£52,500	£53,500	£54,500
2	£55,125	£57,245	£59,405
3	£57,881	£61,252	£64,751
4	£60,775	£65,540	£70,579
5	£63,814	£70,128	£76,931
6	£67,005	£75,037	£83,855
7	£70,355	£80,289	£91,402
8	£73,873	£85,909	£99,628
9	£77,566	£91,923	£108,595
10	£81,445	£98,358	£118,368
11	£85,517	£105,243	£129,021
12	£89,793	£112,610	£140,633
13	£94,282	£120,492	£153,290
14	£98,997	£128,927	£167,086
15	£103,946	£137,952	£182,124
16	£109,144	£147,608	£198,515
17	£114,601	£157,941	£216,382
18	£120,331	£168,997	£235,856
19	£126,348	£180,826	£257,083
20	£132,665	£193,484	£280,221

much it could have earned on the money by investing it elsewhere rather than in you. That cost to the company is then passed on to you as a reduction in the cash sum. The older you are when you take out the plan, the more you will get back for any given value of your home that you sell. For example, a 70-year-old might get say £45,000 for every £100,000 of home they sell, while an 80-year-old might get £55,000.

The reversion company buys a percentage of your home (100 per cent if you sell your whole home) and takes that percentage of the sale proceeds when the home is eventually sold. This means the reversion company, not you or your heirs, benefits from any rise in the value of the part of the home you sold. If house prices rise steeply, the reversion company will make a handsome profit. But the reversion company also takes the risk of a much lower profit if house prices rise only modestly or even a loss if house prices fall.

> ### Case Study **CHRIS**
>
> Chris takes out a lifetime mortgage of £100,000 against his £350,000 home. The mortgage is at a fixed rate of 7 per cent a year with the interest being rolled up and added to the outstanding loan. Chris lives another 12 years. When he dies, the outstanding loan plus interest has nearly tripled to £225,220. But his house has also increased in value to just over £450,000. Once the mortgage has been repaid, £224,780 still remains to be added to Chris' estate and passed on to his heirs after IHT has been paid.

> ### Case Study **ROSEMARY**
>
> Rosemary sells 50 per cent of her home when it is worth £460,000. This raises a lump sum of £101,500. When Rosemary dies nine years later, her home is worth £520,000. The reversion company takes 50 per cent of this, in other words £260,000. The remaining £260,000 remains in Rosemary's estate to be passed on to her daughter after IHT has been paid.

COSTS AND RISKS OF EQUITY RELEASE

Apart from the value-for-money question, there are a number of other aspects to equity release schemes that you should consider carefully when weighing up whether this is the right course of action for you.

 Discuss the scheme with family members so they understand the implications for their inheritance.

 Age UK publish a detailed free guide to equity release, FS65 *Equity release*, available from www.ageuk.org.uk.

The suitability of you and your property

Equity release schemes are designed for people from, say age 60 or 65 upwards. The amount of money you can raise increases with your age at the time you take out the scheme.

To be eligible, you need to have a suitable property. Some providers will not offer schemes on flats. Most will not accept sheltered housing. Usually your property will need to be worth at least a minimum amount and be free of any existing mortgage.

Valuation

With a home reversion scheme, it is crucial that it is based on a fair valuation of your home's current value. It is important that you make sure the valuation is carried out by a valuer who is independent of the reversion company.

Immediate and ongoing costs

Make sure you understand all the costs that are involved in the scheme you choose.

There is likely to be an arrangement fee for a lifetime mortgage – say, several hundred pounds. This can be added to the outstanding loan, but interest will then be charged on it, so you might prefer to pay the fee out of the money you raise.

With a reversion scheme, there is usually an arrangement fee of, say 1 to 2 per cent. Check whether this is a percentage of the value of the home

you sell or a percentage of the amount of money you raise. Do not pay the fee upfront – it should be deducted from the money you raise after the deal is complete.

There will be a survey and valuation fee. The scheme provider might offer to reimburse this on completion of the deal.

With a lifetime mortgage, you may have legal costs. With a home reversion scheme, it is essential that you get advice from a solicitor who is acting for you rather than the reversion company, so allow for these costs.

You will be expected to keep the property insured and well maintained. The maintenance requirements may be particularly detailed with a reversion scheme. So you need to allow for these ongoing costs. Get your solicitor to check the terms of the tenancy agreement carefully.

Check whether there are charges if you want to end the scheme early.

Effect on state benefits

Be wary of taking out an equity release scheme if you are receiving any means-tested state benefits, such as pension credit.

Your eligibility for benefits and the amount you get depends on your income and capital, so raising money from an equity release scheme will affect this. The scheme provider or any independent financial adviser you are using should be able to advise on this or refer you to an appropriate alternative source of information. Your local Citzens' Advice Bureau can estimate the likely effect for you.

Possible effect on tax liability

If you are aged 65 or over and receiving extra personal allowance (age allowance) against Income Tax (see page 109), using an equity release scheme to provide income could result in some allowance being lost and a rise in your tax bill.

This is not a problem where you use a scheme to raise a lump sum. In practice, even schemes providing 'income' are often structured to provide a series of capital sums that are not within the scope of Income Tax. But bear in mind that if you invest a lump sum, interest or other income from the investment could boost your taxable income and reduce your age allowance.

Moving home

Check what happens if, after taking out the scheme, you want to move house. Can you transfer the scheme to another property? What restrictions are there on the type of property you can choose? (Bear in mind that sheltered housing is not usually eligible.)

Sharing your home

If you are married or living with a partner, to ensure their security if you were to die or move into care first, you should take out a joint equity release scheme. This will ensure that

◼ PLANNING POINT ◼

Equity release schemes that you take out at **arm's length** with a commercial company are outside the scope of the POAT – see Chapter 4. But if, on or after 7 March 2005, you arrange your own scheme with, say, a relative or friend, you might be caught. However, bear in mind that a yearly benefit of less than £5,000 does not trigger a POAT bill – see the case study on page 73.

Arm's length The term HMRC use to describe the sort of commercial deal you would make with someone you did not know on the open market as opposed to a special arrangement you might strike with a friend or family member.

the home does not need to be sold until neither of you needs it any more.

Normally, there is no security of tenure for someone who moves in with you after you have taken the scheme out. And you will need to check with the lifetime mortgage or reversion scheme provider whether they will allow someone to move in with you. This could be an issue if, say, you decide to marry late in life or you want a family member or carer to move in with you as you get older.

Family expectations

Whatever your reason for taking out an equity release scheme – to save IHT, to raise income – it will reduce the

To find details of where to find your local Citizens Advice Bureau go to www.citizensadvice.org.uk.

TAX AND YOUR HOME

value of the estate you leave on death. It is generally advisable to discuss this with family members and any others who expect to inherit from you.

HOW EQUITY RELEASE SCHEMES ARE REGULATED

Lifetime mortgages and home reversion schemes are regulated by the Financial Services Authority (FSA) (due to be replaced from 2013 by a new regulator to be called the Consumer Protection and Markets Authority). This means that providers and advisers have to be solvent, competent and abide by good business standards. They must also provide you with adequate information before you buy, including a Key Facts document which sets out important information, such as charges and your obligations, in a clear format that makes it easy to compare one scheme with another. Provided you deal with a firm authorised by the FSA, you are covered by proper complaints procedures if things go wrong, including the independent Financial Ombudsman Service. If you lose money because of bad advice, you may be eligible for compensation from the Financial Services Compensation Scheme.

Many equity release providers belong voluntarily to a trade body called Safe Home Income Plans, which sets standards for its members.

SUMMARY

It is extremely difficult to plan away a potential IHT bill on a home that you need to live in. Before entering into any arrangement that involves giving away your home, or part of it, during your lifetime, think carefully about how robust the arrangement will be if the circumstances of you or someone who will live with you were to change later on.

The lack of tax planning opportunities does not mean that you should ignore your home when it comes to inheritance planning. On the contrary, it is essential to plan if your survivors would need to carry on living in the home after you are gone. The most basic essential step is to make a will.

! Before taking out an equity release scheme, make sure you get advice from a solicitor acting for you and an independent financial adviser (IFA). Make sure the provider and IFA are regulated by the Financial Services Authority (FSA) by checking the FSA Register.

To find a solicitor and IFA, see Useful Addresses on pages 214–17. To check whether a firm is authorised by the FSA, see www.fsa.gov.uk/register/home.do or call 0845 606 1234.

RECEIVING AN INHERITANCE

Inheritance planning does not end when the giver dies. A person receiving an inheritance can also take steps to claim or alter a bequest and possibly minimise the tax paid.

11

YOUR RIGHTS AS A BENEFICIARY

Being named as a beneficiary under a will should be good news but matters do not always run smoothly.

WHAT'S IN THIS CHAPTER?

So far, this guide has looked at giving and inheriting from the perspective of the giver. But there are also important issues for people receiving your bequests or sorting out your affairs. Therefore, this final chapter considers:

- How to find out about and protect your rights as a beneficiary under a will (right and opposite).
- How tax may affect your inheritance(page 203).
- Where you have a choice, whether it is better to accept cash or assets(page 205).
- What to do if you want to refuse a bequest or would like it to go to someone else (page 207).

FINDING OUT ABOUT AN INHERITANCE

One of the jobs of the personal representatives appointed to sort out a will is to trace the beneficiaries named in the will. In many cases, the personal representatives are also the beneficiaries or close relatives of them, so there is no problem letting the beneficiaries know about their inheritance.

If you are named in a will but the personal representatives don't know how to contact you, they must make reasonable searches to try to find you. This might include, for example, checking the deceased's address books, questioning relatives and friends of the deceased, and employing a specialist tracing agency.

In other cases, the will might not name you specifically but perhaps you are one of a class

 Pursuing a claim on an estate after it has been distributed is a difficult area and you will need the help of a solicitor.

of beneficiaries and the personal representatives might not be aware that you exist.

In general, if you were to turn up after the estate had been distributed with a valid claim to an inheritance, the personal representatives would be personally liable to meet your claim. But the representatives can protect themselves by publishing appropriate notices calling for beneficiaries and creditors of the estate to make themselves known. The notices must appear in *The London Gazette* (England and Wales), *The Belfast Gazette* (Northern Ireland) or *The Edinburgh Gazette* (Scotland), a newspaper local to the area where any land in the estate is situated, and any other local or national newspapers that are appropriate given the circumstances. They must give a period of at least two months during which you should get in touch – the notice will give contact details of the personal representatives or their solicitors.

If you have not come forward within the notice period, you no longer have a claim against the personal representatives. However, you do still have the right to pursue your claim to the inheritance and, if it is valid, have the right to try to recover the assets or money involved from the other beneficiaries. If they are sympathetic, they might agree to share the estate with you. If not, you would need to pursue your case

The Gazette

The London Gazette, *The Belfast Gazette* and *The Edinburgh Gazette* are the UK's official newspapers of record. When the law requires information to be published – for example, regarding companies or insolvencies – generally, wherever else it is published, a notice must also appear in the appropriate edition of *The Gazette*. So this is the official publication in which personal representatives, if they wish to protect themselves, must advertise for claimants to an estate. You can view the deceased notices placed in *The Gazette* free on the Gazettes website (see box, below).

through the courts. Even if your claim is established, it might not be possible for you to inherit if the assets or money has already been dissipated and can no longer be traced.

{ In the worst event, after all the expenses and debts, there might not be anything left. }

 To check the notices in *The London Gazette*, *The Belfast Gazette* or *The Edinburgh Gazette*, see www.gazettes-online.co.uk.

PROBLEMS WITH EXECUTORS

While an estate is in administration, the money and property belong to the personal representatives, not the beneficiaries. The personal representatives are not even holding the estate property on trust for the beneficiaries, because until the estate is sorted out, the representatives cannot know how much of the property will have to be used to meet bills and pay off other creditors. In the worst event, after all the expenses and debts, there might not be anything left to share out among the beneficiaries. So, even if you have been left a specific item in a will – 'the ormolu clock', 'my ruby necklace', 'my stamp collection' – you have no right to it until the representatives release it. However, beneficiaries could object if the personal representatives sold a named asset unnecessarily.

Personal representatives are allowed a period of at least a year in which to sort out the estate. Some estates are complex and will take much longer – sometimes many years. But at some point, you might feel the representatives are dragging their heels and should speed up.

Other problems might be the impression that the representatives are taking too much from the estate in expenses or charges, selling assets at less than their full value, or worse.

In general, if you are dissatisfied with the way the representatives are handling their job, your only course of action is to apply to a court for help. A court has a range of possible remedies, for example, requiring personal representatives to seek court approval before selling or distributing assets and replacing or removing personal representatives. You could take out a personal action against a representative for redress or against people you believe have wrongly received assets from the estate.

{ If you are dissatisfied with the representatives, your only course of action is to apply to a court for help. }

TAX AND YOUR INHERITANCE

Inheritance Tax (IHT), Capital Gains Tax (CGT) and Income Tax can all have a bearing on the amount you eventually receive.

IHT

There is no IHT as such on anything you receive under a will. But the estate may have had to pay tax and, depending on the type of bequest you receive, this tax may have reduced the amount you receive as described in Chapter 9.

If you have been left a bequest that bears its own tax (see page 170), a share of the estate tax bill will have been deducted from any cash sum before it is handed over to you. Such gifts are more problematic if you are left an asset rather than money. In that case, you will have to find cash from elsewhere to pay the tax or, alternatively, sell the asset in order to raise the cash to pay the tax.

Even if there is a delay before the estate is distributed, if you inherit an asset (rather than cash), you are treated as having acquired it on the date of death of the deceased at the open market value of the item on that date. This will be the same as the value of the asset as shown in the estate accounts.

CGT

For CGT purposes, you are also treated as having acquired an asset that you inherit on the date of death of the deceased at its open market value on that date.

If the personal representatives sell assets and pay out cash to the beneficiaries, it is the estate not the beneficiaries that is liable for any CGT on the sale due to any increase in value since the date of death. Of course, any tax paid by the estate reduces the amount left to be distributed to the beneficiaries. Usually tax bills will reduce the residue of the estate, but if the residue has been used up, other bequests could be affected.

INCOME TAX

There is no Income Tax on the actual inheritance you get but there could be tax on any income earned by the estate after the date of death and before the estate is wound up. The personal representatives are responsible for Income Tax on any income received by the estate during administration. They pay tax at the basic rate, 10 per cent dividend rate, depending on the type of income.

If any of the income is paid out to you either during administration or when the estate is finally distributed, it counts as part of your income for the year in which you receive it. With the income from a UK estate, you get a tax credit for the tax already paid at the basic or dividend rate. If you are a non-taxpayer or pay tax at the starting rate, you can reclaim all or part of the basic-rate tax credit. You cannot reclaim any of the tax credit with dividends. If you are a higher-rate taxpayer, you have extra tax to pay on the grossed-up amount of the income. (Grossing up means you add the tax credit to the income you received to find the before-tax amount.)

The personal representatives should give you a completed certificate R185 (Estate income) setting out the amount of each type of income, the amount of each tax credit and whether it is reclaimable.

The position is more complicated if you receive income from a foreign estate. In that case, there might be UK Income Tax to pay. You will need to fill in a tax return including the supplement headed 'Trusts etc'. The notes accompanying the supplement give details of what tax might be due and what to enter on the return.

If you were left cash in the will and there is a delay before the cash is paid out to you, you might receive interest from the personal representatives in recognition of the delay. Usually, you will receive the interest without any tax deducted and, if you are a taxpayer, you must declare this income and pay any tax due.

? **Grossed-up amount** When related to Income Tax, this means the net amount of income you receive plus the tax credit or tax already deducted. For example, if you receive £80 from which £20 tax at the savings rate has already been deducted, the grossed-up amount is £80 + £20 = £100. If you are a higher-rate taxpayer, you would have extra tax to pay equal to 20% × £100 = £20.

Case Study SANJAY

Sanjay's uncle died in December 2010 and his cousin, Rajiv, is dealing with the estate. In 2010–11, Rajiv paid out some of the cash from the estate, which included interest that had been earned since the date of death. Sanjay received interest of £80 together with a tax credit of £20 representing tax at the basic rate of 20 per cent, which had already been deducted. Sanjay is a higher-rate taxpayer, so he has extra tax to pay. The grossed-up interest is £80 + £20 = £100. Tax at the higher rate would be 40% × £100 = £40 but Sanjay can set the tax credit against this, leaving £20 tax to pay.

CASH OR ASSETS?

Sometimes you are offered a choice about the form in which you receive an inheritance. Tax treatment is a factor to take into account in making your decision. (If you are not offered a choice but have a preference, you could ask the administrators of the estate if they would be willing to hand over your inheritance in your preferred form.)

YOUR OPTIONS

Typically, an estate will be made up of a mix of cash (bank accounts, savings accounts, and so on) and assets (for example, property, furniture, other personal possessions, shares). Unless you have been left specific items, the personal representatives might offer you the choice of taking your inheritance in the form of cash or some of the assets in the estate.

Substituting assets instead is an example of 'appropriation' (see page 162). The choice has these tax implications:

- **Cash.** The personal representatives sell assets to pay you cash. They are liable for any CGT on an increase in the value of the assets since the date of death and the tax is a bill paid using the estate's funds. The personal representatives are liable for CGT at a single 28 per cent rate in 2011–12. They have a tax-free limit equal to £10,600 in the year of death and the following two years but, after that, falling to half the rate an individual gets (£5,300 in

2011–12). If the asset has fallen in price since death, the representatives could set the loss against other gains made by the estate or alternatively use the lower value to adjust the IHT bill due on the estate. (Since IHT is charged at 40 per cent, significantly higher than CGT at 28 per cent, applying to amend the IHT bill will often be the better option, but is for the executors rather than you to decide.) You, as beneficiary, have no personal CGT liability and cannot make use of any losses, because you receive cash.

- **Assets.** The personal representatives pass the assets direct to you. You are treated as having acquired the assets on the date of death. Therefore you become liable for any CGT on any increase in value since the date of death, but only when you eventually sell the assets. You may be liable for CGT at 18 or 28 per cent (at 2011–12 rates), depending on your personal tax position and have an annual tax-free limit of £10,600 in 2011–12 (see Chapter 3). If the assets fall in value, you can use the loss in the normal way as set out in Chapter 3.

Often the residue of an estate is to be divided among several beneficiaries. If some of the beneficiaries opt for cash and others for assets, the personal representatives need to value the assets in order to ensure that each beneficiary gets a correct share. If the price of the assets changes frequently – as in the case of, say, shares – the personal representatives will set a fixed day on which the valuation will take place.

DECIDING WHAT TO DO

These are the points to consider when weighing up what to do.

Taking cash

Opting for cash could be worth your while if you want to spend some of your inheritance straight away, maybe paying off your mortgage or other debts.

{ Opting for cash could be worthwhile if you want to spend some of your inheritance straight away. }

If you would want to invest your inheritance, taking cash might still be sensible if you expect asset prices to fall or the assets are not the sort you would want to invest in.

Taking the assets to sell immediately

Weigh up the tax position. Would the CGT you would have to pay be less than the amount the personal representatives would pay? Or, if the assets are standing at a loss, could you claim more tax relief than the representatives? Also consider the sale price and any selling costs. Could the personal representatives get a better deal than you? This might be the case if, say, the assets are shares and the personal representatives would be selling in bulk.

Would you benefit from any tax or cost savings made by the personal representatives (because you get a share of the residue) or would the benefit go to other beneficiaries under the will?

Taking the assets to keep

This could be a good idea if the assets are suitable for you and the type you would choose to hang on to. If the assets are investments, you need to consider how they fit in with your overall financial planning and whether they match the level of risk you are comfortable taking.

 To explore financial planning more generally, see *Make the Most of Your Money* from Which? Books.

RENOUNCING YOUR INHERITANCE

You cannot be forced to accept an inheritance if you don't want it. If you simply disclaim the bequest, you have no control over what happens to it. If you want to redirect the gift to someone else, a deed of variation may be more appropriate.

DISCLAIMING YOUR INHERITANCE

Disclaiming an inheritance means you simply give up your rights to receive it. A disclaimer must cover the whole of the item concerned, not part of it. For example, if you were left 'the money in my current account' you could not give up just half of it and take the rest. But where you have been left more than one distinct item, you could disclaim one but accept another.

You cannot disclaim an inheritance if you have already accepted it or started to benefit from it (by, for example, receiving interest from it).

The inheritance effect of the disclaimer is as if your right to inherit had not existed. So, if you disclaim part of the residue of an estate, the intestacy rules take over for the part you disclaimed. Where you were left a specific bequest or legacy, whatever

you disclaim becomes part of the residue and is passed on in accordance with the rest of the will or, if there was no will, the intestacy provisions.

Tax and disclaimers

As far as IHT and CGT go, the disclaimer is treated as if it had been made by the deceased person provided certain conditions are met in which case there are no tax implications for you. (There could be IHT implications for the estate if, say, the bequest to you was a tax-free gift but will now pass as a taxable gift to someone else.) The conditions are:

- The disclaimer is made within two years of the date of death.
- It is made in writing, and
- You do not receive anything in return for making the disclaimer.

 To disclaim an inheritance, contact the personal representatives in writing within two years of the death.

If you do not meet these conditions, you are treated as having made a lifetime gift (usually a PET) to whoever gets the item instead and as having made a disposal for CGT purposes (see Chapter 3).

USING A DEED OF VARIATION

Another way of changing your inheritance is to draw up a 'variation'. In effect, this is like re-writing the will of the person who died, though technically you are not varying the will itself just the gifts made under it.

Unlike a disclaimer, with a variation you decide how the inheritance should be redirected. It can be used not simply to renounce an inheritance (say, in favour of your grandchildren instead of you) but to alter its form (for example, changing an outright gift to a life

> **!** There is no special Income Tax treatment if you disclaim an inheritance or alter it using a deed of variation. This does not normally cause a problem but, if the effect of your disclaimer or variation is that the bequest passes instead to your unmarried child under age 18, HMRC is likely to argue that the anti-avoidance legislation covering parental gifts to children applies (see page 86). This would mean that, if the inheritance produced more than £100 a year income for the child, that income would be taxed as yours.

interest) or save tax (for example, ensuring that the deceased person's tax-free limit is used).

Other differences from a disclaimer are that a variation can be made even if you have already started to benefit and it can affect just part of the inheritance if that's what you want.

A variation must be agreed by all the original beneficiaries affected by the will or that part of it which is to be varied. These beneficiaries must be aged at least 18 and of sound mind. If one or more of the beneficiaries is a child (or an unborn member of a class of beneficiaries), it may still be possible to vary the will but the consent of a court will be required.

A variation cannot be revoked or changed again. But you could vary a will more than once if each variation dealt with different assets under the will.

Tax and variations

Provided certain conditions are met, the variation is treated for IHT and CGT purposes as if the new pattern of bequests had been made by the deceased person. This means there are no IHT or CGT implications for you, but there could be IHT implications for the estate (and this might be a reason for making the variation). The conditions are:

- The variation is made within two years of the death.
- It is in writing, including specific wording to state that the variation is to be effective for IHT and CGT.

- You do not receive anything in return for making the variation, and
- If extra tax is due, the personal representatives must send a copy of the variation to HMRC.

A variation that does not meet the conditions would result in the new 'bequests' being treated as lifetime gifts (usually PETs) from the original beneficiaries to the new ones with the normal IHT and CGT (see Chapter 2) implications.

Case Study COLIN, FREDA AND LILY

Colin died in spring 2011 and left his entire estate of £600,000 to his two sisters, Freda and Lily. The sisters are both elderly and relatively well off in their own right. They do not need Colin's bequests and, by accepting the inheritance, there is a risk of a large IHT bill on their own estates when they die. They agree to draw up a deed of variation that effectively rewrites Colin's will as if he had left his estate direct to his nieces and nephews (Freda's and Lily's children). This does not affect the IHT payable on Colin's estate, but potentially saves tax on the sisters' estates.

SUMMARY

This chapter has looked at some of the issues that you may want to consider if you are the beneficiary of a will, including protecting your rights and renouncing bequests. In the extreme, you can seek a deed of variation that has the surprising result that a person's will and testament is not, in fact, necessarily their last word!

{ The variation is treated for IHT and CGT as if the new pattern of bequests had been made by the deceased. }

GLOSSARY

Administrators: The name given to your personal representatives if you have not made a will. They will distribute your estate in accordance with the law.

Alternative Investment Market (AIM): A junior section of the London Stock Exchange designed for companies that do not qualify for the main market. Generally, AIM companies tend to be relatively new, small and/or growing so tend to be high-risk investments.

Arm's length: The term HMRC use to describe the sort of commercial transaction you would make with someone you did not know on the open market as opposed to a special arrangement you might strike with a friend or family member.

Asset: Anything you own, for example, cash, investments, a house, your personal possessions or anything else. Something you owe to someone else – such as an outstanding mortgage loan – is called a 'liability'.

Bare trust: Arrangement where someone holds assets as nominee for another person who, for tax purposes, is treated as if they own the assets outright.

Beneficiary: A person (or organisation) who may receive property from a trust or who has been left something in a will.

Bereaved minor's trust: A trust set up in the will of a parent who has died to benefit their child(ren). Provided certain conditions are met, special IHT rules apply instead of the normal rules that apply to most trusts from 22 March 2006 onwards.

Capital Gains Tax (CGT): Tax on the gain you make from selling an asset for more than it was worth when you started to own it. If you give the asset away, you are deemed to have made a gain if the asset has risen in value during the time you owned it. In practice, there may be no CGT to pay because you can deduct various reliefs and allowances.

Chattels: A tax term for those of your possessions tht are physical and portable, such as cars, jewellery, furniture, antiques, paintings, and so on.

Capital risk: The risk of losing some or all of the money you invest because the value of the investment can fall as well as rise.

Defined benefit scheme: Pension scheme that promises you a set level of pension. Offered mainly by larger employers.

Defined contribution scheme: Pension scheme where your savings build up a fund for use at retirement to provide a pension.

Disabled person's trust: A trust set up either in life or in a will for the benefit of someone with a disability. Provided certain conditions are met, special IHT rules apply instead of the normal rules that apply to most trusts from 22 March 2006 onwards.

Discretionary trust: A trust set up either in life or in a will where none of the beneficiaries has an interest in possession (see below) and the distribution of the trust assets and any income from them is at the discretion of the trustees.

Disposal: In the context of CGT, ceasing to own an asset, for example, because you sell it or give it away.

Domicile: Broadly the place where you make your permanent home and intend to end your days. However, for the purposes of IHT, you are treated as still UK-domiciled during the first three years after you have acquired a domicile in another country, or if you have been a UK resident for 17 of the last 20 tax years.

Drawdown pension: The practice of leaving your pension fund invested and periodically cashing in small parts of it to provide yourself with retirement income. Unless you have a substantial secure income from other sources (from April 2011 onwards), tax rules restrict the pension you can draw to prevent you running down the pension fund too fast.

Estate: Everything you own at the time you die less everything you owe. For example, your estate includes your home, your furniture, car, personal possessions, savings and investments less your mortgage, tax you owe, unpaid bills, and so on. If you own something jointly with someone else (or have a joint mortgage or other debts), your estate includes just your share.

Executors: The name given to your personal representatives if you have made a will. They will try to ensure that the instructions in your will are carried out.

Gift Aid: A scheme with tax incentives to encourage people to give to charity.

Gift with reservation: This occurs when you give something away but carry on using or enjoying it. For IHT purposes, you are treated as if you still own the asset.

Gross gift: A gift where the person receiving the gift pays any tax due.

Grossed-up amount: An amount you receive with tax already deducted plus either the tax deducted or the tax credit received with the amount.

Immediate post-death interest trust: A trust set up in a will that meets certain conditions and which gives someone – for example, your spouse or civil partner – the right to income from, or use of, the assets held by the trust. Provided all the conditions are met, special IHT rules apply instead of the normal rules that apply to most trusts from 22 March 2006 onwards.

Inheritance Tax (IHT): Tax that may be due on some gifts you make in your lifetime and on your estate when you die. Tax is worked out by looking at the running total of taxable gifts in the seven years up to making the lifetime gift or death. If it comes to more than your IHT-free limit, tax is due.

Intangible asset: Something you own that has no physical presence, such as cash, shares, insurance policies or other financial assets.

Interest in possession: The right to receive income from, or to use, assets held by a trust.

Interest-in-possession trust: A trust set up in life or in a will where one or more of the beneficiaries has the right to receive income from, or to use, assets held by the trust.

Intestacy: Dying without having made a will. The law sets out how your estate will be distributed.

Joint tenancy: A way of sharing the ownership of an asset. All the owners had equal shares and identical rights to enjoy the whole asset. On the death of an owner, their share automatically passes to the surviving owner(s).

Lifetime annuity: Special type of investment where you hand over a lump sum (such as your pension fund) and in return get an income for life. Because the income carries on however long you live, lifetime annuities are a sort of insurance against giving longer than expected.

Net gift: A gift where the person making the gift pays any tax due. The tax paid counts as part of the gift.

Nil-rate band: Another name for the IHT-free limit.

Non-resident and not ordinarily resident: This is likely to apply if you go to work full-time abroad and the following conditions are met: your absence from the UK and your contract of employment both last at least a whole tax year; your visits back to the UK add up to less than 183 days in any one tax year; and your visits back to the UK average 91 days per tax year or less. By concession, a husband, wife or civil partner accompanying their spouse to work abroad can also count as non-resident. If you go abroad for reasons other than work – say, you retire abroad – to count as non-resident, you will need to convince HMRC that you have severed your ties with the UK.

Ordinarily resident: This normally applies if you live in the UK year after year, even if you are away temporarily.

Payroll Giving: A scheme with tax incentives to encourage employees to give to charity.

Personal representative: The person, people or organisation that sees that your estate is distributed following your death.

Potentially Exempt Transfer (PET): A lifetime gift between individuals (or occasionally a trust). There is no IHT on the gift provided the giver survives seven years. If they don't, the gift is reassessed as a taxable gift and IHT on it may become due after all.

Pre-Owned Assets Tax (POAT): Income Tax on any benefit you are deemed still to get from an asset you once used to own or have contributed towards the purchase of. But, if the gift is caught by the gift-with-reservation rules (see above), there will be no POAT to pay.

Power of attorney: A legal arrangement that appoints someone (called your 'attorney') to take over your affairs for you. There are different types of power of attorney, but commonly they are designed to let someone take over in the event that you develop a mental condition that prevents you making your own decisions any more.

Qualifying trust: A trust set up to benefit a person who is disabled, or who has a health condition expected to lead to disability or a trust set up in the will of a parent who has died or under the laws that step in where there is no will (see Chapter 8) for the benefit of a child of the deceased. In general, no IHT charges apply to this type of trust.

Relevant property trust: A trust that does not qualify for any special Inheritance Tax treatment. Therefore, putting money or assets into the trust counts as a taxable gift, there may be an IHT charge at 10-yearly intervals throughout the life of the trust and there may be IHT to pay when money or assets are paid out of the trust.

Resident: You will always count as resident in the UK if you spend 183 days or more of the tax year in the UK. You may still count as resident even if you spend fewer days here.

Residue: Whatever remains of your estate after all your debts, expenses and specific legacies and gifts have been made.

Reversionary interest: The right to receive assets from a trust at some specified time or when some specified event occurs. In the meantime, you have no right to the assets or income from them or use of them.

Settlement: A term that is used in tax legislation to mean most arrangements or agreements that transfers assets with some element of 'bounty' (an element of gift to the recipient). Trusts are also referred to as settlements but 'settlement' includes many other types of arrangement as well.

Tenancy in common: A way of sharing ownership of an asset. The owners have specified shares which may be unequal and which they can sell or give away without the consent of the other owners. On death, an owner's share is passed on according to their will or the intestacy rules.

Taper relief: In the context of IHT, a reduction in any tax due on a PET, which has become taxable because the giver died within seven years of making the gift.

Testator/testatrix: The man or woman whose will it is. You must be aged 18 or over (and of sound mind) to make a valid will.

Trust: A legal arrangement where one or more people (the trustees) hold money or assets (the trust property) to be used for the benefit of one or more other people (the beneficiaries). The trust's rules can set conditions on how the trust property is held and used.

Variation: The process of changing the gifts made under a will after the person who made the will has died.

USEFUL ADDRESSES

Accountant – to find one

Association of Chartered Certified Accountants
29 Lincoln's Inn Fields
London WC2A 3EE
Tel: 020 7059 5000
www.accaglobal.com

Institute of Chartered Accountants in England and Wales
PO Box 433
Chartered Accountants' Hall
Moorgate Place
London EC2P 2BJ
Tel: 020 7920 8100
www.icaew.co.uk

Institute of Chartered Accountants in Ireland
Chartered Accountants House, 47–49
Pearse Street, Dublin 2
Ireland
Tel: (00 353) 1 637 7200
www.charteredaccountants.ie

Institute of Chartered Accountants of Scotland
CA House
21 Haymarket Yards
Edinburgh EH12 5BH
Tel: 0131 347 0100
www.icas.org.uk

Age UK

Tel: 0800 169 6565
www.ageuk.org.uk

England 207–221 Pentonville Road,
London N1 9UZ
Tel: 0800 107 8977
www.helptheaged.org.uk

Wales Units 13–14, Neptune Court,
Vanguard Way, Cardiff CF24 5PJ
Tel: 029 2043 1555
www.agecymru.org.uk

Scotland Causewayside House, 160
Causewayside, Edinburgh EH9 1PR
Helpline: 0845 125 9732
www.ageconcernandhelptheaged
scotland.org.uk

Northern Ireland 3 Lower Crescent,
Belfast BT7 1NR
Tel: 028 9024 5729
www.ageni.org

Charities Aid Foundation (CAF)
Tel: 03000 123 000
www.cafonline.org

Charity Commission
PO Box 1227
Liverpool L69 3UG
Tel: 0845 300 0218
www.charitycommission.gov.uk

Child Trust Fund
Helpline 0845 302 1470
www.childtrustfund.gov.uk

Citizens Advice Bureau – to find your local branch
See phone book

England and Wales:
www.citizensadvice.org.uk

Scotland: www.cas.org.uk

Northern Ireland:
www.citizensadvice.co.uk

Courts

Look in *The Phone Book* under 'Courts'.

England & Wales:
www.hmcourts-service.gov.uk

Scotland:
www.scotcourts.gov.uk

Northern Ireland:
www.courtsni.gov.uk

Discount broker – some examples

AWD Chase de Vere
PO Box 228
Manchester M32 2AJ
Tel: 0845 140 4014
www.awdchasedevere.co.uk

Hargreaves Lansdown
1 College Square South
Anchor Road
Bristol BS1 5HL
Tel: 0117 900 9000
www.h-l.co.uk

Financial Ombudsman Service

South Quay Plaza
183 Marsh Wall
London E14 9SR
Tel: 0800 234 567 or 0300 123 9 123
www.financial-ombudsman.org.uk

Financial Services Authority (FSA) register

Helpline: 0845 606 1234
www.fsa.gov.uk/register/home.do

Financial Services Compensation Scheme

7th Floor
Lloyds Chambers
1 Portsoken Street
London E1 8BN
Tel: 0800 678 1100 or 020 7741 4100
www.fscs.org.uk

Fund supermarket – some examples

Funds Direct: www.fundsdirect.co.uk/
Default.asp?

Funds Network: www.fidelity.co.uk/
investor/research-funds/fund-
supermarket/default.page

SFS Invest Direct: www.sfsinvestdirect.
co.uk/

Vantage: www.h-l.co.uk

Historic share price service

www.londonstockexchange.com

HM Revenue & Customs (HMRC)

For local tax enquiry centres look in
The Phone Book under 'HM Revenue
& Customs'
For your local tax office, check your
tax return, other tax correspondence
or check with your employer

HMRC Trusts & Estates
Inheritance Tax
Ferrers House
Castle Meadow Road
Nottingham NG2 1BB

IHT and Probate Helpline:
0845 302 0900
Revenue Orderline (for forms and
helpsheets): 0845 900 0404
Self Assessment Helpline:
0845 900 0444

IHT Business Property Relief: www.
hmrc.gov.uk/inheritancetax/pass-
money-property/business-relief.htm
Centre for Non-Residents: www.hmrc.
gov.uk/cnr/
Community Amateur Sports Clubs:
www.hmrc.gov.uk/casc/clubs.htm
Find a form: http://search2.hmrc.gov.
uk/kbroker/hmrc/forms/start.jsp
Inheritance Tax: www.hmrc.gov.uk/
inheritancetax/

IHT limits for earlier years: www.hmrc.gov.uk/rates/iht-thresholds.htm
Official interest rates: www.hmrc.gov.uk/rates/interest-beneficial.htm
Pre-Owned Assets Tax: www.hmrc.gov.uk/poa/poa_faqs.htm
Probate forms: www.hmrc.gov.uk/inheritancetax/iht-probate-forms/index.htm
Successive charges relief: www.hmrc.gov.uk/cto/customerguide/page13-2
Tax credits: www.hmrc.gov.uk/taxcredits
Tax rates and allowances: www.hmrc.gov.uk/rates/cgt.htm
Tax return – filing online: www.hmrc.gov.uk/sa/file-online.htm
Tax return – commercial software: www.hmrc.gov.uk/efiling/sa_efiling/soft_dev.htm
Trusts: www.hmrc.gov.uk/trusts/types/index.htm
Trust for a vulnerable person: www.hmrc.gov.uk/trusts/vpe1.rtf

Independent Financial Adviser – to find one

IFA Promotion
www.unbiased.co.uk

The Institute of Financial Planning
Whitefriars Centre, Lewins Mead
Bristol BS1 2NT
Tel: 0117 9345 2470
www.financialplanning.org.uk

MyLocalAdviser
www.mylocaladviser.co.uk

Personal Finance Society(PFS)
www.findanadviser.org

Institute of Professional Willwriters
Trinity Point, New Road
Halesowen
West Midlands B63 3HY
Tel: 0345 257 2570
www.ipw.org.uk

Insurance broker – to find one

British Insurance Brokers Association
8th Floor, John Stow House
18 Bevis Marks
London EC3A 7JB
Tel: 0870 950 1790
www.biba.org.uk

Law Societies

The Law Society (England and Wales)
113 Chancery Lane
London WC2A 1PL
Tel: 020 7242 1222
www.lawsociety.org.uk

The Law Society of Northern Ireland
Law Society House
96 Victoria Street
Belfast BT1 3GN
Tel: 028 9023 16 14
www.lawsoc-ni.org

The Law Society of Scotland
26 Drumsheugh Gardens
Edinburgh EH3 7YR
Tel: 0131 226 7411
www.lawscot.org.uk

Legal Ombudsman
PO Box 15870
Birmingham B30 9EB
Tel: 0300 555 0333
www.legalombudsman.org.uk

The London Gazette
(also Belfast and Edinburgh Gazettes)
www.gazettes-online.co.uk

Money Advice Service
Helpline: 0300 500 5000
www.moneyadviceservice.org.uk

National Association of Valuers and Auctioneers
Arbon House, 6 Tournament Court
Edgehill Drive
Warwick CV34 6LG
Tel: 0845 250 6004
www.nava.org.uk

National Savings & Investments (NS&I)
Tel: 0500 007 007
www.nsandi.com

Probate Registry (England & Wales)
To obtain probate forms, leaflets and information
Your local Probate Registry. See Phone Book under 'Probate Registry'
Probate & IHT Helpline: 0845 30 20 900
www.hmcourts-service.gov.uk/infoabout/civil/probate/index.htm

Probate and Matrimonial Office (Northern Ireland)
Royal Courts of Justice (Northern Ireland)
Chichester Street
Belfast BT1 3JF
Tel: 028 9023 5111
www.courtsni.gov.uk

Scottish Legal Complaints Commission
The Stamp Office
10–14 Waterloo Place
Edinburgh EH1 3EG
Tel: 0131 528 5111
www.scottishlegalcomplaints.com

Solicitor – to find one
Contact the Law Societies above or Society of Trust and Estate Practitioners below
for a list of members

Society of Trust and Estate Practitioners (STEP)
Artillery House (South)
11–19 Artillery Row
London SW1P 1RT
Tel: 020 7340 0500
Fax: 020 7340 0501
Answerphone for list of members:
020 7340 0506
www.step.org

Stockbroker – to find one
Association of Private Client Investment Managers and Stockbrokers (APCIMS)
22 City Road
Finsbury Square
London EC1Y 2AJ
Tel: 020 7448 7100
www.apcims.co.uk

London Stock Exchange
Follow this path on website: Prices and markets/ Stocks/ Tools and services/ Find a broker
www.londonstockexchange.com

Tax adviser – to find one
The Chartered Institute of Taxation
1st Floor
Artillery House
11-19 Artillery Row
London SW1P 1RT
Tel: 020 7340 0550 or 0844 579 6700
www.tax.org.uk

Web use giving sites
www.goodsearch.com
www.everyclick.com

Which? Books
www.which.co.uk

Which? Legal Service
www.whichlegalservice.co.uk/our-services/make-a-will

Will Aid
The next Will Aid campaign takes place in November 2011
www.willaid.org.uk

INDEX

Other books in this series

NEW EDITION
Pensions Explained
Jonquil Lowe
ISBN: 978 1 84490 110 4
Price £10.99

Whether you're setting up a pension for the first time or approaching retirement age, this practical and accessible book will help you navigate the pensions maze. *Pensions Explained* covers state, personal and company pension funds, and offers practical advice on plugging gaps and maximising savings. It also examines 'auto-enrolment' that will affect all employees from 2012, explains what to do if your circumstances change and looks at pension investments and how to protect your income.

NEW EDITION
Tax Handbook 2011/12
Tony Levene
ISBN: 978 1 84490 119 7
Price £10.99

Essential reading for all UK taxpayers, the no-nonsense advice and practical tips in *Tax Handbook 2011/12* show you how to cut through the red tape and easily navigate the current tax system. This book explains how to complete your tax return, how to check your tax code and use National Insurance Tax Credits to boost the family budget, as well as giving advice on online self-assessment. Fully updated to include the 2011 Budget and how it affects you.

Finance Your Retirement
Jonquil Lowe
ISBN: 978 1 84490 057 2
Price £10.99

Finance Your Retirement is the essential step-by-step guide to a secure retirement, providing advice on saving for your pension, whether to opt for an annuity, how to access your money if you retire abroad and the basics of Inheritance Tax. There are helpful tips for maximising your budget using state benefits and investments, such as unit trusts and OEICs, plus guidance on how to make your property work for you.

Other books in this series

NEW EDITION
Divorce & Splitting Up
Claire Colbert
ISBN: 978 1 84490 107 4
Price £10.99

Divorce & Splitting Up gives comprehensive, clear advice to help you get to grips
with the legal and financial complexities of finishing a relationship, whether you
are married, cohabiting, or in a civil partnership. Fully updated with changes to
the CSA, this book offers practical assistance on minimising unnecessary conflict
and costs, choosing a solicitor and going to court, and also looks at the needs of
children, maintenance settlements, parental responsibility and legal rights.

NEW EDITION
What To Do When Someone Dies
Anne Wadey
ISBN: 978 1 84490 072 5
Price £10.99

Dealing with bereavement is never easy, and arranging funerals and financial
administration can be complex. *What To Do When Someone Dies* helps you
make informed decisions, plan for costs, and manage the process right up to
applying for probate. This book includes advice on registering a death and
notifying relevant parties, making funeral arrangements, sorting out tax,
property and finance, and covers the whole of the UK, including Scotland
and Northern Ireland.

Wills & Probate
David Bunn
ISBN: 978 1 84490 070 1
Price £10.99

Now in its fully revised 13th edition, this is an invaluable guide for anybody
making a will or charged with administering an estate, helping to avoid delays,
disputes and excessive legal bills. *Wills & Probate* explains the basics of making a
will and how to avoid common mistakes, how to reduce your inheritance tax bill,
and hassle-free steps to setting up a trust. Covers the UK including Northern
Ireland and Scotland.